# API'S BERLIN DIARIES

# API'S BERLIN DIARIES

## MY QUEST TO UNDERSTAND MY GRANDFATHER'S NAZI PAST

Gabrielle Robinson

SHE WRITES PRESS

Published 2020
Printed in the United States of America
ISBN: 978-1-64742-003-1 pbk
ISBN: 978-1-64742-004-8 ebk
Library of Congress Control Number: 2020905902

For information, address:
She Writes Press
1569 Solano Ave #546
Berkeley, CA 94707

She Writes Press is a division of SparkPoint Studio, LLC.

*To Mike and Benedict,*
*the best companions on my journey*

# 1

# OH MY GOD!

I never wanted to write this memoir. As a child growing up in Germany in the 1950s, I heard a few family stories about the war, but mainly there was silence. We did not talk or ask about the recent past. We wanted to forget it. The stories I did hear merge in my imagination with transient memories like half-remembered dreams. I see my mother and myself on a crowded railroad station platform, jostled by hundreds of people. I am two and a half years old, wrapped in a brown double-breasted coat against the winter cold. I can't see beyond a wall of suitcases pressing around me and more feet than I have ever noticed before. The shrieks, sobs, and shouts that fill the air scare me. I do not understand why my mother repeats constantly, sometimes shouting above the noise all around, "Don't let go of the suitcase handle. Never let go. Keep your little hand tightly on the handle." She herself is loaded down with luggage and has no hand free to hold on to me. It was February 6, 1945, and we were fleeing from Berlin after being bombed out of our apartment for the second time. None of us would ever live in Berlin again.

Another, much clearer memory comes from the winter after the war. We lived in one and a half rooms of a tiny farmhouse in

Suderburg, Lower Saxony, to which my mother, my grandmother, and I had fled. The cottage did not have indoor plumbing. I remember not so much the cold and hunger of that time as the delight when Farmer Ohlde, who owned the cottage, dug into the pig trough to fish out the moist morsel of a potato for me. Even better, sometimes his old mother got up from her spinning wheel to dip the potato in salt. Whenever Herr Ohlde had no handouts for me, my grandmother—I called her Nyussi, for reasons I can't remember—took me outside. We passed the compost heap on the right and the pigs on the left to look for the beavers under the woodpile. Somehow we always just missed them. So Nyussi told me stories about their life. I can still hear her melodious, slightly accented German—she was a native Hungarian—and see her lively dark eyes as she began her story: "You see, Brielchen," a pet name my grandfather invented, "the beavers are just beneath where we stand now, and they have warm and cozy burrows and a big larder stuffed with good things to eat." I wondered whether they, too, enjoyed potatoes with salt. As I looked all around for the sight of a beaver, Nyussi went on: "The beavers don't care how cold the winter gets, for they always have this cozy hideaway." I stared at the woodpile till my eyes hurt, but I never spotted a single beaver. When I got too chilly, Nyussi took me back inside and I crawled under the table, pretending it was a beaver burrow. I loved the beavers and their adventures underground. Nyussi's stories always delighted me and made me forget that I was hungry and cold. It was only much later, when I was in my forties, that my mother mentioned casually in a conversation that Nyussi had made up the beaver stories. There never were any beavers there at all. Even after so many years, I felt a pang of sadness and loss that has not entirely left me even now.

Apart from such snippets of memories, World War II was not part of my world and the silence about it did not bother me. When I was older, I realized that my mother, then my only surviving relative, did not want that subject brought up. Then, sixty years after the end of the war, I made two discoveries that reawakened the past and changed everything. The first brought the past back into my world in terrifying detail, and the second opened the floodgates to a torrent of questions about my grandfather, the Nazi era, and me.

In the summer of 2005, after my mother's death, my husband, Mike, and I vacationed in her Vienna apartment. We had returned from a hike in the hills above the city, stopping at vineyards along the way. I was pleasantly tired and just wanted to relax with a book before going to bed. As I plucked *Effi Briest*, my favorite Theodor Fontane novel, from high up on the bookcase, two small objects tumbled to the floor. Picking them up, I saw that they were two notebooks bound in faded green cloth with AGENDA stamped in gold at the top of each. Curious, I flipped through the pages. They were covered from top to bottom in penciled writing. I immediately recognized it as my grandfather's hand.

Seeing his tiny, precise lettering after so many years brought back a flood of memories. I had spent the happiest years, all too few, of my childhood with him, until his death in 1955. Api, as I affectionately called him, took me in when my mother could not look after me anymore. My father had been killed in the war, shot down over England in 1943 in his single-engine fighter plane, and my mother worked full-time in Vienna. I had been passed around and stayed with an aunt, with my paternal grandparents, and finally in an Ursuline boarding school in Vienna, where I fell ill with scarlet fever. Even though at age sixty-four he himself was struggling to rebuild an existence in rural northern Germany, Api gave me a loving home and, for the rest of his life, was both father and grandfather to me.

I thought of the poems he had written for me to recite and the corrections he had made to my Latin grammar. I pictured Api as I had known him, a thin and tall man with cropped white hair who walked with a slight stoop. His bright blue eyes always seemed to be laughing, and his thin lips echoed the smile in his eyes. I do not remember that Api ever raised his voice at me in anger. He invented all sorts of affectionate names for me, calling me Gabruschken, Brielchen, his little sunshine. When we had nothing after the war, he built me a dollhouse out of matchboxes with tiny doll figures made of bits of silver paper he had saved. It even had a hospital room where I was Api's head nurse. I was delighted when he joined Nyussi and me at teatime for "the length of a cigar," wearing his white doctor's coat and filling the room with his good spirits.

However much he surrounded us with laughter and play, Api was chiefly concerned with teaching me the importance of learning, and of giving my whole attention to whatever I was doing, whether it was work or play. He had been brought up in the Prussian tradition of work and discipline, and he tried to instill these values in me as well. The only time he chastised me was when I was doing nothing, wasting time, without thought or feeling. I remember one summer Sunday afternoon outside our apartment in Bevensen when I was eight or nine years old. I felt hot and lazy, and none of my friends were around. So I picked up a stick and dragged it along our dark brown slatted fence, listening to the *rat-tat-tat* it made against the wood. When Api saw this, he was upset. He scolded me, not for playing or for damaging the fence, but for doing something without engagement. And then he offered to build a kite with me.

Caught up in memories, I was not tired anymore. Sitting on the couch Api had bought for my mother when she got married in 1941, and which somehow had survived the war, I started to read. The diary began on April 21, 1945, in Berlin, where Api, age fifty-seven, served as a military doctor, with the rank of major. He was stationed in the central district, what the Nazis called the Citadel, near the Reichstag, the Brandenburg Gate, and Hitler's bunker. Almost instantly, the enjoyable nostalgia of life with my grandfather was swept away by the terror he faced day by day. He lived under the howling of bombs and the heavy rain of grenade splinters. The familiar streets lay buried under mountains of rubble, twisted wires, burned-out streetcars, and bomb craters. Acrid smoke and dust made it hard to breathe and transformed day into night. Together with other gray, emaciated survivors, many of them refugees from the East, Api tried to forge a path through this wilderness.

Without sanitation, and without water after they had drained the last drops from the heaters, he felt almost helpless to assist the wounded and dying in the medical bunker. The only light came from a few Hindenburg candles, bits of tallow in cardboard, and everyone took care to scoop up and reuse every fallen drop. Over all hung the stench of decaying bodies and excrement. Unimaginable. "Just now I have been looking for spaces where one can at least have the sick sit down or lay them on the ground for the night, without doors or windows, but at least protected from rain and safe from grenade splinters, although cold without padding. Corpses lie in a chapel of the Ziegelstrasse Clinic, for the most part without clothes, men and women together in layers."

Reading late into the night, I felt as if, years after his death in 1955, Api was there, speaking to me and helping me understand him much more intimately. I now saw him at his most desperate, when his existence had shrunk down to paralyzing anxiety, with only the slenderest ray of hope to keep him going. On almost every page I also saw his love for me, his three-year-old fatherless granddaughter, and I anxiously followed his mental and physical deterioration. Witness to daily horrors, he was driven to the point of collapse. And he felt so desperately alone, unable to communicate with us. His best company was the swifts and swallows he watched circling over the ruins. They, too, had become homeless.

Finally, long after midnight, worn out emotionally, I had to stop reading. But I resolved to translate the diaries and tell Api's story. Of course, I was aware that my grandfather was not an important historical figure, just an ordinary German who lived in central Berlin at a crucial time. But his experiences would, I hoped, add firsthand details to one of the most dreadful times of the twentieth century. So, when we left Vienna, I carefully wrapped up the diaries and took them with me to South Bend, Indiana, where I would have time to read and transcribe them.

Back home, I set to work immediately. Always a writer, Api had furnished an eloquent testimony of his experiences in 1945. I began to understand how his diary was an attempt to cope with the horror of war and a refuge in the maelstrom of chaos and death. It served as a lifeline to a saner and more humane existence, a world that was all but lost. He clung to the hope that at some happier time in the future we would be able to read these notes, "although," he admitted, "they are paltry in relation to the shocking force of my inner experiences."

I followed the days and weeks of Api's nightmare. The war finally ended on May 9, but his situation did not improve. The Soviets took over central Berlin, and the misery, fear, and starvation continued. They who had suffered so much at the hands of the Germans and who themselves were destitute plundered and raped their way through the ruin of a city. It was at this point, even more than during the inferno of the war, that Api was at his most desolate. Even his faith, which had always been strong, deserted him, and he contemplated suicide. He was not alone in this despair. It got so bad that the newly installed gas lines in a suburb east of Tempelhof Airport had to be shut down again because too many people used the gas to kill themselves. According to historian Ian Kershaw, 3,881 people committed suicide in Berlin in April and May 1945.

As I worked my way through the diaries, an abbreviation appeared more and more frequently. It was two letters: *Pg.* I recalled dimly that this might—no, must—mean *Parteigenossen*, party members. Surely not my grandfather?

And then I made my second discovery. Api had been a *Pg*, a member of the Nazi Party, the National Socialist German Workers'

Party. I had not known this. It had never been mentioned in my family. I sat there with a pounding heart, saying to myself over and over in the crudest and most shocking terms, "Oh my God, Api was a Nazi!"

*Api's Diary*

*Reichstag, 1945*

*Berlin street, 1945*

*Api in 1945*

*Api and Gabrielle, 1944*

# 2

# YOU MADE SOAP
# OUT OF MY AUNT

I could not go on. In tears, I could not talk about it, not even with
my husband, Mike, or my son, Benedict. I hid the green notebooks
again, burying them deep in the bottom drawer of my desk. I had
wanted to tell the story of the diaries for their historical value and
also as a tribute to my Api, who loved me and played with me, who
taught me Latin, and showed me how to build a kite. I had not foreseen that this supposed tribute to him would lead to a painful reeval-
uation of my family, my life, and my nationality.

Until then, I had thought of myself as not so much a victim of
war but a lucky survivor. Although I had heard about the bombings
where we lost everything and about the hunger in that cruel winter
after the war, it was all mainly stories for me. I have preserved from
that time a love for potatoes with salt, but no scars. I never knew my
father, but then, many of my classmates were fatherless. There were
two million of us half orphans in Germany.

As a small child, I was moved from place to place. A symptom
of my itinerant existence is that, originally baptized Protestant in
Berlin, I was rebaptized and confirmed Catholic in Vienna, and

eventually Protestant again in northern Germany. Out of necessity, I learned to fit in anywhere, and our family's social standing gave me, despite initial poverty, a good start in life. And then, for five years until his death, Api gave me a stable home.

After Api died in 1955, my transitory life began again: a boarding school on the Baltic; summers with an aunt in Munich or wherever Nyussi happened to be. When my mother remarried, I lived with her and my stepfather in Darmstadt, where I graduated from the gymnasium in 1962. Then we emigrated to the United States.

All along, the silence about the Nazi regime endured and I did not feel implicated in any of it. Of course, I was aware of the atrocities of the concentration camps. I had seen pictures and documentaries of the six million murdered Jews—the emaciated bodies; the heaps of bones, hair, teeth; men, women, and children crowded into cattle cars, deported to their deaths in gas chambers. I often could not bear to look at the images on the screen and have never visited any of the concentration camps. The German mood of the 1950s helped me in this escape from reality—everyone just wanted to forget this ever happened in our country. But I am afraid that to this day I have tried to avoid direct confrontation with the Holocaust. Even as recently as 2005, I walked out of Roman Polanski's movie *The Pianist*. Mike and I were watching the film together with a Polish couple, when I became ever more frantic at the powerful images of suffering in a concentration camp. Before I knew what I was doing, I rushed out of the theater. I could not bring myself to return and waited numbly in the lobby until the movie was over.

Living in the United States, I felt the burden of having to admit my German background. I tried to hide it and silently agreed when people pegged me as Scandinavian. I often claimed to be Austrian, but that hardly improved the situation. When I was a graduate student at Columbia University in 1965, a fellow student told me with a smile, "You know, you made soap out of my aunt." He saw it as a clever opening line, but I could only run away horrified. And yet even that did not make me reflect on German guilt. For the burden of my German origins was not so much the result of guilt as of embarrassment. I felt a little like Emperor Otto III in *Dr. Faustus*, who, in Thomas Mann's words, "was a prize specimen of German self-contempt and had all his life been ashamed of being German." I have read somewhere that it is easy to avoid the patriotism that shows itself in a foolish national pride, but much harder to give up the kind that makes you feel ashamed for your country.

However, the discovery of Api's Nazi membership hit much closer to home. Now at last I had to confront the guilt that people thought I should have felt when I was twenty. Sins of the fathers and grandfathers, going back generations, suddenly made sense. I knew little of my grandfather's life before the war and nothing about the reasons why he joined the Nazi Party. But now I felt implicated in the horrors of the Hitler regime and thought that I may well have survived because of his membership.

I asked myself how I would have acted if I had lived at that time. It is impossible to judge from a distance, and I could not come close to imagining what it must have been like to live under a brutal totalitarian regime, cut off from the outside world. Even listening to the BBC on the radio could bring a death sentence. What choice did most people have but to watch the crimes of the government in paralyzed horror while trying to carve out their own lives as best they could? As Ian Kershaw, whose fascinating accounts of the Nazi era I was soon to discover, notes, "Passivity and cooperation—however sullen and resentful—were the most human of responses in such a situation."

Then, more than a year and a half later, on the first balmy spring day, Mike and I drove to St. Joseph, Michigan, to have breakfast at Tozzi's, our favorite coffeehouse near Lake Michigan. Although the fields were still brown and the trees bare, the sky was washed a transparent blue and the sun was hot on our faces. When we entered the little café, it was empty except for a group of middle-aged women in one corner who were celebrating a birthday. Suddenly, unexpectedly, my secret came out. As soon as Mike and I sat down, the whole story just spilled forth, together with my tears.

"My grandfather was a member of the Nazi Party. Of course, I cannot publish the diary. It's a betrayal of the grandfather I loved. I am silenced by shame." I further thought that it was a betrayal not only of a grandfather long dead, but also of my son, Benedict. I remember our looking at an old picture album when he was a teenager. He was shocked to spot my father and grandfather in Nazi air force and army uniforms with little swastikas on their badges. Brought up in the United States, he had seen these uniforms only in films, worn by the enemy, brutal Nazi men. He had not expected to see them on members of his own family.

At that moment, I fully sympathized with a cousin of historian Edward Ball, who responded angrily to Ball's project of writing about the slaves their family had owned and in the process uncovering the many cruelties and crimes that were part of that heritage: "To do this is to condemn your ancestors! You're going to dig up my grandfather and hang him!" He seemed to be speaking for me.

As I surreptitiously wiped away tears with my Tozzi's napkin, hoping the birthday women would not notice, Mike insisted, "Now you really have to write your story and the story of the diary. I thought it interesting before, but this makes it much more complex and significant. You can either walk away from this or come to terms with it. It may be more convenient to ignore history than to confront it. But it is also more dangerous and no help for the future. We need to understand how ordinary people get caught up in totalitarian regimes. We need to understand the human condition in a richer and more nuanced fashion. You have to write about this. You have to get started."

For weeks I returned to that conversation and eventually followed

Mike's advice. I dug out the diaries from my desk drawer. Although I still had doubts about releasing Api's story to public scrutiny, I thought that after all he might approve. He treasured these diaries and often mentioned that he hoped they would be read. He was thinking of us and talking to us, but he also was aware of them as historical documents, and they were carefully crafted. In times of particular danger, he made certain that the diaries were in safe hands, once with the minister of his church that lay in rubble, another time with the head nurse at the North Sanatorium where he worked. Therefore, I told myself, I had some reason to hope that this story, written with love, complied with my grandfather's wishes.

# 3

# A CLASH OF MEMORIES

Once determined to go forward, I began to read about the Nazi period. I acquired books on the fall of Berlin, on German guilt, and memoirs of that time by children and grandchildren. I was drawn in particular to studies that combined individual stories with social and historical analyses, like those by major historians Ian Kershaw, Antony Beevor, and Richard Evans. Gradually I built a whole new library next to my books on drama and literary theory. And it seemed to me as if many books were urging me on with my project. Writer after writer insisted on the importance of personal stories for a fuller historical picture. There is even a special designation, *Alltagsgeschichte*, history of everyday life, which Kershaw termed "a most fruitful approach." Journalist and German exile Sebastian Haffner justified his own autobiographical account by saying, "Decisions that influence the course of history arise out of the individual experiences of thousands or millions of individuals." Therefore, he believed that "by retelling my private, unimportant story I am adding an important, unrecognized facet to contemporary German and European history—more significant and more important for the future than if I were to disclose who set fire to the Reichstag."

David Stafford's book about Berlin in 1945 added further arguments. "Behind and amid all great events lie individuals, their experiences, and their actions, and it is only through understanding these that we can fully grasp the larger picture." Api's diaries could furnish another facet in this larger picture.

Until the twenty-first century, not many stories of the war from a German perspective have been published. As A. C. Grayling noted in 2006, "The guilt felt about the Holocaust by most individual Germans of the immediate postwar generation . . . for long made it impossible for them to see the catastrophe they experienced in 1945 as anything other than deserved punishment." The passage of time, however, has changed attitudes. "The descendants of the bombed have begun to raise their voices and ask questions about the experience of their parents and grandparents." Mark M. Anderson emphasized that such personal accounts are necessary because what we learn "is the importance of individual historical experience that resists the either/ or of victimhood."

So now I am one of these voices. I began to think about Api in a way I had not done before, not as my grandfather who was always there to help and support me but as a vulnerable and fearful man who had come close to total collapse and also as a member of the Nazi Party. I realized that we never talked about politics, a subject that did not seem to interest him, although it had dominated his life almost from his birth in 1888. Despite all that had happened, Api, I began to see, was a loyal German of a generation who would not have shared or understood the shame of being German that Thomas Mann attributes to Emperor Otto III. Yet the Nazis derided and destroyed everything Api treasured about his country. He wrote that when he saw the reality of Hitler's intentions, he criticized the regime to colleagues and patients, even when it was dangerous for him to so. In the diaries, he referred to Hitler and his group only as criminals and executioners.

But he did not leave the Party. It would have taken extraordinary courage and not only self-sacrifice but also the sacrifice of his family to get out and risk falling into the hands of the Gestapo, the German secret police. Certainly, he paid dearly. He lost his only son and his son-in-law, my father; bombs destroyed his apartment and practice; and his family was forced to flee their home. He himself survived only barely, in cellars and attics, and he still tried to help others. He was, after all, a doctor. Yet he was also a Nazi.

In May and June 1945, when denunciations of former Nazis ran wild among the German population, Api often thought about this. "Now, if such members, who were such only because they could not get out, and who more or less condemned and rejected everything in the government and spoke against it more openly than many others, if now all those should be looked upon as liable to punishment, then one is on exactly the same path of irresponsible injustice and brutality as are held against the Nazis." He seemed to be thinking about himself, and I wondered why he used this displacement on an imagined other group. At other moments, however, he did talk directly about himself when he voiced his regret: "Oh, if only we could have done something on our part against the crimes and mistakes of the government which we recognized years ago!" He felt "well-knowing but impotent."

I realized that if I were to make sense of Api's life and his experiences in 1945, I needed to find out more about him. Only by putting the six terrifying months of the diary into the context of an entire life could I hope to piece together a clearer picture and perhaps answer some of the questions that kept me awake at night.

Serendipitously, just around that time, my stepfather brought me a wooden box that had been in my mother's possession. When I undid the lock, I found a yellowing stack of documents, letters, and photographs. Many of the letters were in Api's handwriting and covered a period from the 1920s to 1945. Several were written at the same time as the diary. Desperate to contact us, Api kept giving letters addressed to us to anyone who was leaving Berlin. None of the earlier letters made it through, but some of the later ones did. At the bottom of the box, I uncovered several passports and military records, including Api's *Wehrpass*, which documented his military positions and stations in both World Wars. I was particularly touched by a note Api had written me for my third birthday, on October 17, 1945, in which he told me, "Be proud and strong, devout, and good to all men."

The sepia-colored pictures I found in the box allowed me glimpses into my grandparents' life. I saw snapshots of family picnics and parties. They seemed larger, more flamboyant versions of what I remembered of my life with my grandparents in the early 1950s. I noticed several photographs of the family with a group of friends that must have been taken on New Year's Eve, for everyone was in costume, holding up champagne flutes and laughing into the camera.

When I was with my grandparents, we enjoyed quieter celebrations among just the three of us. But we still dressed up, and Nyussi helped me put together my costumes. At midnight on New Year's Eve, Api lit the candles on the Christmas tree, and I stood beside their warm glow and recited the poem he had written for that year. They all dealt with love, peace, and faith and expressed profound gratitude for what we had. In one picture, I am dressed up as a gypsy girl with a shiny red turban on my head. I am holding Theodor, the teddy bear a British airman brought me from London in 1946.

Picnics were another of Api's favorite leisure-time activities. As I studied the pictures of the 1920s and '30s, my mind drifted to similar scenes in the heath landscape of northern Germany. The old pictures invariably featured not only the family but whatever new Buick Api had bought. It was the chief luxury of his life. The first one, in 1926, was a boxy car with wooden spokes and a wide, curving running board. In the 1950s, our pictures showed the much more modest Grey Donkey, a secondhand Opel Olympia. Yet Api delighted in this car. It was a sign that, in his sixties, he had once more managed to climb out of poverty. It also meant no more visiting his patients on a bike.

Continuing to read about the Nazi era, I came back again and again to the question of why Api had joined the Nazi Party. I knew that he cherished stability and order, which Hitler promised, and speculated that Hitler's religious bearing at the time may have been attractive to Api, a strong Lutheran. In his early public appearances, Hitler liked to pose as a conservative and religious man who was committed to reviving the Prussian values Api held dear. Richard J. Evans says that Protestants provided "the broadest and deepest reservoir of support for the Nazi Party in all social groups." In many ways, Api fit the profile of people who joined the Party at that early stage. Like he was, they tended to be older, conservative, Protestant, and veterans of World War I.

Many troubling questions remained, however—questions not only about Api's guilt but also about myself and my telling his story. How could I measure Api's personal suffering in view of the suffering of millions of innocent victims of that regime? For whatever he had to go through cannot compare to the agonies of Holocaust victims. And how could I even begin to discuss these questions separate from my love for my grandfather and the picture of him I had cherished all my life? I felt doubly disqualified to take this on, at once too close to Api and too removed from any similar terror. Finally, did the question of German guilt also involve me, since my family may well have benefited from Api's Nazi membership? Would I have acted differently in Api's situation? Was I responsible after all for "making soap out of my aunt," as that young man in New York suggested many years ago?

This led me to questions about collective guilt and political responsibility that are important today as well. We all act politically, even by doing nothing. As Martin Luther King wrote on April 16, 1963, in his Letter from Birmingham Jail, "We will have to repent in this generation not merely for the vitriolic words and actions of the bad people, but for the appalling silence of the good people."

When I found Api's diaries, I thought I could simply tell his story, and I was glad to rescue them from their sixty-year hiding place. At the same time, I thought that this memoir would allow me to examine my own past, now that I was at a period in my life where I was ready to look back. But I had barely begun this process of memory when a larger issue interfered with that intention. Api was a Nazi, and now I was forced to deal with a guilt I had not confronted throughout my life. I cannot resolve this clash of memories, but I also can't hide from it any longer. What I can do is raise questions and break the silence.

At the end of his history of slaves in his family, Edward Ball concludes, "We're not responsible for what our ancestors did or did not do, but we're accountable for it." By learning more about that time and my grandfather's life, and by raising questions, perhaps I can arrive at some degree of accountability.

*On picnic with first Buick, 1926*

# 4

# GROWING UP PRUSSIAN

Shortly before committing suicide in 1941, the writer Stefan Zweig said about his and Api's generation in his autobiography, *The World of Yesterday*, that "each one of us has been churned up in his innermost being by the almost uninterrupted volcanic eruptions of our European world." To place Api's actions in a broader context, I have to try to understand how these eruptions affected him throughout his life. Throughout this journey, I have realized that the tremors Zweig mentions still reverberate with me in the third generation.

Api was born in the pivotal year 1888, when Emperor Wilhelm I died and, after the three-month reign of Friedrich III, his son Wilhelm II ascended the throne. The death of Wilhelm I signified the end of the old Prussian era. He had thought of himself more as king of Prussia than as emperor of Germany. Known as the "soldiers' king," he was the embodiment of Prussian values of military discipline, obedience, and thrift. He regarded rubber tires on his carriages as an unnecessary luxury and refused to have hot-water baths installed in his palace. Wilhelm II, by contrast, saw himself as the leader of a new and powerful German empire. He was a flamboyant, autocratic ruler. Despite his withered left arm, he loved public appearances. Historian Christopher Clark refers to him as the first "media monarch." The emperor's absolutist and vainglorious attitude about Germany's supremacy, coupled with his reactionary ideology, did much to precipitate his country's involvement in World War I, which in turn paved the way for Hitler and World War II.

However, in Marienwerder, where Api was born on January 22, 1888, the spirit of the old soldiers' king still prevailed. The West Prussian town was situated on the Liwa River, 250 miles northeast of Berlin and 50 miles south of Danzig/Gdansk. The Weichsel/Vistula River runs just two miles east of town. In 1888, Marienwerder had about eight thousand inhabitants.

Marienwerder has a war-torn history, divided between Eastern and Western influences. It was founded in 1233 by the Teutonic Knights, a German Roman Catholic military order that engaged in crusades under the direction of the pope. Their very appearance was meant to terrify the native Prussians as they swooped down on horseback, dressed in white cloaks that dramatically displayed a large black cross and a black eagle with red claws and beak. The knights, however, found their match in the Prussians, who for centuries had repelled any intruders. Chronicles say that they "roasted captured brethren alive in their armor like chestnuts." The knights retaliated by giving the Prussians the option of baptism or death. In the long run, that method prevailed. The knights established a sovereign monastic state from which they colonized the area.

The Teutonic Knights' reign lasted less than two hundred years. In 1410, a Polish-Lithuanian army defeated them in the Battle of Tannenberg, and Marienwerder became a Polish fiefdom. (By an accident of history, the first action Api saw in World War I was another Battle of Tannenberg where Hindenburg defeated the Russians.) During the Reformation, Marienwerder turned Lutheran, and, starting in 1523, Lutheran bishops administered it. In 1618, the Hohenzollerns inherited Marienwerder as part of the Duchy of

Prussia, and it became the administrative center of the new district of West Prussia.

In the early nineteenth century, the population of Marienwerder was largely Polish. But this majority was steadily reduced by a policy of enforced Germanization. In 1871, when Bismarck forged the German Empire out of its many separate states, duchies, and kingdoms, Marienwerder became part of the empire, and the *Kulturkampf,* the cultural battle that Bismarck initiated, was directed against the remaining Polish Catholic population. By the time Api was born, Marienwerder was more than 80 percent German and Lutheran. Today, Marienwerder, now Kwidzyn, belongs to Poland once again.

Api is descended from a line of artisans and small-business owners that I traced back to the sixteenth century. The Freses originally came from Korbach in Westphalia. In my mother's box, I found a 1910 postcard of Korbach's tree-lined, triangular marketplace surrounded by half-timbered two-story houses. In the bottom-right-hand corner, I discovered the name Carl Frese affixed above the front door of a store. Grocer Carl probably was a relative, but by 1910 Api's family had long left. Like many people in the mid–nineteenth century, Api's grandfather Ferdinand Hermann Frese, a teacher, emigrated to the rapidly developing east and settled in Marienwerder. All I have is some dates. Ferdinand was born in Korbach on April 4, 1823, and died in Marienwerder on May 2, 1909.

Api's father, Max Frese, likewise became a teacher and stayed in Marienwerder. By then the family had become thoroughly Prussianized. The only picture I found of Max shows him in 1927, two years before his death, sitting in the sun by the wall of a house. He is wearing a three-piece suit and the stiff choke collar called the *Vatermörder,* the father slayer. His hair is cropped well above the ears, but the very top is longer and parted in the middle, and he has a short beard. He sits a little hunched, with his legs crossed at the ankles and his hands folded in his lap. He does not look at the camera but seems to be staring straight ahead. I can recognize Api's features in the shape of his head, but not in his dejected posture and expression. Max was a staunch royalist and conservative. Although himself not a military man, he taught at the royal noncommissioned officers' school in his hometown and believed in the military ethos of discipline and obedience to authority. The army was Prussia's foremost institution, its values deeply ingrained in everyday life. Military parades and regimental music formed an important part of the town's activities. Whether for the dedication of a monument to the 1871 victory over the French or the emperor's birthday on January 27, soldiers marched through Marienwerder resplendent in their Prussian blue uniforms. The men were made taller by their shiny pointed pickle helmets, which bore the gilded Prussian eagle on top. Swords and bayonets flashed in the sun, and the population cheered, waving the black, white, and red imperial flags. As the comte de Mirabeau (an eighteenth-century statesman) put it so wittily, "Prussia isn't a country that has an army; it's an army that has a country."

Max Frese married a young woman from the neighboring town of Garnsee. Emma Riegamer's father owned a hotel, the Black Eagle, on the market square there. Api was their first child, followed by his brother, Werner, and his sister, Lisbeth. My mother kept Api's birth certificate in her box of memorabilia, showing that the midwife Karoline Toepfer delivered him. Api may have been his mother's favorite. He certainly was strongly attached to her and remained a devoted son all his life. In 1929, after Ohchen, as everyone called her, was widowed and had moved to Berlin, she became a constant presence in family outings. I have pictures of her sitting up, straight and unsmiling, at outdoor cafés or on picnics in the Grunewald. Her white hair is combed back into a bun, and she almost always wears a jabot, a little cascade of ruffles down the front of her blouse. Nyussi told me that Api never could do enough for his mother, who was quite spoiled and demanding. She thought nothing of calling them at night to say that she had a taste for champagne. Without hesitation, Api rushed over a bottle to her.

Api's family embraced the Prussian work ethic. Their motto was "*Erst kommt die Arbeit, dann das Vergnügen*"—that is, work before play. Max Frese, son of a teacher and a teacher himself, believed in education as the main asset he could hand down to his children. Although his salary was not large, he made sure that all three children attended the local gymnasium, the highest level of secondary school, where they were taught Greek, Latin, and French, as well as mathematics, science, ancient history, and the German classics.

Religion was the other cornerstone of the Frese family. Max instilled in his children a commitment to translate the teachings of the Bible into their every thought and action. They were encouraged to be modest, self-disciplined, and tolerant and to check their hearts carefully for any slips away from these virtues. The family attended Lutheran services every Sunday in the large redbrick cathedral, where Api's attention was invariably drawn to three ancient stone memorials to the Grand Masters of the Teutonic Order.

Api absorbed all this, the discipline and devotion, the belief in education and hard work, as well as the pietistic Lutheran tendency toward introspection. They became his guiding principles, to which he stuck throughout his life, refusing to adapt to the free-spirited, pleasure-oriented ethos of Berlin in the "gay '20s." As Zweig observes, "What a man has drawn into his blood from the air of the time cannot be expelled."

# 5

# SEVEN KILOMETERS OF DOCUMENTS

Until Mike and I visited the Humboldt University archives in 2007, this was the limit of what I knew of Api's early life. But Frau Ilona Kalb, the archivist with whom I had corresponded before our departure for Germany, assured me that she could provide additional information. There were, after all, she said, "seven kilometers of documents stored here," and she would search for Api's employment record at the Charité Hospital, his applications, and his study at Friedrich Wilhelm University.

As soon as we reached Berlin, I called the helpful archivist. Frau Kalb told me that she had found several volumes documenting my grandfather's life, and that we could come right over to inspect them. We took the S-Bahn, the city rail, from the busy Friedrichstrasse station to go north to the university archives. As we mounted the broad stone staircase to the station, I thought of Api's shock when he saw two officers executed there by SS at the end of April 1945, just days before the end of the war. Their corpses were left as a "deterrent" to others who might not want to fight anymore. Now the rebuilt station was crowded with commuters and stalls heaped with fruit and flowers. We bought some shiny, tart Balaton cherries from Hungary for our journey.

When we got off the S-Bahn at Eichborndamm in the far north of Berlin, I was full of anticipation. We found the archives near the station, in a converted Nazi munitions factory whose low buildings stretched for blocks along the avenue. On the outside, the old red brick was left as it had been, but inside all was light, modern, and functional. Its high walls had been subdivided to create ample space for the seven kilometers of documents. We were directed to the reading room, whose large, southwest-facing windows let in the June sun. It was furnished with rows of modern desks in light-colored wood. As soon as we were settled near a window, Frau Kalb brought us three bulky volumes that gave off little puffs of dust as she deposited them in front of us.

Putting the materials in chronological order, I saw from one of his applications that Api had started at the gymnasium in 1896, at age nine. He must have been a diligent student, for he graduated in March 1906, released from the dreaded oral examinations of the baccalaureate. Api wanted to become a doctor, but his family did not have the funds to send him to university, so he applied to Kaiser Wilhelm Academy for military doctors in Berlin. If accepted, he would be guaranteed a first-rate education, although for every semester of study he had to commit himself to one year of military service. Api must have thought that what amounted to ten years of service was well worth the opportunity to attend this premier institution that was linked to the university and the famous Charité Hospital. In 1906, the year Api applied, fewer than 40 students were chosen from among 150 applicants from all over the country.

While waiting to hear, he volunteered with the 4th Queen Augusta Guards Grenadier Regiment, stationed in Berlin Tempelhof. Ostensibly, these were specially chosen soldiers whose job it was to serve as bodyguards for the emperor, but mostly they showed off their fancy regalia in parades and on festive occasions.

The archives revealed mainly facts and dates. But Api's acceptance was no doubt overwhelming, and I can picture that, at eighteen and from the provinces, he felt at once excited and forlorn. When he enrolled, the academy was still housed at Friedrichstrasse 140, near the large station that had been built in the 1880s for the rapidly growing city. Friedrichstrasse also was Berlin's red-light district. Garishly lit nightclubs and bars attracted customers of all sorts. Prostitutes and street vendors wandered among the throng of visitors, amid laughter and shouting everywhere. In contrast with the vivid nightlife, by day the street looked bleak and tawdry.

In 1910, the new academy, located a few blocks north at Invalidenstrasse 48–49, was completed. It was an imposing, turreted neobaroque structure of red brick and beige stucco topped by a steep, red-tiled mansard roof. At its center was a park. Above the main entrance, in large gold letters, shone the inscription SCIENTIAE, HUMANITATI, PATRIAE: To Science, Humanity, Fatherland. The academy is one of the very few buildings in Berlin Mitte that survived the war with little damage. It now houses the Federal Ministry of Commerce and Industry.

*Gabrielle on top of Reichstag,*
*former Emperor Wilhelm Academy in background*

Api never talked to me about his time at the academy, but I found a book that described its curriculum and atmosphere at the time he was there. Students took courses not only in science and medicine, but also in philosophy and art. They had to complete one semester of riding and fencing lessons and do weapons training in a Berlin regiment. Their education ended with a course on medical ethics. The academy emphasized what Api had already learned at home: duty, discipline, obedience, and hard work. But it also aimed to create a spirit of comradeship among its students. There was a "Kasino" where students could party and relax, no professors allowed. The book has a picture of Dr. Kern, the director during Api's stay. In fact, he reminded me of Api, a tall and thin man with a mustache who looked at once stern and appealing. He had the military bearing of a Prussian officer, and the Iron Cross was affixed prominently to the choke collar of his uniform, but he also exuded warmth of character. Dr. Kern's educational vision, the book said, was to foster men "of thorough knowledge, a chivalrous cast of mind, and an honest character." I imagine that Api liked and respected him.

The practical training was done at the Charité Hospital. The Charité was founded in 1710 as a pest house for plague victims but changed to a hospice for the poor, as well as an academy for military doctors, when Berlin was spared an outbreak of the plague. In the eighteenth century, three large wings were added so that patients had plenty of fresh air and "the bad fumes would be blown away." Rooms faced a long, arcaded balcony where patients could recuperate out of doors.

*Perhaps*, I thought, *this is where Api learned the healing power of fresh air.* I smiled at the memories of Api walking with me in the rain. "Notice how fresh the air smells," he would say. "We may not get many hot and sunny days here in the north, but this is beautiful, too, and the fresh air will do us good." His lesson stayed with me. I love to be outside in any weather and have a fondness for moist and foggy days.

The afternoon sun streaming in the window brought me back to my research. By the time Api attended the Charité, it had become the medical school of Berlin's Friedrich Wilhelm University, today renamed Humboldt University, and had achieved an international reputation. Although Api was no doubt overawed by working in this illustrious place, the architecture happily reminded him of home. The Charité was built of red brick, and each building featured the step gable front he knew from Marienwerder. It was a larger version of his gymnasium and the academy where his father taught.

Like most of his fellow students, Api joined a fraternity. I know that the academy gave students a choice of three *Corps*, but all my efforts failed to identify the one to which he belonged. All I have is his *Commersbuch*, the songbook students used. It was one of the few possessions he kept throughout the war and that I also cherished when I lived with him. The book features a mix of folk songs, patriotic songs, and fraternity songs, like, "Oh Old Fraternity Glory." Whether they were in beer halls or on hikes, fraternity brothers sang together from their *Commersbuch*. Often the book is decorated with the colors of the fraternity. But here again I was unlucky, for Api's book had no such inscription that could tell me his *Corps*.

There were, and still are, two groups of fraternities in Germany, the *Burschenschaften* and the *Corps*. Both developed out of the *Freikorps*, the freelance soldiers who fought against Napoleon. The Corps tended to be more elitist and more conservative—the emperor himself was a member of one. *Corps* required more fencing bouts than Burschenschaften, although Api did not have a *Schmiss*, the gash on his face that was regarded as a sign of distinction. I am sure, however, that he believed in the ideals of his *Corps*. As soon as he was settled after World War II, he joined a club of *alte Herren*, old gentlemen, who had been fraternity members.

Fraternity life was much like military life. It had strict rules about everything from greeting a fellow member to defending one's honor. There were uniforms for special occasions and a billed cap with the fraternity colors on the band for everyday use. Belonging to a fraternity was a status symbol, and members regarded themselves as the ideal of German manhood. They made sure to educate new recruits—foxes, as they are called—in fortitude, self-control, and patriotic idealism. Although it involved much drinking, singing, and partying, the fraternity saw itself as a school to build character.

I imagine that above all, Api valued the comradeship of the *Corps*. He often talked to me about the beauty of friendship, and Schiller's "Die Bürgschaft," an ode to friendship, was one of his favorite poems. I will never forget the time when we listened together to a reading of it on the radio. I must have been ten years old. The poem is set in ancient Greece, where Damon is condemned to death for trying to assassinate Dionysius, the tyrant of Syracuse. His best friend willingly stands in for Damon, who has promised to relieve his friend, but all kinds of terrible obstacles loom in the way of Damon's return. Finally, people tell him to turn back. It is too late to save his friend; now, he can save only his own life. Damon ignores the advice. If he cannot save his friend, at least he will die with him. He arrives just as his friend, who never doubted Damon, is being strung up, and the two embrace in tears. The tyrant is so moved that he lets both of them go, asking only to be a third in their union.

During the reading, Api stood a little behind me, with his arm on my shoulder, and I remember how embarrassed I was when, toward the end, I noticed a single tear of his fall on the polished dark wood of the radio and glisten there for the rest of the recital.

In 1911, Api joined the regiment Freiherr Hiller von Gaertringen of the 4th Posen Regiment Nr. 59 to fulfill his military service requirement. It was stationed in Deutsch Eylau, an ancient town picturesquely situated on a peninsula of Lake Geserich. But I am sure the main attraction was that it was only thirty-one miles from his hometown. On May 27, 1913, Api passed his state medical examinations and was qualified as physician. He moved to the Deutsch Eylau garrison for his ten years of service. He was twenty-five years old.

# 6

# THE SHOT HEARD
# AROUND THE WORLD

No archives were necessary to tell me that on June 28, 1914, the shot heard around the world blew up Api's quiet existence. Every newspaper carried the screaming headline "Archduke Franz Ferdinand of Austria and His Wife Murdered by a Serb in Sarajevo." I suspect that Api, whose patriotism could only have been strengthened by his recent military education, was caught up in the euphoria that swept across Europe that summer. Even nonmilitary recluses, like the philosopher Ludwig Wittgenstein and the poet Rainer Maria Rilke, joined in the celebration. Looking back a few months later, Sigmund Freud wrote, "We saw war as an opportunity for demonstrating the progress of mankind in communal feeling . . . a chivalrous crusade."

Api accompanied the third battalion of his regiment as doctor. His first engagement—also the most spectacular of his military career—took place thirty miles south east of Marienwerder and only about eighteen miles from his headquarters in Deutsch Eylau. This was the Battle of Tannenberg, August 26–31, 1914, where, under the leadership of two Prussians (Paul von Hindenburg and his chief of staff, Erich Ludendorff), the Russian First and Second Armies were decimated.

In the archives, I found a two-page résumé Api had written after the war as part of his application for an assistantship at the Charité. It contained another revelation. Only three months into the war, Api had suffered a nervous breakdown. He explained that in October 1914, while at the Eastern Front, he contracted a severe case of dysentery, followed by nervous complications that developed into polyneuritis, paralyzing both his legs. Api was hospitalized in the nerve station at the Charité from October 1914 until January 1915, where just months before he had been a student. He was released in January 1915 but had to continue outpatient treatment until June. This news shocked me. To me, a child buffeted about until I lived with him, Api had always been a tower of strength and stability. But in the course of looking into his life, I came to regard him as a highly sensitive and vulnerable person. This breakdown also helped me to understand Api's anxiety in 1945, whether he would hold out under that terrible stress. By contrast, Nyussi, whom I had known only as a frail woman with severe rheumatoid arthritis, turned out to be the powerhouse in the family.

The full record of Api's service is listed in his *Wehrpass*, his military passport, issued under the Third Reich. It is a field-gray document with the German eagle clutching a swastika on the front, the same emblem embossed on each page. The *Wehrpass* lists all his engagements and recognitions during World War I. In July 1915, Api rejoined the third battalion. By then it had moved to Galicia, which the Russians had conquered. Now, combined German and Austro-Hungarian forces were pushing the Russians back again in a series of fierce skirmishes. Api served in a field hospital. Most of the wounded were maimed by trench mortars, grenades, and machine guns. In August 1915, Api was promoted to senior medical officer and moved to Division 101, Medical Company 101. He was stationed in Lugos on the Timis River, now Lugoj, in southeastern Hungary, and next was moved to various posts along the Macedonian front. In later life, Api occasionally thought back to places he had seen in the war, but he never spoke of the traumas that, as his breakdown shows, had deeply wounded him.

I was surprised to learn that even on active duty Api was able to continue work toward a doctor of medicine at Friedrich Wilhelm University. But I was told that this was not unusual at the time. In 1916, Api completed his dissertation, "A Case of Bridgekolobom of the Chloroida," with a grade of A. He had to go to Berlin for the oral examination, which he likewise passed with an A. On November 14, 1916, Api was promoted to doctor of medicine as an ophthalmologist. The following day, he took the vow "to fulfill conscientiously, loyally, and humanely the duties of my profession toward those who seek my help, as well as toward my colleagues."

Immediately after his promotion, Api was sent back to the front, first at the Greek border and then again in Macedonia. He earned the Iron Cross, both First and Second Class, for acts of bravery and leadership. The second-class medal was fairly common, awarded to about five and a half million soldiers during World War I. Only about 220,000, however, received the Iron Cross First Class. Pictures of Api in dress uniform show him proudly wearing both medals, the second-class medal on a ribbon among others on the left side of his chest, and the first-class medal pinned directly to his tunic below that. While in Greece, Api earned the Gallipoli Star, awarded by the Ottoman Empire for gallantry in battle. I found this medal in my mother's lockbox. In addition, he had been awarded the Iron Cross for frontline soldiers and the Order of Franz Joseph. The *Wehrpass* states also that he had a medal for wounded soldiers. It was black, which signifies a one- or two-time injury, which I assume was related to his breakdown in 1914.

In the summer of 1918, Api was on leave in northern Yugoslavia, which then belonged to Hungary and the Austro-Hungarian Empire. That stay changed his life when he visited Mezőhegyes, the largest imperial stables, and met his future wife, my grandmother Elizabeth Döhrmann. Her father, a colonel in an imperial and royal hussar regiment, was commander there. When I was with them in the 1950s, Api still fondly remembered their first meeting. He told me that he was immediately struck by her black eyes, by her slim figure, and most of all by her high spirits. Erzsi, as everyone called her, was almost as tall as he was. She wore her hair pinned in two rolls, "snails," on each side of her head. When she laughed, he noticed the little gap between her front teeth, which made her look charming and mischievous. The middle child between two brothers, she was well able to hold her own and loved to romp about and ride, but, Api said, he soon found out that she could stand up for herself also in conversation. She was witty and highly educated, fluent in German and French, and she played the piano. Api loved music and was quite competent on the violin. So, he thought, in every way, they would make a perfect duo.

For Nyussi, too, it was love at first sight. She was taken by the tall young man with the fine nose, the little mustache over rather thin lips, and the deepest blue eyes she had ever seen. His dark blond hair was shaved close to his head. And although he may have looked like a stiff Prussian officer, she soon realized that he was a romantic at heart who wrote poems to her.

The end of the war brought a collapse of the old order and of Henrik's world. He lost both his position and his title. Luckily, his wife, Alice, owned an estate around Nagykörös, forty miles southeast of Budapest. Although they had just lost a fortune in war bonds, the Farago family was still able to live comfortably on the lease income from their land. Pictures show her as a small, rotund person with a friendly smile. But her husband never adjusted to civilian life or to the easygoing ways on the Farago estate. I have several pictures of him from before and after that cataclysmic change. As commander, he looks into the camera with confidence, wearing the richly braided uniform of the hussars, with three stars on the choke collar, and sporting a magnificent mustache turned up at the ends. In photos from the 1920s, Henrik still has his straight military bearing but now wears civilian dress, three-piece suits with high, stiff white collars. His mustache is much smaller, and he never smiles. My mother remembered him as a stern and taciturn presence in the house. But when I consulted Dr. Georg Kugler, research director at the Lippizaner Museum in Vienna, I learned that Henrik Döhrmann had been a well-known hippologist, author of hundreds of articles on horse breeding as well as a book that had been translated into French and German. I now have that book, in addition to a painting of one of Henrik's favorite horses.

After the end of the war, Api was back in his regiment in Deutsch Eylau, and in August 1919 he was released from further military duty, having served nearly six of his stipulated ten years. Api immediately returned to Marienwerder to obtain a passport to Hungary and Erzsi.

This passport, a small, dull-brown document with the German eagle embossed on its front, is something of a historic oddity. The top of the right inside page bears the inscription "German Empire" and beneath it "Kingdom of Prussia." By 1919, however, both had ceased to exist. But then the passport was valid only for a return trip from Marienwerder to Nagykörös via Passau between August 20 and October 27, 1919. The passport is a testimony to the chaos that reigned in West Prussia after the war. The Treaty of Versailles had ceded much of the former West Prussia to Poland. Only the city of Danzig was declared a free city. Its port, however, was Polish, so that Poland could have access to the Baltic Sea. To complicate matters further, some districts, like that of Pomesania, which included Marienwerder, were ruled by an interallied commission until a plebiscite was to decide whether it would become Polish or stay German. In the interim, there was much Polish and German agitation and guerilla fighting. Finally, on July 11, 1920, the plebiscite went over-whelmingly for Marienwerder to stay German and become part of East Prussia. However, a strip of land on the east side of the Weichsel/ Vistula River near Marienwerder became Polish, so that Poland could maintain the sovereignty over the river that Versailles had accorded it. The town thus became a Protestant German community marooned in the new Polish republic.

The picture on the inside front cover of the passport shows Api in civilian dress in a double-breasted suit that looks too big for him, adorned with a white kerchief in his left pocket. He wears a homburg hat and still sports his thin mustache. He looks at the camera with a serious, somewhat diffident expression fitting for someone with a passport from a vanished kingdom.

*Nyussi (second from left) and family, Hungary, 1917*

*Passport from a vanished kingdom, 1919*

# 7

# TRACK 17

My grandparents were married on September 29, 1919, in Nagykörös when Api was thirty-one and Erzsi, twenty-five. Their wedding announcement said that Dr. med Herbert Frese was a retired medical officer and an assistant at the Charité. Now that he had a wife to support, Api was eager to put behind him the war experience that had brought him close to collapse. I do not know how well he succeeded in overcoming the traumas—it was not something that our family talked about—but his 1945 diary shows how much he relied on my grandmother for emotional support and how lost he was without her. However, he was also determined to succeed. Falling back on his childhood lessons of thrift and hard work, Api set out to make a civilian life for himself and support his wife in the manner to which she was accustomed.

It was an inauspicious time to build the foundation of a new life. Although still one of Europe's foremost clinical centers, Berlin was a violent and chaotic place. The Weimar Republic under the first German president, Friedrich Ebert, was powerless to prevail against the many warring political parties and deal with extremists on both the right and the left. Germany had lost two million people in the war, and four hundred million were wounded. Much of the country felt betrayed by the conditions of the Versailles peace treaty, which stipulated a loss of 14 percent of Germany's territory and crippling reparations and attributed to Germany sole responsibility for the war. Unemployment and inflation further fueled the fires of unrest. The result was political and social chaos, including almost daily reports of street shootings, assassinations, and other outbreaks of violence. Infamous were the 1919 assassinations of Rosa Luxemburg and Karl Liebknecht, founders of the radical socialist Spartacus League, and that of foreign minister Walther Rathenau in 1922. In March 1920, *Freikorps*, radical veterans' groups, took over the government in the so-called Kapp Putsch. The Ebert cabinet fled to Weimar, but before leaving, they called a general strike that turned Berlin into a ghost town. The insurrection lasted not even a week. However, the anger and despair of the population was not so easily put down.

Api did not join any of the *Freikorps*, but he did become a member of the Stahlhelm, literally Steel Helmet, which had replaced the pickle helmet in World War I. This was another surprise turn in my journey to find out more about his life. But as I learned about the organization, I could see why Api was attracted to it. Founded in 1918, the Stahlhelm called itself the League for Frontline Soldiers. It was a conservative organization but opposed to any form of political radicalism and violence. Its initial protocol asked to continue "the spirit of loyal comradeship practiced on the battlefield, and give mutual support regardless of social and class differences or party loyalties." In 1925, the Stahlhelm campaigned for Hindenburg, of Tannenberg fame, helping him get elected as Germany's second president. As to what party Api voted for, I can only guess that it may have been the Deutschnationale Volkspartei, the German National People's Party, led by Alfred Hugenberg. Its platform included a return to Christian and family values, and it appealed to the civil service and military establishments. Richard Evans calls it "the quintessential Protestant Party," which would be further reason for Api's joining.

My grandparents found an apartment on the ground floor of a villa in the leafy suburb of Dahlem, about three miles southwest of the Brandenburg Gate. I had often heard them talk nostalgically about their "Dahlem apartment" and its beautiful surroundings of woods and lakes, but I could not picture it. So I was excited when Mike and I boarded a double-decker bus that took us to Dahlem. To have the best view, we climbed to the top, and I noticed that in Dahlem we went down Koenigsallee, where, eighty-five years earlier, Walther Rathenau had been assassinated by a right-wing anti-Semitic *Freikorps* group.

The bus let us off at the top of Fontanestrasse, and we walked past large villas set among huge beeches, sycamores, and oaks. I wondered whether any of them had been around when my grandparents lived here. Their house at Fontanestrasse 14 was a handsome villa of white painted stucco with a red tile roof. It was flanked by a spectacular red beech on one side and a chestnut on the other. The dense hedge and iron fence made it hard to see much of the ground floor where my grandparents had lived, but it looked quiet, spacious, and comfortable. Api must have loved the view of the trees.

A short walk to the end of the street brought us to a little station. It looked picturesque and peaceful. Its swooping red roof with a pointed clock tower in the middle and an arched entryway seemed modeled on a castle gate. We walked through the gate into a long tunnel, from which stairs led up to the various tracks of the S-Bahn. Mike spotted a sign that said To TRACK 17. He ran up the stairs two at a time, and I had trouble catching up with him. At the top, we found ourselves alone in a place surrounded by overgrown saplings and even trees. It was completely and eerily quiet. Obviously, no trains left from here anymore. Puzzled, we moved along the platform. Then we noticed that something was written at its edge. It was a date, a number, and a destination. Going farther, we found many more such inscriptions etched in cast steel. And then it hit us like a punch to the gut: These were the dates, the concentration camp destinations, and the number of deportees that had left from that track between October 1941 and February 1943. On some of the spots, visitors had left flowers, stones, and even little notes.

Mike and I remained there a long time, absorbing the still atmosphere, so different from the terror of sixty-five years earlier, when old men and small children, pregnant women, and wealthy businesspeople, all Germans like the rest of us, had been crowded together in cattle cars and shipped off to die. Standing on that empty platform, I was all of a sudden ambushed by the perhaps fanciful notion that this haunting track before us led to my past in a way I could not have imagined when I eagerly set out for Dahlem earlier that day. It struck me as providential that it was number 17, since 17 is the day of my birth and 1942 fits right in the middle of the dates of deportation.

To my relief, no train had left from there on October 17, 1942. Although I recognize this reaction as selfish and sentimental, I still was relieved that my birth date was not etched into the station platform, with its gruesome news. I thought of all the trains that had been a defining part of my childhood. My earliest memory is of the crowded and noisy platform at Lehrter station in Berlin when we were fleeing the city. When I was six, there was the straw-covered wagon of a Kindertransport. Trains continued to feature prominently in my life, going to and from boarding school, traveling to stay with relatives. The happiest train rides were those daily ones from Bevensen, the small town where I lived with Api and Nyussi, to Lüneburg, where I attended the first years of the gymnasium. They made me feel grown-up and adventurous. Then there were all those melancholy train rides into the late afternoon when I was reluctantly leaving Nyussi to return to boarding school on the Baltic Sea. I do not, of course, think that my experience in any way compares to that of the people on Track 17. My trains may have brought me to loneliness and cold, but they also led to life. Track 17 led only to a terrifying death. Still, in my mind, that track of the Dahlem station, so near to where my grandparents had once lived, became a link to me, my past, and my German guilt.

Leaving the station, we noticed a plaque to the left of the building partially hidden by trees. We read, In memory of the more than 50,000 Jewish citizens of Berlin who, between October 1941 and February 1943, were deported from here by the National Socialist state to its death camps and were murdered there.

After Track 17, it was hard to bring my mind back to the early 1920s, when my grandparents had lived in Dahlem. At that time, even the brutal killing of Walther Rathenau, just about on their doorstep, cannot have given them any idea of the murders that were to be perpetrated starting from their pretty station. I imagine that Api's mind was preoccupied with the dire economic situation and worry about how to feed his growing family. My mother was born in 1920 and my uncle in 1923. It was a time of galloping inflation, when at its peak a loaf of bread cost 100 trillion marks. Such gargantuan inflation created not only economic but social chaos. Raimund Pretzel, a young journalist in Berlin at the time—after his emigration to England, he adopted the name Sebastian Haffner—noted, "No other nation has experienced anything comparable to the events of 1923 in Germany. . . . None but Germany . . . has experienced the gigantic carnival dance of death, the unending, bloody Saturnalia, in which not only money but all standards lost their value." Age and experience counted for nothing, and adventurous young people could grow wealthy one night and lose it all the next day. People who had saved lost everything, and those who had debts did well. Historians acknowledge that this went far beyond a monetary crisis. In his portrait of Berlin in the 1920s, Otto Friedrich finds that "the fundamental quality of the disaster was a complete loss of faith in the functioning of society." In November 1923, the mark finally stabilized at one new reichsmark equal to one trillion former marks.

# 8

# BETTER TIMES

In the brief respite of the "golden '20s," Germany's economic situation improved dramatically. This was true also for Api. In the mid-'20s, the family left Dahlem for Berlin Mitte. Their new apartment, in which they were to remain until 1945, was at Luisenstrasse 41, directly across from the Charité, in the heart of Berlin's medical district. From their balcony they could see the cupola of the Reichstag. Luisenstrasse is the continuation across the Spree River of Wilhelmstrasse, Berlin's Whitehall or Pennsylvania Avenue. Karl Marx lived on Luisenstrasse when he was a student, as did my favorite Prussian novelist, Theodor Fontane, behind whose novel *Effi Briest* I had found Api's diaries.

I knew that the move to Luisenstrasse turned out well for Api's career, but I was to make another disturbing discovery about his relationship with the Charité and his boss there, Privy Counselor Greeff, director of the university eye clinic. The sun was already low in the sky and I was just about finished with those three large volumes of documents when Frau Kalb, the archivist, rushed into the quiet room, visibly excited. She handed me a slim booklet with "Dr. med Herbert Frese" handwritten on the mottled gray binding and whispered, "I just found this. Look, it's not even been cataloged yet! You are the first to read it."

My joy at this find soon turned to shock. The booklet contained correspondence between Api and Dr. Greeff concerning Api's dismissal from the Charité, effective September 30, 1924. I did not understand. All I had ever heard was that our family was proud of Api's connection to that illustrious institution. I carefully read Dr. Greeff's letter, in which he said that Api was let go because he had set up his own practice while still employed at the Charité and had done so "right in front of our gates." In much longer responses, Api vigorously defended his action. He claimed that the director had expressly permitted, even advised, him to start a private practice so that he would not be penniless when his term as assistant ran out. It was commonly allowed, he argued, for longtime assistants to start a practice before their term was up so that they had a chance to get established. He added that the first assistant had done just that and no one had objected. So when the opportunity for a practice came up, Api jumped at it, even though Dr. Greeff happened to be on vacation. He vehemently rejected that he was acting secretly. All his colleagues knew about it. Furthermore, one could hardly speak of secrecy when he had put up a sign where people from the Charité passed by every day. Api added that his office hours never conflicted with his duties at the Charité. Dr. Greeff grudgingly admitted that Api had mentioned something about starting a practice, but said he assumed that Api had been talking about some point in the future and that he would not choose Luisenstrasse, right next to the Charité, as his place of operation. This back-and-forth continued until May 1925. It may have been fueled by malice on the part of Dr. Greeff's first assistant, who kept accusations alive and may well have been at the heart of the controversy.

On the long S-Bahn ride back into Berlin, I remained uncertain whether Api had merely upset some people or committed a grave offense. I remembered how often my mother had talked with pride about her father's association with the Charité. During a sleepless night at the hotel, I continued to ponder what I had read. Api clearly felt treated unjustly, but his arguments could not sway his boss. I considered also that in 1924 Api was already thirty-six years old, with two small children, and must have felt an urgency to strike out on his own, especially since the Charité job was about to end anyway.

The university archives had been useful, if disconcerting, but that, I thought, was almost inevitable when one unearthed one's family's past. Back in South Bend, I was eager to write up my findings and certain that we would have to return to retrace more of Api's steps, no matter what other surprises that might bring.

In the meantime, I sorted through more family pictures. Shortly before she died, my mother had put together an album in which she also noted dates and people in her forceful and legible handwriting. Together with stories I remembered, this would, I hoped, help me to round out a picture of Api's life in the 1920s.

Just as they had done on Fontanestrasse, from which I have a couple of rather dark pictures and one standing lamp that made it through everything to end up with me in South Bend, my grandparents furnished the new apartment with large and comfortable leather sofas and chairs, fringed lampshades, old-fashioned desks, and tables with lacy coverings and long fringes. The parquet floors were decked out in colorful Oriental rugs. Two French doors with windows at the top opened from the library into the dining room. It looked cozy, if a little heavy and *altväterisch*, in the style of our fathers. But the sun streamed in the tall windows to spread light.

I studied the photos more closely to look at the dark floral wallpaper and the pictures in ornate gilt frames. I still have two of Api's favorite oils, painted by the contemporary Berlin artist Adolf Hinzpeter. I do not know how the two large paintings made it out of destroyed Berlin, but they have always been part of my life, first in my grandparents' home and later in my mother's. The larger one shows the Chiemsee, south of Munich, a quiet scene of water, sky, and reeds, with the Alps hazily in the background. The other depicts a mountain path dominated by tall firs. Whenever Api was at his lowest, this painting of dark green trees with pale blue mountains in the background reminded him of the many walking tours he and Nyussi had taken in "better times."

Api's reputation grew in the 1920s, and with it, his practice. He conducted surgeries at various hospitals and wrote articles in medical journals. He also maintained his connection with the nearby university eye clinic, which was part of the Charité. He must have established a good reputation, since in June 1945 the clinic's professor Walther Löhlein invited Api to assist in his first postwar lectures.

Api worked hard, almost without rest. Nyussi took the children on vacation, mostly to Hungary but also to famous spas like Karlsbad in western Bohemia and Bad Elster in Saxony. Api joined them for a few days, but only when he could find a substitute for his practice. He did, however, take time off each afternoon to have coffee with my grandmother, preferably on the balcony, even when it was chilly. He continued this little break when I was with them, appearing in his white doctor's coat, laughing and looking forward to his cigar. On weekends, he made time for a picnic. I remember the glee with which he planned these weekly outings for Nyussi and me when he was already in his sixties and can imagine with what bustle and excitement they all set out, well prepared with sandwiches and looking forward to their ride in the Buick and an afternoon in the woods and lakes around Berlin. Api, no doubt, was singing and joking with the children, and Nyussi was watching the road, a little intimidated by the power and speed of the big car. In one of the pictures, taken in the summer of 1926, Api stands in a clearing in the woods, perhaps the Grunewald, dressed in knickerbockers and cardigan, his favorite leisure-time outfit. Leaning on a walking stick, he stands close behind Nyussi, who sits in the grass, wearing a light blouse with a little dark bow tie. In the top left corner of the picture is the first Buick with the Buick ornament on the still-rather-small hood. My mother stands on the running board, dressed, it seems, all in white, while my uncle Dieter leans nonchalantly against the car.

Next to picnics, most of the pictures are of family parties, especially New Year's Eve parties, since everyone is dressed up in costumes. In one of them, Api postures as a pirate, and in another, as a Turkish pasha. Nyussi looks fetching dressed as a man about town, her dark hair stuffed under a cap, yet with high-heeled T-strap shoes peeking from beneath her suit. There are about a dozen people crowded around a table laden with glasses and wine bottles and the special jam-filled doughnuts that are part of any Berlin New Year's celebration. The candles are lit on the tree, which glitters with tinsel. My mother, who is about seven, wears a pointed cap, and my uncle Dieter, at the age of four, has a small pickle helmet on his head. I recognize Ohchen front and center, not in costume, and Api's brother, Werner, to one side, with pipe and little round glasses. Nyussi is holding Api's hand, and Api, who has obviously just set the timer, looks expectantly at the camera.

Seeing his expression triggered my memories of Api setting up a tripod in the woods when we were out together. After he had carefully adjusted everything and we were arranged to his liking, he pushed the timer, which was on a short flexible cord. He called this a *Schnippedolderich*, a nonsense word that he either had invented or perhaps remembered from his boyhood, for he worked the apparatus with childish delight. Then he rushed or jumped to join us and looked at the camera with just the expression of gleeful expectancy that I saw in that New Year's Eve picture.

Letters from my mother's lockbox add information the pictures alone cannot convey. Whenever Nyussi was away, Api wrote to her every day. I am curious but will never know whether the handful of letters I now have were saved especially by my grandmother, or whether they survived by chance and somehow made it out of burning Berlin and the many moves that followed. In none of them did Api say anything about the current political battles, although the 1920s were a turbulent time. Instead, he summed up Sunday's sermon or a recent book. He talked about his patients, what operations he had performed, how he cared for complicated cases, and how much money he had made. In the summer of 1927, he mentioned that in one week he had earned 320 and in another 450 reichsmark. The following summer, he said that he had made 100 and 133 reichsmark in two weeks, even without performing any operations. Statistics show that physicians' gross income at that time was 13,741 reichsmark per year, and it seems that Api was somewhat above that. It was a considerable amount of money. A secretary could expect to earn no more than 30–50 reichsmark per week. Evans has a different scale for the 1930s, saying that a doctor's average gross earnings were 9,000 reichsmark for 1933 and nearly 14,000 in 1937.

Api was proud of the comfortable life he could offer his family, but he also tended to be thrifty to a fault. He was *knauserig*, penny-pinching, as they often teased him. One of the letters to Hungary offers an amusing example of this trait. On the occasion of my mother's birthday on July 24, Api could not stop himself from writing to his wife, "I enclose 20 marks in case you want to buy something for her (but nothing silly)—I am sorry, kiss—I mean nothing that's superfluous." He knew Nyussi was not a spendthrift and that there was no point in saying this, and yet he still had to voice it. I can see Nyussi smiling as she read this all-too-familiar admonition.

Despite his growing wealth, Api lived simply, his Buicks of course excepted. He enjoyed the country meals of his West Prussian childhood. When I was with him, he still loved *Schustertunke*, cobbler's dip, brown sauce over potatoes. In summer we had fruit soups, which

I loved. There were, however, two meals of his I hated with a passion: beer soup and chopped lung. I remember sitting, long after everyone had finished, over what I thought was an evil-smelling mess. Api, who didn't allow us to waste food, insisted I eat it up, although in the end he took pity on me and, to my infinite relief, the plate was removed. But Api also was in charge of many of my favorite treats. He brewed the egg liqueur at Christmas and made marzipan tarts, which he decorated with tiny flowers. In summer he made what we called "sour milk," possible only before pasteurization. On warm days, which did not come that often in northern Germany, he set out a large earthen bowl filled to the brim with rich, fatty milk. He carefully checked each day until the milk was thoroughly thickened, much like yogurt today.

Apart from the car, the chief luxuries in their life were opera and theater. All four of them regularly went to the opera on Unter den Linden and to the Deutsches Theater on Schumannstrasse, around the corner from their apartment, where they saw the productions of the illustrious director Max Reinhardt. My mother liked to talk about going to the Deutsches Theater as a girl. She remembered the fantastic world Reinhardt created in such grand style. Especially popular was his presentation of *A Midsummer Night's Dream*, which conjured up a fairy-tale world far removed from the everyday. Reinhardt's spectacles appealed to all the senses, a fantasy of color, music, and movement. Reinhardt, who was Jewish, fled Germany in 1933.

Since my field was modern drama, I wished I could have seen some of these famous productions. In 1986, I spent a semester as a faculty visitor at the Max Reinhardt Seminar, the academy for acting and music that Reinhardt founded in Vienna. It is located just a few buildings down from our Vienna apartment. Reinhardt is still a formidable presence there, and professors discuss his productions with their students. Walking the halls or enjoying the rather wild garden with a view of Schönbrunn Castle, the summer residence of the Habsburgs, I often thought about my mother and grandparents, who had actually witnessed Reinhardt's work.

One picture I found shows Api and Nyussi just before setting out for a party or performance. He is wearing a smoking jacket, and she is in a straight and lacy flapper dress with an orchid pinned at her shoulder and a long necklace. I recognize the pendant. Nyussi never went out without this favorite piece of jewelry, which was passed down in her family for centuries and now has come down to me: a ruby snake coiled around an emerald, with emerald and ruby drops hanging from its mouth and tail. Nyussi's hair is parted in the middle and swept back into a knot at the nape of her neck, much like her mother wore hers. I have seen only one picture in which Nyussi's hair was cut short, as was the fashion. But when an even shorter cut became popular, the "man's cut," she let her hair grow long again.

Nyussi wore slouch hats and low-waisted, slim-line dresses that fell to just below the knee and Api proudly drove his Buick, but at heart they both remained traditional and conservative, true to their small-town upbringing. It seems to me that they created an island of Wilhelmine order and values in the midst of political turmoil and the amoral trendiness of avant garde Berlin. It was as if they did not want to accept that 1918 had marked the end of an epoch, that the world was changing with the speed of the new airline traffic, and that they, too, were part of this turbulence.

Stefan Zweig recognized that the glitter of Berlin was covering something more troubling. He saw beyond the wild gaiety and seemingly limitless freedom to a rather desperate desire for order and stability. In *The World of Yesterday*, Zweig calls Berlin "the Babylon of the world." He describes scenes he saw daily: "Along the entire Kurfürstendamm powdered and rouged young men sauntered and they were not all professionals; every high school student wanted to earn some money and in the dimly lit bars one might see government officials and men of finance tenderly courting drunken soldiers without shame. Even the Rome of Suetonius had never known such orgies as the pervert balls of Berlin." But Zweig concludes that this orgiastic world was just a disguise beneath which "the whole nation, tired of war, actually longed only for order, quiet, a little security, and a bourgeois life."

# 9

# MAY DAY, MAY DAY, MAY DAY

Order of sorts did come, but not in any way Zweig or my grandparents could have foreseen, even in their worst nightmares.

In 1929, the world was steeped in an economic crisis, followed by widespread unemployment. By 1932, Germany had 6.1 million unemployed, which amounted to more than 40 percent of the workforce. Banks collapsed, and the stock market had to be closed for more than a month. The newly democratic constitutional system of the Weimar Republic was under increasing strains, and the president felt forced to rely ever more on his emergency powers.

With manifold promises to establish peace and prosperity, Adolf Hitler came to power on this wave of disorder and discontent, but he also played on German longings for national unity and fear of communism. Hitler never forgot the euphoria of the summer of 1914, the delirious wave of patriotism and national pride that he longed to re-create in his day. In 1932, the Nazi Party no longer attracted only radical youth but became legitimized in traditional circles, especially among older voters like Api. They were persuaded by Hitler's assurances, such as those he made in his speech of February 1, 1933, where he outlined his Four-Year Plan. He promised to replace "turbulent instincts" with "national discipline," to cherish "Christianity as foundation for all our morality, and the family as germ cell of our people and our state."

At the opening of the Reichstag on March 21, 1933 in Potsdam Hitler was inaugurated as chancellor. In his speech he promised to restore both order and national pride under the auspices of Prussian values. Api may well have listened to the ceremony, since it was broadcast in full over the radio. The cheers from the crowd around the Brandenburg Gate must have drifted up to him in nearby Luisenstrasse. Hitler, for once dressed soberly in black tails, bowed his head, both literally and figuratively, to Field Marshal Hindenburg, saying that this day demonstrated "the marriage between the symbol of old greatness and young strength." Evans notes that the event was held at the Garrison Church, "in order to underline the symbiosis of Protestant religion and Prussian tradition."

Somewhere, Api got a commemorative postcard of this so-called Day of Potsdam, and it has survived in my mother's lockbox. The card shows the Garrison Church he so loved. It had the Prussian eagle on the tower and the tomb of Frederick the Great under the cupola. At the bottom of the card are the profiles of Hindenburg and Hitler, as if on a coin. The main color effect comes from two flags draped around the two heads and wafting up to the church: the black, white, and red flag of the empire, and the swastika in the same colors. The black, red, and gold flag of the Weimar Republic, which goes back to the revolution of 1848, is nowhere to be seen.

Api joined the NSDAP on May 1, 1933, only six weeks after Hitler had become chancellor. Many Germans from the social and professional elite became members that day, among them the industrialist Fritz Thyssen and the philosopher Martin Heidegger. After 1933 there was a steady decline in membership from that group, but in 1933 the National Socialists were not regarded as an extremist party.

I will never know for certain what motivated Api to join the

Nazi Party, a decision that was to haunt him and that now keeps me awake at night. I come back to this fateful step again and again. Hindenburg's decision to appoint Hitler as chancellor must have been a major factor for Api. The field marshal was probably one of Api's heroes, even though at that time he was in both mental and physical decline. And after the Day of Potsdam, Api may well have believed that Hitler would usher in a new era of German unity and welfare. Like everyone else, as Zweig had recognized, Api longed for order and a sense of normalcy. In addition, Alfred Hugenberg, leader of the conservative German National People's Party—which may have been the party Api voted for—became part of Hitler's first cabinet. That alone might have inclined Api to join, although just a month later Hugenberg's party was forced to dissolve itself. Or perhaps Api saw it chiefly as a matter of professional necessity, for the pressures the Nazis exerted were both powerful and subtle, and physicians were the largest professional group to join the Party. Like Api, many doctors who did so had participated in World War I. Many also were members of the Stahlhelm, which, too, the Nazi Party took over. One reason to suspect that professional considerations, rather than personal conviction, were instrumental in Api's decision is that Nyussi never did become a member of the NSDAP.

Once in charge, Hitler wasted no time in weaving Nazi ideology into the fabric of everyday life—*Gleichschaltung*, the Nazis called it, literally putting everything on the same electrical circuit, a totalitarian coordination of every aspect of German life. Previous professional associations were disbanded, and Nazi versions took their place. Loyal Nazis replaced professors, lawyers, and judges, and opponents were held, tortured, and often killed in the first secret concentration camps in Berlin. In June 1935, the government altered the penal code, which meant the dissolution of law in Germany. No aspect of German life escaped Nazi surveillance and control. There was to be no distinction between public and private life. Individuals were important only insofar as they contributed to the national good. Children were brought up with Nazi ideology in schools and trained in the Hitler Youth. Nazi holidays replaced Christian ones so that the year was structured around the Day of National Solidarity; the Day of the Führer; the Day of the Worker, the Farmer, the German Mother. To help the war effort, Hitler instituted enforced charities like Winter Help and *Eintopfsonntag*, the simple stew to replace the Sunday roast. Nazi officials, from the Gestapo down to the block warden, made sure everyone participated. International newspapers were forbidden, and the minimum penalty for listening to the BBC on the radio was twenty-five years in jail.

I know little of Api's life between 1933 and 1945. It is one of those subjects about which not much was said. I imagine, however, that, apolitical as he was, he withdrew even further into private life. Historians found this to be true of many Germans. But, I wonder, how far could that have been possible? Already on June 30, 1934, during the Night of the Long Knives, a wave of violence swept through Berlin and other cities. Ostensibly directed against the SA, execution squads made up of the Gestapo, together with the black-shirted SS—the *Schutzstaffel*, a Nazi military organization under Himmler—hunted down and murdered everyone on the Reich's list of unwanted persons, including former chancellor Kurt von Schleicher. Afterward, there were daily reminders of Nazi atrocities against Jews and other minorities. But I do not know how my grandparents reacted to any of it. Then, however, the world did not take notice, either. "Notoriously, a joint 'Statement on Atrocities' issued by Churchill, Roosevelt, and Stalin in October 1943 did not even mention [the fate of the Jews]," as Ruth Franklin notes.

Almost one-third of the physicians disappeared from the Charité, and the world-famous professor Ferdinand Sauerbruch, who was in charge, played an equivocal role. He condemned the persecution of the Jews that affected him so painfully among his colleagues, but at the same time he participated in a letter "to the physicians of the world," saying that German doctors and scientists supported the NSDAP. Then again, he publicly protested the euthanasia and eugenics teaching at his institution. At one point, he even speculated that Hitler might become "the most insane criminal in the world." Yet he accepted Nazi honors. At the Nuremberg doctors' trial, eight physicians from the Charité were found guilty.

Although I have many photos of the 1920s and before, I found only a few from the 1930s, and none of parties and picnics. The only one with Berlin in the background shows my grandmother, mother, and uncle walking along Unter den Linden in 1936, the year of the Olympiad. The avenue looks bare. The beautiful linden trees are all gone, replaced by poles with huge swastikas.

Then, on the night of November 9–10, 1938—exactly fifteen years after Hitler's failed Beer Hall Putsch in Munich—erupted the horror of Kristallnacht, the Nazi pogrom during which Jews were arrested, their businesses and places of worship set on fire. Api must have had firsthand experience on the streets of central Berlin. One of the targets was the beautiful redbrick synagogue near St. Hedwig Hospital, where Api did surgeries. It was a ten-minute walk from his home.

The fateful year 1939 began with the inauguration of the New Reich Chancellery, designed by Hitler's chief architect, Albert Speer. Built in the *Einschüchterungsarchitektur*, the "architecture of intimidation" that the Nazis favored, it had frontage on the north side of Voss Strasse that was a quarter mile long. Four square stone columns towered at the entrance, and above them loomed an eagle in half relief. Inside, the Marble Gallery stretched 480 feet, twice the length of the Hall of Mirrors in Versailles. Twenty-five feet of steel and concrete below was the elaborate bunker system where Hitler committed suicide in 1945. After the war, the Russians demolished the badly damaged building. Today, there is nothing but a patch of grass where the bunker was, with a simple sign—nothing to commemorate and turn into a shrine for neo-Nazis.

On September 1, 1939, Nazi Germany invaded Poland, and three days later Great Britain and France declared war on Germany. Joseph Goebbels tried to inspire "a mobilization of the mind and spirit in Germany," as in 1914, but, as journalist William Shirer notes, this time there was "no excitement, no hurrahs, no cheering." Nevertheless, many Germans believed that Poland, not Germany, was the aggressor and were angry at Britain and France for declaring war.

According to his *Wehrpass*, Api had already been called up as reservist medical officer in Berlin on July 20, 1939. He was fifty-one years old. He was assigned to hospitals but could live at home. Despite blackouts and ration cards, life in the city continued almost unchanged. "You may call me *Meier*"—a colloquialism that means "stupid"—famously boasted Hermann Göring, "if one single enemy plane ever enters German airspace."

*Memorial postcard, 1933*

# 10

# WEDDING BELLS

My mother attended the Staatliche Augusta Schule in Berlin Schöneberg, a humanist gymnasium much like Api's, where they started with Greek and Latin and later added French and English. "There was no room for Nazi ideology," one of my mother's classmates reminisced when I contacted her in 2005. "Even our art room was decorated until the end with the forbidden *entartete*, degenerate, impressionists." In school photos I could always spot my mother because she was dressed most fashionably, with little ankle boots and jaunty hats, her hair cut short—no Germanic costumes or braids for her. Her best friends were the international "triumvirate," as they liked to call themselves, made up of her, a classmate from Italy, and her best friend, who was Greek. Writing about growing up in Nazi Berlin, Peter Fröhlich, now Peter Gay, a Jewish boy, also said that he experienced no bigotry in his school.

However, when I was looking at school pictures with my mother shortly before her death, her veined hand pointed to a fellow student and she said, "One day, she was not there anymore." She had never mentioned anything like that before, but I did not dare question her, knowing how agitated she became when I brought up the past.

As Api had learned from his father, so he taught his children to put work before play. He also instilled in them a love of literature and music and an appreciation of classical learning. In all of this, he was more successful with my mother than with my always easy-going, playful, and lighthearted uncle Dieter. It was schooling that stayed with her all her life. Until her death at age eighty-four, she read voluminously in French, German, English, and Hungarian. After her death, I found a copy of Jacques Lacan in the original French on her bedside table.

After my mother graduated in 1939, she had to fulfill her work-force requirement. Her fluent Hungarian got her a job as secretary in the Hungarian section of the foreign office. Then, in the spring of 1940, she met my father, Kurt Hevler, at a *Tanztee*. Tea dances were popular with young people, although the Nazis denounced them as un-German. They decried the swing and jazz played there as "Jewish vagabondism," and the entire ritual of a five o'clock tea as British. Good Germans had coffee and cakes at four in the afternoon, as did Hitler himself with great regularity in his favorite hotel, the Kaiserhof.

Kurt, the son of a general in the Austrian army, had joined the air force, which the German Luftwaffe took over after Austria's annexation in 1938. No doubt the pressures of war accelerated and intensified their courtship. Perhaps my mother thought of her parents, who also fell in love during war and did not wait long to decide on marriage.

My parents got married on September 29, 1941, the day of my grandparents' wedding in 1919. I have a whole album dedicated to wedding pictures. The dinner, for sixteen family and friends, took place at the fashionable Hotel Esplanade near the Tiergarten. The table was decorated with flowers, and there were three glasses—for champagne, red wine, and white wine—in front of each guest. My mother wore a long dress of white lace with a gauzy veil in her dark hair that trailed to the floor from a tiara-like headdress. The groom was in his air force uniform. On his right breast was the silver Luftwaffe eagle, and on his left the Front Flying clasp and the Iron Cross, with the fighter pilot's badge below it: an eagle holding a swastika in its claws, its wings spread out over the edges of the oak-leaf wreath. From the black-and-white photos I cannot tell whether the wreath is bronze, silver, or gold—that depends on how well he did in pilots' training. Api wore his tailcoat and white tie, which my mother thought suited him so well. It was to be the last time in his life that he appeared in this finery. Nyussi had a high-necked, dark silk dress decorated with her favorite pendant.

Kurt's Viennese parents, Maximilian and Thea Hevler, came to Berlin for the occasion. Maximilian was a small and thin man with deeply etched features and dark eyes that looked huge behind his thick lenses. At the end of his career, he was a general in charge of supplies; I have several of his articles about this job. But I think his heart was always back in Kalinovik, in the Zagorje, south of Sarajevo, where, as a young lieutenant, he was stationed for four years. He loved to talk about how he roamed that wild area, fitted out with a dagger, a revolver, and a pickax. He also carried a shotgun he called a triplet, explaining to his little granddaughter that it had one rifle barrel and two shotgun barrels. I still have his silver dagger from that time. It has a decorated sheath that I dare not remove because the blade is so very sharp and pointed. He once sent me a sketch of the area and included the lines he had written in what he called a memory book of Kalinovik, dated 1907, the year of his departure: "Bare, melancholy Zagorje. For four years my tired feet staggered in the endless gray of barren rock. And yet, when I have sweet dreams, I want to dream of you, sunny Kalinovik."

His wife, Thea, a concert pianist, cut an imposing figure at his side. Taller and more corpulent than her Mackl, as she called him, with bright blue eyes and a halo of white hair, she looked more martial than her husband. When she was young, she not only appeared in concerts but founded music courses for women. After the war, she supported the family with music and language lessons.

Although marriage between a Prussian and an Austrian seemed like a union of opposites, the two families had a lot in common. Maximilian and Api both had been stationed and wounded in the Balkans during World War I, and Nyussi, of course, had grown up in the Austro-Hungarian Empire, in which her father was a colonel. Both men also had married above their class. Maximilian's wife came from a wealthy industrialist family in Prague, the Stiasnys, who, however, had lost everything at the end of World War I. My paternal grandmother may have been Jewish, which may have led her husband to lose his position after the annexation. I was told that eventually he was reduced to selling leather straps from door to door. My grandmother's Jewish origins were another discovery on my journey, although I have not been able to verify this. My mother denied it. Yet when I was looking up their Vienna apartment, an old neighbor of theirs told me, "in secret," "Thea was Jewish. No one was supposed to know, but we did. That's why Herr General lost his job."

The wedding was the last big family celebration, during which everyone tried to cling to the hope of a better future. In 1941, there had been a lull in the bombing of Berlin, yet "there was a scent of disaster in the air, a feeling that calamity lay just around the corner." The one person everyone missed painfully was my uncle Dieter, who at age eighteen, had been drafted as a private and sent to the brutal eastern front in a tank division of the Sixth Army's armored regiment. Germany's invasion of the Soviet Union had begun in June 1941.

My mother's lockbox contained a postcard she had written to her brother from her honeymoon. I marveled at what odd bits and pieces survive and how much that card had traveled. It had gone to Stalingrad and back and had somehow been taken along on many moves my mother made, out of Berlin to Suderburg and Bevensen; then to Vienna, Hamburg, and Darmstadt; and, finally, to Champaign-Urbana, Illinois. But here it was in the box, and it told me that my parents spent their honeymoon at the Grand Hotel Pupp in the famous spa Karlsbad, now in the Czech Republic and of James Bond's *Casino Royale* fame. My mother loved the place, for in peacetime she had spent vacations there with Nyussi.

On a bitterly cold January day, Mike, my son Benedict, and I had coffee at the Grand Hotel Pupp. In the center of the spa, it was once again restored to its glory, with chandeliers and red carpet. The spa town, spread out in a deep and narrow valley along the Tepla River, was lined with fancy boutiques and, most of all, jewelry stores. We watched Russian ladies walk by in stiletto heels, wrapped in mink and sable coats. Although much of Karlsbad may have outwardly look the same, it seemed worlds apart from what my mother and grandmother must have experienced.

After a short reprieve at the Pupp, my father returned to serve as pilot in *Jagdgeschwader 77* and my mother to her parents in Berlin. On December 11, 1941, Germany declared war on the United States. Early in 1942, Api was called up to serve full-time in Berlin auxiliary military hospitals—*Reservelazarette*, RL for short. These were set up wherever space could be found in schools, hotels, and other public buildings that had not yet been destroyed. Finally, they were moved into cellars. Nyussi and my mother were left in the apartment. Between trips to the cellar whenever there was an air raid warning, they tried to live as normally as possible. But most of all, they were waiting for mail from my uncle Dieter, in Stalingrad, and my father, stationed somewhere in France.

# 11

# LITTLE NOODLE

Among the letters I found in my mother's lockbox was one of the most emotionally charged of my discoveries, a stack of blue Feldpost envelopes held together by a ribbon. I did not recognize the tall and straight handwriting. They turned out to be letters my father had written to my mother between 1941 and 1943. Here again were the dates I had seen on Track 17. These letters are the first and only direct information I have about my father. As I read, I saw that he was allowed to reveal very little of what he was doing or where exactly he was stationed. All my mother had was a number, and that changed four times in the letters indicating his reassignments. His last one was L44889A.

Just as I was working on the copyedit of this manuscript in November 2019, Clint Mitchell, administrator of the Luftwaffe Research Group, provided astonishing details about my father's life and death as a fighter pilot. In 1940, he served as a lieutenant with carrier group 186, which was set up especially to operate onboard the *Graf Zeppelin*. However, the carrier remained unfinished and my father was moved to other fighter groups, stationed for a time in Norway but mostly in northern France.

From there, he wrote my mother that he lived through almost constant air raid warnings, as RAF planes were flying missions into France. During day attacks, everyone ran for shelter, for "then it thumped powerfully," but at night they just slept through the raid. Once, as he was writing to my mother, he heard a particularly heavy explosion, which made him comment that "the Tommys hit their targets pretty well after all."

He also told her how, when he was flying over a particularly lovely spot, his thoughts drifted into daydreams. He imagined the two of them lying together in the fragrant meadow in a world where there was no war and no separation. "Do you think that this will ever really happen? We both have to believe in this absolutely, have to be totally convinced that this time will come. Otherwise one's entire life would be in vain and for naught."

I was born on October 17, 1942, when the war was turning to inevitable defeat for Germany. My father saw me no more than a couple of times. He could only write admiringly of the pictures my mother sent him. He dispatched parcels with oranges, a rarity, for me and asked in each letter about his "little noodle." Any food he sent was most welcome, because since April 1942 Berlin had instituted the most serious cuts yet in food rations. His own reports, however, became increasingly hopeless.

I have several pictures of my father in front of his Messerschmitt 109, with Margit, my mother's name, painted on the fuselage. The single-engine, single-seater plane is hardly taller than my father, who stands on one of its wheels, his hands in his pockets. He is wearing his combination suit with straps hanging from the inflatable flight vest, knee-high leather boots, and his peaked cap.

Not long after I was born, our family suffered a series of disasters. On December 3, 1942, Uncle Dieter's tank was hit and he sustained a lung injury. However, my grandparents heard from their son only when he was safely in an Erfurt military hospital. In a way, he was lucky to be injured before the final encirclement of the Sixth Army in Stalingrad, what the Russians called "the grave of German youth." On March 1, 1943, we lost our apartment when an incendiary bomb hit the building. This was even before the Battle of Berlin had begun in earnest. One of the few things my mother ever told me about her war experience was how Api and she had banded together with the other tenants to form a chain from the ground floor to the attic. They passed water buckets and sand from hand to hand in an effort to contain the blaze. They often had to warn each other to pat out sparks that threatened to set them alight as well. Everyone worked feverishly in the smoke until the water supply ran out. Luckily, no one was hurt, but the apartment was destroyed. I was told later that we had found another place to live, but I never knew the location, except that it was also in Berlin Mitte and that a bomb had demolished it, too.

It was becoming all too clear that by 1943 the German air force was overtaxed and underequipped, nor were enough experienced fighter pilots left, and none of them, my father included, had ever dropped bombs. Nevertheless, Hitler ordered the resumption of bomb attacks against England, with the aim of damaging the takeoff and landing places of RAF bombers. This meant that fighter planes that had not been intended for bombing missions had to be outfitted for them.

On what was to be his last reassignment, starting in April 1943, my father was stationed in a castle. He had time to write almost daily, since they were flying training missions by day but could rest at night. He was training pilots to fly the FW190, the Focke-Wulf plane called the Würger, the Shrike. Like the Messerschmitt 109, this was a single-seat, single-engine plane, but it was the powerhouse of the fighter planes. He now was part of *Schnellkampfgeschwader 10*, a specialized unit for fast and dangerous "tip and run" bombing raids. New to this group, my father missed his former comrades, with whom he had become close. He felt a stranger there, and that, combined with his ever more perilous missions and constant anxiety about his wife and baby daughter, made him at times despair of the future.

All during the spring of 1943, my father kept trying to call Berlin but could not get through. So he wrote letter after letter expressing his worry about what was happening there and how we dealt with the air raids. When he wrote again, on May 15, 1943, he realized only when he was almost finished that it was Mother's Day. He had forgotten all about it. He promised that he would rush out to buy flowers and decorate my mother's and my picture with them. Less than two weeks before his death, he wrote, "But one is so completely in the dark and there is nothing that suggests in the least the end of our separation. One just always and always has to continue to wait and hope. . . . At some point it has to come." I understand why the Lale Andersen song "*Es Geht Alles Vorüber, Es Geht Alles Vorbei*" had been so popular. So many people must have shared the hope of the song that "all will be over, all goes away." As it was, most of my parents' brief marriage was by correspondence.

His last blue Feldpost envelope bore a stamp with a special message urging women to volunteer in the post office: "Women and girls report to help at the Reich Post. It connects front and homeland." Inside was only a scrap of paper. My father hastily informed my mother that he could not give specific information except to say that "very shortly it will start" and that "it's directed toward England."

My mother told me later that my father was well aware that his missions had become suicidal. It was obvious to him and his colleagues. The plane had to carry a 550-pound bomb and a 66-gallon drop tank in order to fly longer distances. Luftwaffe general Theo Osterkamp saw it as "completely insane to hang bombs under the bellies of my fighters." As a result of the extra weight, the planes were slow, and had difficulty reaching even five thousand meters in height. Nevertheless, the "tip and run" maneuver was enormously complicated. Approaching their target, pilots were to fly low to get under British radar, then quickly climb to five hundred meters. Once above the target, they had to dive down suddenly and, at great speed, drop their bomb and hurry back to safety.

One of the most emotional pieces of information from that lockbox is a letter from Captain Schumann, dated June 5, 1943. He wrote to my mother that her husband had not returned from their mission to the city of Eastbourne, on the southeast coast of England, on June 4, and had to be counted as missing. Kurt, he explained, was his *Rottenflieger*, or wingman. In the two-man formation called a *Rotte*, the wingman flies behind and to the side of the leader. "At our destination we came under intense antiaircraft fire. We were no more than 20–30 meters high! Kurt probably got a direct hit on his engine, since a trail of black smoke poured out from behind. He was last seen when, already at an altitude of 250–300 meters, he veered off over the English mainland, probably just about ready to bail out. We all hope that this supposition is correct, for in the short time we have been together, we all have got to know Kurt as a dear and honest colleague whose loss would hit us very hard."

My family knew that my father's plane crashed over Bexhill-on-Sea on June 4, 1943. But now Clint Mitchell provided a photo of that crash. It was a shock for me, even seventy-five years later, but I was also grateful for the information. Mitchell analyzed the crash site and explained to me that the plane suffered relatively little damage, an indication that my father came close to making a textbook belly landing. "He very nearly made it, but at the last minute one wing touched the ground and the plane flipped over, thus killing your father. But he appeared to have been in complete control of the aircraft until that wing touched the ground."

Effective June 1, my father was promoted to *Hauptmann*, or captain. The war diary of the Armed Forces Chief Command, which gave daily logs of activities, had just one note for Luftwaffe 3 over England on June 4: "11:27 attack on Eastbourne by 15 FW 190."

My father is buried in Cannock Chase, Staffordshire. I went to visit the large military cemetery shortly after its opening in 1967, the result of a collaboration between the German and the Commonwealth War Graves Commission. The cemetery lies in a quiet valley of birch and pine trees, far from the noise of traffic and the bustle of Birmingham. As I looked out over the sea of markers where close to five thousand German servicemen from both wars are buried, I despaired of ever finding my father's grave. An old attendant was walking among the stones. Hesitantly, I asked him about Kurt Hevler, a fighter pilot. His eyes lit up as if I had inquired about an old friend. Without hesitation, he took me to one of the rough-hewn granite stones deep in heather. And there it was, my father's grave, with his name etched into the stone.

The attendant stood with me. We talked a little; he knew all the names in this section where many other fighter pilots lay buried. He talked about their bravery and how they deserved this quiet resting place. To him they were no longer enemies who, just over thirty years earlier, had dropped bombs on his country. Judging by his age, I thought he had most likely served in the war himself. Now he tended his former enemies' graves with love and care. He was glad I had come and that we could share this peaceful moment together. I was moved to tears by the kindness and compassion of that old man, even more so than by the gravesite of a father I had never known.

*Kurt's crashed Focke Wulf 190, June 4, 1943*
*Andy Saunders Collection*

*Wedding picture of Gabrielle's parents, 1941*

*Kurt Hevler with his Messerschmitt 109, 1942*

# 12

# CHRISTMAS TREES

The Battle for Berlin began in November 1943. As Martin Middlebrook says, "No other Second World War bombing campaign against a single target was pressed so hard, for so long, and at such cost as the attempt to destroy Berlin." Sir Arthur Harris, marshal of the Royal Air Force and head of Bomber Command, had high hopes that it would bring Germany to its knees. He wrote to Churchill in November 1943, "We can wreck Berlin from end to end. . . . It will cost us 400–500 aircraft. It will cost Germany the war." Altogether, he ordered 14,562 sorties over Berlin. The raids destroyed much of the center, killing thousands of Berliners and rendering hundreds of thousands homeless, yet they failed to provide the knockout blow "Bomber" Harris had hoped for. The Battle of Berlin was costly not only to civilian life but also to the RAF, which lost 2,690 crew members and 625 bomber planes—chiefly, four-engine Lancasters, which carried a twenty-two-thousand-pound bomb known as the Grand Slam. An observer riding the Stadtbahn wrote in March 1944 that "from Alexanderplatz to the Zoo you can see nothing but ruins. . . . Despite this, they all try to live in the ruins and cellars, dirty, sick, and desperate, or rather apathetic and stupid."

Like all Berliners, my family established an eerie routine around the clockwork bomb attacks. Radio announcements reported enemy planes, and everyone got used to the military terminology: "*Achtung, Achtung. Wir geben eine Luftlagemeldung.*" "Attention, attention. Here follows a message about airspace." Or "*Achtung, Achtung. Gefechtsstand der Flakdivision Berlin.*" "Attention, attention. Combat situation of Flak Division Berlin." The howl of sirens, swelling and subsiding three times, made everyone scramble for shelter. They had about ten minutes between the first alarm and the attack. People scampered out of buses and streetcars, looking for the nearest bomb shelter; they ran down stairs of apartment buildings, clutching a few treasured items. A suitcase or two always stood ready at the door for these daily descents. Secretaries grabbed their typewriters and bundles of papers, trying to carry on business as usual, and hospital staff maneuvered patients into medical cellars. Thousands sheltered in the S-Bahn tunnels under the huge dome of Anhalter station. Only a few people, either fearless or apathetic, stayed where they were and waited out the attack. The city was suddenly a ghost town. Then came the droning of planes just above roof level, the whistle and hiss of bombs, followed by the *boom, boom, boom* of explosions and the staccato hammering of antiaircraft missiles.

Even if one's building was spared a direct hit, it shook and groaned, windows and doors were splintered by the air pressure, and debris rained down in the cellar. Marianne MacKinnon describes what she experienced when the building across the street from her was demolished. "A gargantuan force lifts us off the floor, dumps us again. Heads and bodies crash against each other in the dark, my ear drums stretch painfully. . . . And now, half blind and coughing, we do not wait for the all clear, but follow the beam and the warden's reassuring voice, holding on to each other's sleeves or coat tails, stumbling up the dust-clogged cellar staircase amid choking and spitting noises. . . . [T]he view across the street is laid bare: a mound of rubble and twisted steel steaming with dust in the light of a gauze-veiled moon. . . ."

Conditions in bunkers grew ever worse: damp, dusty, dark, and overcrowded. Whenever possible, my mother took me to the Charité bunker, which was in better shape than the Luisenstrasse cellar. She told me that I, just over one year old, was not much bothered by any of this. I clapped my hands, saying, "Boom!" whenever I heard an attack.

At night the sky was lit by marker bombs, popularly known as Christmas trees because of their red, yellow, and green cascades of light, which slowly spread as they drifted to earth. The beautiful spectacle identified bombing targets. Novelist Boree describes it as "an overture to the play about hell which yet always delighted again." Berliners, known for their sarcastic wit, joked that the situation was not critical until you could reach the front by underground.

In October 1943, Api was promoted to *Oberstabsarzt* in reserve, with the rank of major. Next to surgeons, eye doctors were in special demand because of the many eye injuries flying shrapnel caused. He served in an auxiliary military clinic in Berlin Steglitz, directly south of the center. In January 1944, he earned the *Kriegsverdienstkreuz*, the War Merit Cross, for acts of bravery not directly connected to frontline action.

One of the very worst air raids occurred on February 3, 1945, when American B-17 bombers, the Flying Fortresses of the Eighth Air Force, dropped 2,272 tons of bombs on the center of Berlin, creating two-mile-high smoke columns. This was probably when we lost our second apartment, and that convinced Api that Nyussi, my mother, and I had to leave Berlin. It made no sense to flee to the east, since the Soviets were already driving thousands of refugees west toward Berlin. But Nyussi had distant relatives in Lower Saxony, 160 miles northwest of Berlin. Her grandfather had emigrated from there to Hungary. Once again, the lockbox helped with information—a torn and creased piece of paper headed *Abreisebescheinigung*, certificate of departure. I was astounded that even at this eleventh hour, German bureaucracy was still churning away. Ian Kershaw points out that "the regime was sustained to the end by a sophisticated and experienced bureaucratic machine." As late as April 1945, the mayor of Berlin announced that no new dog licenses would be issued that year and that the old ones remained valid.

# 13

# UNWELCOME GUESTS

Nyussi, my mother, and I were assigned to one and a half rooms in a small farmhouse belonging to the Ohlde family in Suderburg, less than two miles from Holxen, where our relatives the Steinkes lived. We could not stay with them, since their house was already overcrowded with refugees. The Ohldes were poor, had no land of their own, and made a sparse living with chickens, bees, a couple of pigs, and a sheep. Their cottage stood right at the end of the village, next to the cemetery, with its huge old oak trees. We were not welcome guests. The family was forced into giving up space to city strangers when they had hardly room enough for Farmer Ohlde, his wife, their daughter, and Herr Ohlde's mother. At first we could hardly communicate with the family. They spoke the Low German dialect, Plattdeutsch, which is closely related to Dutch and English. But I soon learned to speak Plattdeutsch like the locals.

Altogether, the villagers of Suderburg were not happy about city refugees crowding their homes. The cottage next to us housed refugees from the Hamburg bombings. It belonged to the Klapproth family, who, like the Ohldes, were poor. The father served as both church warden and gravedigger. One of his jobs was to ring the bells of the ancient Suderburg church. Hearing the church bells toll in the evening, we always thought of old Herr Klapproth up there in the medieval tower, pulling the bell ropes.

The Ohldes' cottage was primitive. The low entry door gave onto a dark, narrow corridor that led to the kitchen in the back of the house. When they were not working outside, the Ohldes spent most of their time there. To the left of the entry was the *gute Stube*, the fancy parlor, which was rarely used, except for the spinning wheel of Farmer Ohlde's mother. To the right of the entrance were our rooms; the larger was no more than ten by ten feet, and the smaller one had just enough space for a bed and dresser. That room was especially cold; thick black mold grew on its two outside walls. There was a stove in the larger room, but often we had nothing with which to heat it. Its two windows looked out onto a sandy road and fields beyond with a wooded hill in the distance: the *Blauer Berg*, the Blue Mountain. The bedroom window overlooked the village cemetery. "At least I know my next move," quipped my always witty grandmother. She and I slept in that little room, while my mother had to create a makeshift bed with some blankets in the outer room.

The old farmhouse had no indoor plumbing. The outhouse was in the back, across the unpaved farmyard, past the pigsty. It had a little heart-shaped hole in the rickety wooden door. To the right was a compost heap higher than I was, as well as the woodpile, which I checked for beavers whenever I passed. Chickens and a rooster scratched in the sand of the yard. At the very back were a vegetable patch and Farmer Ohlde's beehives. We had to fetch water from a well by the back door. I loved to help pump it with the big, curved iron handle that always squeaked noisily.

The Steinkes gave us a little electric cooker, on which my mother prepared our watery soups and heated the chicory coffee we called *Muckefuck*. The term, I learned later, has been used since the Franco-Prussian war of 1870–71. It derives from the French *mocca faux*, false coffee. For Germans, *Muckefuck* is any variety of substitute coffees made from grain or chicory. Even with donations from our relatives, food was a problem. Although both Nyussi and my mother made sure I got more than they did themselves, I was always hungry. Nyussi thought up ever new ways to distract me. When we weren't out looking for beavers, she told me stories and invented adventures for my doll.

On Sundays, we walked together to the ancient village church. It was built of red brick and timber, like most of the houses of the area, but its tower stuck out incongruously. Round and squat, barely taller than the church itself, it was constructed from rough gray fieldstones. The tower dates back to 1003, the last remnant of the Suder Castle, after which the village is named. Its little pointed roof, decked in red tiles, was added much later.

Unlike the inferno of the Berlin we had left, here everything was quiet, almost eerily so, as if there were no war. Farmer Ohlde fed his chickens and pigs, although he had some trouble with these chores, as the fingers on his right hand were missing two joints where a circular saw had cut them off. His wife planted cabbage, carrots, potatoes, and peas, just as she had done in peacetime.

# 14

# A DEATH IN PRAGUE

Api's first entry in the green diary is just one word, "Prag," under-scored painfully hard several times; below it is a penciled iron cross. The date is February 14, 1945. It is the day my uncle Dieter was killed during an air raid on the Charles Bridge in Prague. We had left Berlin just over a week before, so Api was alone when a telegram told him of the death of his only son. Except for a few lists and a brief note, Api wrote nothing more until April 21, 1945.

Dieter had survived Russia—first the heat of the steppes, then the rain and mud, and finally the snow and ice. He had written how they had not enough warm clothing, not enough food, but more than enough lice, fleas, ticks, and mice. He was among the endless lines of Tiger tanks that were the first to reach Stalingrad, the industrial city that stretched for miles on the western bank of the Volga River. For weeks he had been stationed on the river north of the city, sleeping in a hole under his tank. The Germans destroyed Stalingrad before they were annihilated in turn. Vasily Grossman, who was following General Zhukov, described the destruction in these words: "Stalingrad is burned down. Stalingrad is in ashes. It is dead." But Dieter had survived Stalingrad, only to be killed by a stray bomb almost at the end of the war.

Two of his letters, which both Api and Nyussi had read so often that they had memorized them, helped me to understand the depth of their loss, as well as the changes the war had wrought on my previously carefree uncle. Both were written from Prague. One was dated December 3, 1944, exactly two years after Dieter had been wounded in Stalingrad. Part of the letter says, "The war has taught us to ignore appearances. In my mind an inner connectedness appears far more beautiful than a mere physical existence side by side. Such thoughts could—I believe—make it easier to bear even an eternal separation." Dieter also assured my mother that she was not to worry about her and my future. He was going to take care of us. And he himself was only twenty-two years old.

In the other letter, Dieter writes that he is looking forward to the moment when he will be able to express his gratitude in more than words. "It will be wonderful when I can help so that you can enjoy peace after a rather agitated life (even I begin to think of mine that way) in a way you have always desired. And that will happen—dead certain." That "dead certain," written only weeks before his death, must have struck them as a particularly ghastly coincidence.

Over the weeks following this dreadful news, Api fell ill. I found a yellowed and creased document in my mother's box that said that Api was unfit for duty and had been granted sick leave from March 11 until April 10, 1945. The troop physician's certificate was handwritten on the back of some form and hand stamped at the top "Army Commander Troop Physician." It seems that after his son's death, Api had suffered a nervous collapse somewhat like the one that struck him down at the beginning of World War I.

Dieter's remains were transferred to a cemetery in Cheb in 2008. He is buried in a grave with four other fallen men. The simple stone cross shows that two of them are unknown soldiers.

# 15

# LEAVE

Api's next entry comes on March 10, 1945. It is another single letter, this time a "U" written in bold over a list of errands and people to see. The "U" stands for *Urlaub*, or leave, in anticipation of his trip to us the following day. Beneath it, already feeling closer to Nyussi, he added in Hungarian, "One more day and then the one single uniquely fortunate day." Api's diary is silent about that month in Suderburg, but I can piece together the main events from what he recorded when he was back in Berlin, from his letters, and now, for the first time, also from my own memory.

Api had been unable to send us word of his imminent arrival. On Sunday evening, March 11, he knocked on one of the low windows of our room. We were just sitting down to a meager dinner. Api was pale and tired from the long journey. His major's uniform was dusty and crumpled. But his eyes shone with anticipation. It was the happiest reunion, he wrote later, although we could celebrate only with soup made from the dense stand of nettles that lined the road.

Api relished the days of our togetherness. We gathered wood from the forest and what Api called *Schuckchen*, pinecones, for the stove. They were not easy to find, since other refugees were hunting for them as well. On clear evenings, always intent on my learning new things, Api took me outside to study the night sky and point out the constellations. When we came back, the grown-ups gathered around the table to play cards and drink *Muckefuck*. I went to sleep in the little room, curling up in the middle of the bed so that my grandparents would have room on either side of me.

One of Api's first actions was to ask the minister whether we could hang a funeral wreath for my uncle in his church. He readily agreed, and every Sunday on entering, Api greeted the spot between the north windows, and we tried to sit near it during services.

The day of departure must have come all too soon. On Monday evening, April 9, Api took a last stroll arm in arm with Nyussi, discussing once again what to do. The road skirted the oak-darkened cemetery, and they could just make out where it curved up a mild incline to the village of Holxen and the big farmhouse of Nyussi's relatives. As they walked on the sandy path, they looked south to the Blue Mountain. In these few weeks, Api had come to love that tranquil vista, and in days to come he would often think back nostalgically to it. It was not really a mountain at all, just a barely perceptible rise out of the fields, across from the swift-moving Hardau creek where my mother rinsed our washing until her hands bled from the cold. The mist that was part of the northern German climate made the hill shimmer in a pale blue light.

The air was heavy and moist, as it always was, even in summer, in this northern part of the country. Nyussi could not get used to the dampness and fog. Her hands and feet were already becoming crippled with rheumatoid arthritis, although she tried to keep herself warm with memories of her home in Hungary, the vineyards, peach trees, and sun-ripened melons. But on this evening the two hardly felt the damp as they talked and wept together, going over the same issues again and again. What if Api declared himself still unfit to serve, as he believed he was? What if he simply refused to return to the inferno? But then how could he support us in this tiny place when this terrible war, which they knew could not last much longer, was over? Their few belongings and his precious instruments were in Berlin. And there Api was well known as an eye doctor and surgeon, so he could rebuild his practice after the war. The final argument, was that it was his duty as medical officer not to abandon his post at a time when he was needed most. However often they revisited their sad options, they came to the same terrifying conclusion: Api had to go back to Berlin.

Neither Api nor Nyussi got any sleep that night, and even I was restless sensing their unhappiness. They dreaded their separation and worried about the ever more fragile and uncertain future. Although neither voiced it out loud, one question was always on their minds: Would they ever see each other again? Lying awake and trying not to think of the morning, they turned their thoughts to their past happiness. They remembered how they had played duets or sat on their balcony, unaware of the terror to come. Often that night they wept for their son, who had fallen in Prague less than two months earlier.

The next morning, no one said much, except to look forward to our reunion as soon as the war was over. Alone in Berlin, Api often dwelled on that dreaded hour of parting: Tuesday, April 10, at 5:15 p.m. precisely. He never forgot that day, the deathly sadness among us and the irony of the laughing spring day above, a rarity in these parts. My grandmother quickly slipped him a little parcel from our treasured supplies, a few zwiebacks, a piece of bread, and, best of all, a little piece of speck, the fatty bacon we like to eat on dark bread. The speck was a donation from the always generous Steinkes. Api took a last look at Nyussi, my mother, and me standing in front of the cottage, said a silent farewell to the peaceful Blue Mountain, and was gone. We would not hear from him again for many months. During that time, Api often asked himself whether this was not the worst decision he had ever made in his life.

As soon as he left us, Api tried to relieve his anxiety by jotting down details of his journey. Perhaps it was the beginning of a letter to us that never could be sent, yet the scrap found its way into my mother's box. The trip was stressful for its endless delays and even more so for the torturous cycles of his mind. He was lucky to find any trains at all, and when he climbed aboard the first one, in Uelzen, he was not surprised to see that it was filled to bursting. He had to change trains many times and once take refuge in an air-raid shelter. But what bothered him most were the choices he had to make about his route. From here on out, doubts about any one of his decisions, big or small, plagued Api and drove him to distrust himself completely. To calm himself, he unwrapped Nyussi's provisions, thinking gratefully of her care and her strength. When they drew near to Magdeburg, Api, like everyone else aboard, tried to avoid looking out in order not to see the destruction beyond the windows.

But for Api the most difficult part about that long journey was the unrelenting stream of agonizing thoughts from which he was unable to free himself. He kept asking himself the same questions. *Should I have stayed in Suderburg after all? But then what about my practice, which is the foundation for any future existence? And what about my duty as a doctor and officer?* No doubt shaking his head, he wrote about his "silly, exaggerated sense of duty." He knew that he could not act differently, that he had to return.

# 16

# RUSSIANS AT THE GATES

For close to five years, Api had known Berlin as a war zone, but just a few days after he returned, it became the front line. The city that had continued to function through thousands of air raids and years of carpet bombing finally ground to a halt. Factories closed; streetcars stopped running; mail delivery and trash pickup ceased. The Russians were at the gates.

Starting Saturday, April 21, 1945, Api began to write a detailed daily entry. Each started with love and greetings to us far away and then talked about what he saw and heard and feared. He gauged the progress of the Red Army by the sound of the shelling. In those last days of April, forty thousand tons of Soviet artillery shells pounded the city, at the end one shell exploding every five seconds in the government district.

On his return to Berlin, Api tried to report back for duty, but there was no one left who could tell him where to go, so he went to work in the bunker on Albrechtstrasse, one block east of his home, whose cellar housed the auxiliary military clinic RL 104. Conditions were bad and soon grew worse. They had light for only half an hour a day, and even then the Hindenburg lamps, candles made of tallow, threw only the dimmest rays. "Again and again we had to make the old spent ones usable by reusing the fallen drops of tallow." Api was frustrated how little he could do for the injured. There were far too many of them, and many more had to be turned away altogether. But even the "lucky" ones inside were lying on the bare and cold floor. Dust and chalk rained down on them from the ceiling, as explosions shook even that sturdy bunker. Toilets did not function, and a lack of water or bandages meant that injuries had to stay largely untended. Groans and the whimpering of babies filled the air. Blood and grime ran down the surgeon's rubber apron. It smelled of excrement and old blood. Api had only one wish: "When—then I beg it only to be quick."

April 21 was a spring day of sunshine and showers, although down in the cellar Api did not see any of it. I wonder whether he heard Goebbels's last 11:00 a.m. news conference from the Zoo tower in the nearby Tiergarten, in which Goebbels announced that he would stay in Berlin until victory. He added, *"Aber wenn wir abtreten, dann soll der Erdkreis erzittern!"* "However, if we step down, the whole earth shall tremble!" Meanwhile, Hitler was hunkered down in his steel-reinforced bunker below the New Reich Chancellery. He was in a state of collapse, either raging or whimpering. Sunk into himself, his left hand shaking uncontrollably, he shouted, "Politics! I have nothing to do with politics anymore. That just disgusts me."

On the second day of Api's diary, April 22, it had turned cold, with a high barely reaching forty-five degrees Fahrenheit. Chilled and hungry after a sleepless night, Api went to see what was left of his former home on Luisenstrasse. In the distance he could hear long-range artillery fire. Although it was Sunday, stores had been ordered to stay open to distribute crisis rations of sausage, lentils, sugar, and even a little coffee. Berliners jokingly called them suicide rations, and no one was surprised when they did not materialize. Api checked the Pommer and Vorkastner stores where Nyussi used to shop and found one closed and the other besieged by hundreds of people, its shelves almost bare, so he continued on to his apartment building. He could no longer use the front stairs, but the back stairs were navigable up to the second floor, where his practice had been. The place smelled of smoke, dust, and decay, but the ceiling appeared to have held, although there was no floor left above him.

As he surveyed the damage, a grenade hit the building next door at the level where he was standing. The impact made him jump into the air, but he had a moment of hope nevertheless. It seemed to him that the attack had come from the west. That must be the Americans! It was the only hope left that they would reach Berlin before the Soviets. Little did he know that the Americans were nowhere near Berlin. Already, on March 28, General Eisenhower had reportedly told Field Marshal Montgomery to advance to the Elbe River and stop there. "Berlin itself is no longer a particularly important objective," he telegraphed in response to Montgomery's plea for permission to lead a "powerful and full-blooded thrust toward Berlin."

From the moment he saw his surgery, Api cherished the hope that he could rebuild his practice. He left the apartment still hungry but with plans for the future. He decided to go across the street to the Charité, a walk he had taken so often in peacetime. Although the hospital's main buildings had been camouflaged, most of them had suffered heavy bomb damage. On his way, he met a young colleague, Dr. Heinz Kraaz, who had only recently finished his doctorate as a gynecologist. He came to Api's rescue by inviting him to share his lunch.

During the next weeks, they became fast friends. Heinz's visits helped to shore up Api's failing energies. The young man did not have a wife and children to worry about, and he also was possessed of a positive, supportive, and, even in this crisis, hopeful disposition. He helped Api at his most desperate times, and the two enjoyed long, often philosophical talks, which, as Api noted frequently, were not political. Otherwise, politics was what most people talked about, endlessly debating rumors and suppositions and fears. Although more than thirty years separated the two men, they shared a love for their profession and for helping people, a strong religious faith, and a fundamentally conservative outlook. They also shared a joy of the heart, which, however, was all but extinguished in my grandfather at this time. But in Heinz's company he could even laugh sometimes.

That Sunday night, April 22, Api saw the east of Berlin in flames. "Grenades roared through the blood-red sky and fighter planes attacked even in the darkness." He also heard a new noise: machine-gun fire coming from the east and the north, but very near. He reckoned that the Russians were as close as the Schloss, the royal palace, at the east end of Unter den Linden. Despite the noise, he dropped off, for he had not slept for seventy hours.

When he was not at the Albrechtstrasse bunker, Api's other destination was the university clinic at Ziegelstrasse 5–9, turned into a military hospital, RL 135. It was not far, just across the wide Friedrichstrasse and a little to the north, but it always took Api a long time to get there. He had to find his way over heaps of rubble, past abandoned tanks and streetcar rails stabbing the sky. Here and there, one wall of a smoldering building was still standing, and Api could see right inside a kitchen or a bedroom, with its scorched furniture and torn wallpaper. It was like a doll's house wrecked by a giant. With bitter agreement, he noticed a homemade poster attached to a shell of a house. Das danken wir dem Führer: "For this we thank the Führer." In the last days of April, he saw two officers hanging from a lamppost at the Friedrichstrasse station. Each had a bit of cardboard around his neck. On it was scribbled that all cowards would meet the same fate. Fanatical SS had executed the two for wearing civilian clothes over their uniforms.

The early morning of Wednesday, April 25, between 5:30 and 6:30 a.m., saw some of the heaviest bombardment of the inner city, burying the familiar paths through the ruins. Api, of course, was not aware that this attack had even reached Speer's monumental New Reich Chancellery. The ventilation system in Hitler's bunker had to be turned off, since it no longer drew in fresh air, only sulfur and smoke.

Api found the Ziegelstrasse clinic more than half destroyed by this attack. As he walked along the wall of crumbling brick, he noticed the sandstone half relief of a Berlin bear just beside the entrance to one building. The bear has been the symbol of Berlin since the Middle Ages, and this one had remained intact, although the city it represented was in ruins.

The clinic was abuzz with eyewitness reports by people who had managed to come in from outer areas of Berlin. They told Api that the Russians had already taken the northern suburbs of Wittenau, Tegel, and Reinickendorf. The first wave of attack was made up of Katyushas firing phosphorous rockets that set everything aflame. The Germans called them *Stalinorgeln*, Stalin's organs, because going off they made a roaring sound like organs playing. The Katyushas were followed by tanks, which easily broke through the flimsy barricades. After the tanks came the infantry with grenades, submachine guns, and rifles.

Then Api witnessed something that he had to report in his diary right away, perhaps to ease his mind a little. "Just now chief medical officer 135 has buried 12 naked dead in a mass grave in Monbijou Park." The once beautiful park by the Spree River, aptly named My Treasure, was at the end of Ziegelstrasse, just across from the auxiliary clinic. Most parks in the city now served as burial sites, and over the next days Api saw this scene repeated over and over in different locations.

Api was disappointed when he was told that he could not stay at the Ziegelstrasse clinic. Although damaged, it still had more resources than the bunker. This left him no choice but to return to Albrechtstrasse. There, he noticed even further deterioration, although he had been gone only a few hours: "We drink the last water that comes out of the heaters. Now people start to drink water from the Spree River without being able to boil it. Then epidemics without hospitals, yes, even without possibility of any quarters at all. Every child knows what happens then."

He then vented his impotent frustration at what he had seen on his way:

> *One can hardly walk the streets. People die in the streets without there being any way of carrying them anywhere. Military clinics and hospitals have to reject everyone because of complete overcrowding, without water, without light. In some places I met up to 100 unattended heavy casualties with only two surgeons. Citizens are hungry and thirsty. Epidemics will not fail to come—a mass dying without any chance of improvement, an intoxication of the blood, a madness. Millions of furious people, in a powerless rage and despair, rebel against a brutality of tyrants which has never existed like this before, and they die helplessly!! Useless! An end, an end!! . . . The cellars can no longer sustain the heavy bombardment. . . . No quarters whatsoever, no bandages, and no food. . . . Dead horses are cut up in the midst of bombardment, the meat eaten almost raw. No way of cooking, no water, no light! God take pity!!*

Two and a half million Soviet soldiers circled the inner city. They had taken Tempelhof Airport in the southeast and Spandau in the northwest. Alexanderplatz and Potsdamer Platz, both just a few minutes from Api's location, were under heavy attack, and the once bombastic government buildings on Wilhelmstrasse had been reduced to rubble. The whole inner city was smoldering from fires. Sulfurous yellow smoke hung heavy in the air and made breathing difficult. A thunderstorm on the morning of April 26 dampened everything but hardly cleared the air. At night, heavy artillery fire kept Api awake, and in the morning he confided to his diary, "I don't know how I will get through this time. Despite a huge expense of energy, I can hardly work at all. I am constantly shaking with cold so that I can hardly write."

On April 26, Api decided to make an attempt to reach the Command Center Jebenstrasse. Perhaps there he would at last receive a proper assignment. The command center, immediately across from the Zoo tower, was a four-story, neoclassical building of the early twentieth century that had served as officers' mess of the *Landwehr*, the local military. Now it was the home of Major Pritsch's headquarters for the defense of Berlin.

It was an arduous and debilitating journey across the wasteland of the Tiergarten Api so loved. The park was devastated by bomb craters, the trees charred and broken, a nightmare landscape. The command center was barely functioning. The formerly showy interior, once covered in colorful wall and ceiling paintings, lay in ruins. Windows were broken, and papers blew about in the draft. The chief physician, Dr. Pellnitz, who also was an eye doctor, could only tell Api to go back to Albrechtstrasse. He himself had no idea where he would go, since he assumed that his headquarters would soon be moved. He had only sad stories about fellow doctors who had committed suicide.

Back in the Albrechtstrasse bunker after this futile excursion, Api assessed his own psychic state at "point zero." He wrote, "I have lost all confidence in myself and my initiatives. The conditions are horrible: no quarters in military hospitals and no transport for the sick. . . . Deplorable disorganization. Impossible to imagine. Impossible to describe."

# 17

# ABYSS BETWEEN THEN AND NOW

To get a better idea about the places mentioned in the diary, Mike and I retraced Api's steps in Berlin. Of course, in the reunited city, once again the booming capital of Germany, we were working under entirely different circumstances, crowded by tourists, rather than soldiers and refugees, and bombarded by the noise of traffic, instead of exploding artillery shells. We strolled past fashionable stores, while Api had made his laborious way through smoke and ruins, facing death at each step. "Towards evening, the sky to the east is a ghastly sea of smoke. I creep out at ten o'clock at night to the clinic under whistling grenades and bombs, a wilderness of fire and dust, behind it, although already high in sky, the blood-red moon." Nevertheless, we found reminders of the war and saw places in the former East Berlin that still showed its wounds.

Our first destination was Luisenstrasse 41, a ten-minute walk from the hotel. My mother had told me that it was under historical landmark protection and had been rebuilt exactly as it was when she grew up. And indeed the stucco was freshly painted a pale yellow and the red tiles shone on the steep roof. I looked at the nameplates for the fourth floor. The only name listed was a social and religious discussion group. I found it in the telephone book and called to ask whether we could look at the apartment, explaining that from 1924 to 1945 my grandparents had lived there. Frau Bug, the woman in charge, readily agreed, and we climbed up the sunlit stairwell to the fourth floor. Api must have used it a thousand times, and I imagined my mother running down on her way to the streetcar that took her to school.

Frau Bug let us in and explained that the apartment had been split into two, so what we saw was only half of my grandparents' place. Then she allowed us to wander around on our own. The apartment was equipped with functional modern furniture, so unlike what I had seen in pictures of my grandparents' time. Yet as we looked out the front windows we could see the cupola of the Reichstag, although the balcony they had enjoyed so much now belonged to the other apartment.

The view from the back was even less changed. The windows gave onto the first inner courtyard, done in stucco and painted yellow like the front of the building. Typically, Berlin apartment buildings had a series of back courtyards that became successively smaller and darker, made of exposed brick, instead of painted stucco, as the inhabitants got progressively poorer. In this way, every building contained a mixture of social classes, living under very different circumstances but in close proximity.

There was nothing more to see in this shiny new apartment. After thanking Frau Bug, we left to inspect the neighborhood. Right across from the building, I found the little triangular park, the Karlplatz, my mother had told me about, which was just outside the gates to the Charité. On a pedestal at its center stands a bronze sculpture of professor Rudolf Virchow (1821–1902), founder of the field of social medicine and known as the father of pathology. The monument, which has survived World War II, shows a man fighting a lion, perhaps to symbolize the great physician conquering the wild animal of disease.

Luisenstrasse had been in communist East Germany, just east of the Berlin Wall. Now, twenty years after reunification, the area was slowly becoming Westernized and gentrified. We noticed a wine bar and a tapas restaurant, and I bought a wonderfully light and flaky almond horn, a *Mandelhörnchen*, one of my childhood favorite treats, in a bakery nearby. New buildings had filled in most of the east side of the street, where our apartment was, but on the western side we noticed weed-grown and empty lots.

Next, we went in search of my mother's elementary school on Albrechtstrasse, one block east of Luisenstrasse. We scanned both sides of the short street for a small house, since I remember my mother telling me that her school was an old building nestled between taller apartments. And there it was, on the east side of the street, a low and narrow structure of yellow brick, squeezed in between larger ones. It had survived the onslaught of rebuilding during the *Gründerzeit*, the founders' period at the turn of the nineteenth century, and, even more remarkable, wartime bombing.

After taking pictures, we walked farther up the street, not looking for anything in particular. Suddenly, a massive gray block of reinforced concrete loomed in front of us, five stories high, with rows of slit openings, instead of windows. It sat there, huge and somewhat sinister, looking out of place among the apartment buildings, coffee shops, and bakeries that lined the street. It seemed like a dinosaur from a different age. In a moment of excited recognition, I exclaimed, "This must be the bunker Api has written so much about. I never expected to see it." Looking at it more closely, we noticed that the bunker had been converted into a museum of contemporary art and that a penthouse with roof garden had been added. We could see greenery peeking out at the top. But this did little to soften its somehow threatening aspect and brought me closer to Api's time.

We next crossed the broad Friedrichstrasse and turned into Ziegelstrasse. On our way to the former clinic, we got perhaps just a hint of what it must have been like in 1945. Here, the war still left its traces. Although only a few blocks north of elegant and bustling Unter den Linden, Ziegelstrasse was shabby and deserted. On the south side it was flanked by the old brick buildings of the university that stretched for almost its whole length, and we spotted the Berlin bear Api had described. On the north side, we saw broken-down structures, still showing the bullet holes of decades earlier, and empty spaces of rubbish and weeds where once had stood buildings. The street made a dilapidated, abandoned impression and showed how long it takes for the scars of war to heal over.

In the afternoon, Mike and I followed Api's journey from the bunker to the command center, but under much happier circumstances. Before we set out across the park, we enjoyed a glass of wine at the lavishly refurbished Hotel Adlon, next to the Brandenburg Gate. Sitting by the marble fountain, we talked about the Adlon's illustrious history. Before the war, it was a favorite meeting place for journalists, diplomats, film stars, and fashionable ladies out on a *Linden Bummel*, a linden promenade. In 1945, the Adlon was the last of Berlin's grand hotels left standing and served as refuge for the sick and wounded. The barbershop in the basement had been fitted out as an operating room, and the dead were deposited in the once beautiful Goethe garden in the rear. At the end of April 1945, the hotel opened its famed, 250,000-bottle wine cellar to the public. Waiters in their dusty tuxes served wine and champagne, gingerly stepping over debris and shards from the chandeliers. Although heavily damaged, the Adlon survived the war, but on May 3, 1945, the grand building finally collapsed in a fire.

As we sat in luxury, we found it difficult to picture the desolation Api had seen here. We left the Adlon and stepped out onto Pariser Platz, where a bustle of tourists taking pictures of the Brandenburg

Gate met us. My mind wandered to the thousands who had stood there in 1914, cheering and sticking flowers into the gun barrels of young soldiers, much like Api must have been. Less than twenty years later, the square was filled with brown-shirted SA Stormtroopers carrying torches and chanting the Horst Wessel song to celebrate Hitler's becoming chancellor. Then, at the time of the diary, dead and wounded soldiers took up the square, followed by Soviet soldiers roasting an ox to celebrate victory.

From the Brandenburg Gate, we set out across the Tiergarten. It was a cool but sunny afternoon, and we enjoyed the hike through tree-shaded paths, much like Api and Nyussi had before the war. But when we left the park to turn onto Jebenstrasse, I felt once again a little closer to Api's experience. At first I almost did not want to go down that narrow and empty street bounded on one side by the Zoo tower wall. I could just make out a group of men and women farther down, perhaps waiting for a soup kitchen to open. The gray, official-looking buildings on the other side still had a prewar air about them, although they had been renovated.

We found the former command center, now turned into a museum of photography. Even the showy ballroom, the Kaiser Saal, Emperor's Hall, had been restored to its former splendor. It brought home to us the impossibility of bridging the abyss between then and now.

*Nyussi with children in front of apartment, 1927*

*Former Albrechtstrasse bunker, 2008*

# 18

# BLOCKED ON ALL SIDES

Although hopeless and worn out after his futile journey to the command center, Api was too anxious to do nothing. He felt that he had to obtain a definite assignment, preferably at an eye clinic, "where I could do some good even in my condition." All day he worried about this, until, at eight o'clock at night, he rushed out in search of the chief physician. Under heavy bombardment, he had to duck from cover to cover to make his way. The streets were deserted. He reached his destination, which he did not specify, but was told that the chief physician was gone. To his surprise, however, someone else authorized his move to the eye station of the auxiliary military clinic RL 112 in Wilmersdorf. Even a car and driver would be standing ready at four in the morning to take him there. And, incredibly to him, he was offered another option, which had been denied just the previous day. He now also was given permission to work at Ziegelstrasse RL 135 under Professor Löhlein.

Api may have known the professor from before the war, since he had been in charge of the eye clinic at Ziegelstrasse, which was connected to the Charité. They were almost the same age. Professor Löhlein was born in 1882 in Berlin, the son of a professor of gynecology. He was a tall man who wore his hair very short and parted on one side, as did Api. He had a high forehead, a thick white mustache, and penetrating blue eyes. Professor Löhlein had been Hitler's personal ophthalmologist. Ever since his eye injury in 1918, Hitler feared for his sight and needed the reassurance of the specialist. If Api was aware of Professor Löhlein's role, he did not mention it in his diary.

Suddenly, Api had not one but two options, and it threw him into a new quandary. Not trusting his decisions, he did not know what to do. "Well, now again a conflict: the 112 eye station already lies within the HKL [*Hauptkampflinie*: main battle line] and will therefore be run over earlier. If I connect with Ziegelstrasse I can stay in my relatively safe cellar for the time being and can remain close to my apartment and my instruments." At night, Api decided to venture out once more "under whistling grenades" on his way to Ziegelstrasse to make doubly sure that they would have him there.

He reached the clinic unhurt, and the staff confirmed that he could work there. Nevertheless, on his way back, he kept thinking about his options, unable to make up his mind. "At the last minute I decide to stay and go to military hospital Ziegelstrasse. Give God that for once I should have chosen correctly, even just because of you, whom I love above all, above all. God be with you!!" Yet he was unable to stick with his choice. Terror and exhaustion had enervated him and taken away any initiative. As soon as he had opted for one solution, his lack of self-confidence led him to reverse himself. This back-and-forth served only as further proof that he was right in doubting himself. He was correct, however, about Wilmersdorf's already being in the main battle zone—in fact, the Red Army took it just two days later, on April 28. Still, he so wanted to work at an eye station, where he could be of more use. Just before dropping into a weary sleep, he reassured himself that Ziegelstrasse was the right decision after all. "I am a terrible fellow, torturesome indecision impersonated."

He slept restlessly and got up in time for the four o'clock car. "Remain undecided, back and forth. Finally I drive after all. Artillery bombardment small. But all of Berlin a field of ruins more so than after the heaviest bombardment. Streets full of holes and rubble. Hardly navigable, wires, trees, and such a dust that one can hardly keep one's eyes open. All the bridges are barricaded."

Blocked on all sides, Api and the driver decided to motor straight across the paths of the Tiergarten, where, ironically, the tall Victory Column was still standing. Since 1941, it had been camouflaged with netting and the winged golden goddess on top, whom Berliners called Golden Elsa, covered with brown paint. Burned-out tanks surrounded the monument, and the dead lay unburied. Trying not to look too closely, they made it to the other end of the Tiergarten, to the big square then called the Knie, which, Api remembered, had been created in 1902 as the western end station of the first underground. Today, the square is called Ernst Reuter Platz.

At the Knie, they came under low-level attack from Soviet planes, "sewing machines," strafing the city. When it was over, they drove on and finally reached the command center by the Zoo tower. It had taken the driver almost three hours to cover a stretch of about two miles. Api found Dr. Pellnitz, who still held out there, although he had lost contact with his clinics. He showed Api the latest copy of *Der Panzerbär*, the *Tank Bear*, "Combat Paper for the Defenders of Greater Berlin." Its cover always displayed a bear holding a *Panzerfaust*, literally a "tank fist"—a small antitank weapon even the children and old men of the Volkssturm, the People's Militia called up at the eleventh hour, could hold in their hands. Despite all evidence to the contrary, the April 27 copy carried the headline "Bulwark Against Bolshevism. Berlin: Mass Grave for Soviet Tanks." Both Api and Dr. Pellnitz could only shake their heads in disbelief.

Soon after they left the command center on their way to Wilmersdorf, both Api and the driver realized that they could no

more reach their goal by car than Api had been able to on foot earlier. "Impossible to get there. All the streets buried under rubble; the
enemy at the Circle Line Wilmersdorf. Caught in the midst of bat-
tling troops, we are sent back." At this point, the driver left, but Api
did not say anything about the man's plans.

Now what to do? Go back to the decision he had made the previous day? Or stay just north of where he had gotten stuck and report to
the military clinic RL 151 on Nikolsburger Platz? Since it was close to
impossible to return on foot, Api decided on the military clinic. The
medical officer, Dr. Siebert, agreed to have him stay, "but because of
an absolute lack of space he wants to house me on the second, totally
evacuated story, and then once again a heavy high-caliber bombardment gets under way."

During a lull, Api inspected the place. "The corridors and the
middle hall are for untended wounded; fourteen corpses wrapped in
oil paper are dropped in the park, a little earth on top!! No water. The
stink of toilets. Unusable. If only I could get back!! . . . Against urgent
warnings, I decide on a foot march."

Api set out from the devastated Nikolsburger Platz. Only a couple
of blocks from his starting point, the trouble began. He later recorded
it in a breathless and simple language unusual for him. "Already in
Pariser Strasse, increasing bombardment with high-caliber weapons.
At Rankeplatz I thought my last hour had come! Two heavy ones fifty
meters to my right. I try to run across the square, two heavy hits fifty
meters in front of me. Houses only ruins. I crouch, together with a
Volkssturm guy, behind a suburban fence. Again, four heavy ones
right near us. I must try to move forward into Rankestrasse. After
thirty paces, two of the heaviest a hundred paces ahead of me. When
I turn back into Joachimstalerstrasse, again two heavy ones seventy
meters ahead. Three cars of a parked convoy in high flames."

Then he spotted a small car with two officers and a woman. "I
immediately cross the street, force them to stop, and jump in. Straight

through the sea of flames—my brows singed—without sight for 50 meters straight ahead. When we are out, again two pot hits on the old spot. Car drives across Friedrichstrasse. I knew the only usable path and got through, uttering the most heartfelt prayers while grenades continually exploded."

Api's path across the ruins may well have been the same that the last people to flee Hitler's bunker took a few days later, on May 1. That night, a group of Hitler's personal staff, among them his bodyguard, dietician, and young secretary, attempted a last-minute break out of Berlin. The first thing they saw after they left Hitler's bunker was the bloody horror of the emergency clinic under the old Reich Chancellery, where doctors sawed off legs and arms without anesthesia and the dead and wounded lay about in mangled heaps, together with scattered body parts. Next, they crawled through pitch-black subway tunnels toward Friedrichstrasse station, their feet often slipping on something soft, a person either dead or unconscious. But they moved on, hoping not to lose the others in the darkness. They avoided crossing the Spree River at the heavily guarded Weidendammer Bridge, one of the main ways out of the city. Instead, they crept around Friedrichstrasse to Ziegelstrasse and from there to the Charité.

One member of that group was Ernst-Günther Schenck, who had served as physician in the Reich Chancellery. He described how, sweating and bruised, they inched their way through that labyrinth in the ruins. "The path which we now entered was completely hidden and had obviously been forged by pioneers through an entire district. . . . It used old courtyards, cellars, parts of demolished apartments, darted sideways around larger ruins, ran along a small street, and wound its way up and down over rubble and crumbled walls. The path looked lost and yet could not be missed."

The location Schenck describes tallies exactly with where Api was going on his return from Nikolsburger Platz to the Albrechtstrasse cellar. When he finally collapsed there on that Friday, April 27, it felt almost like home. "Arrival!! . . . Luckily, a few old peeled potatoes. Potatoes, dry bread, no water!"

# 19

# WRAPPED UP IN THE FLAG

When we returned to Berlin the next year, Mike and I visited Nikolsburger Platz, in the district of Berlin-Charlottenburg. We sauntered along the tree-lined streets west of Kurfürstendamm where Api had tried to evade grenades. It once again had become an upscale neighborhood, away from traffic yet close to the center. Mike read the menus at the inviting restaurants and wanted to try each one. I admired the pastries in the bakery displays and the fine food in the grocery stores, wishing we could have just one such deli in South Bend.

However, on this day of June 29, 2008, the usually quiet streets were packed with young people. Many wore big, fuzzy hats and had their faces painted in the red, yellow, and black of the German flag. It was the day of the final of the UEFA European Football Championship, between Germany and Spain. Although the game was played in Vienna and started at 8:00 p.m., by 4:00 p.m., five hundred thousand fans had gathered by the Brandenburg Gate and the square had to be closed. We stayed well away from that area. But Mike observed how much better it was to have the Brandenburg Gate besieged by soccer fans than by Stormtroopers, or even the crowds cheering soldiers in the summer of 1914.

I agreed, but all the German flags still perturbed me. They were everywhere I looked, on cars, on buildings, in restaurants and bars. Everyone who strolled the streets carried at least one flag, waving it in the air or even wrapped up in it. It made me feel uncomfortable to walk among all that black, red, and gold. My generation had been taught to avoid the flag. It was seen as a sign of a dangerous nationalism that had led to Nazi terror. My school had no German flag, and when we gathered for ceremonial celebrations, such as the beginning of the school year or graduation, the national anthem had no part in it. Instead, we sang "Ode to Joy" from the end of Beethoven's Ninth Symphony, with the lines "All men become brothers where your soft wing dwells." Today, "Ode to Joy" serves as the anthem of the European Union. While I lived in Germany until the early 1960s, I did not once hear or sing the German national anthem, and to this day I do not like to be surrounded by flag-waving people, of any nation, but especially Germans.

Weeks later, I talked to a young German acquaintance and happened to mention my unease about seeing Berlin blanketed in German flags. To my surprise, she responded that, on the contrary, she thought it was healthy that Germans now could wave their flags like other nations without feeling troubled about the past. "We cannot always live in the shadow of Hitler." I had never thought of it that way and can appreciate its value for a new Germany. Perhaps it signifies a sort of liberation, another step away from the Nazi period. But that does not mean I can overcome my discomfort about flag displays.

I also believe that some of my concern still clings to Germany, as its national anthem indicates. Dating back to the revolution of 1848 and adopted by the Weimar Republic, it has been reinstated after the war and now is sung on festive occasions in Germany. However, only the third stanza has been designated as the legal anthem. It begins with *"Einigkeit und Recht und Freiheit"*—that is, "Unity and Law and Freedom." The first stanza, the infamous and misunderstood

"*Deutschland über alles,*" is not allowed to be sung. However, as the revolutionaries of 1848 used it, the *über alles* did not mean that Germany should rule above all other nations. Rather, it meant that a unified Germany should be the goal above all else, for only then could there be law and freedom for all. But today few people remember the idealistic and revolutionary significance of this über alles. Hitler's insane attempt to set up Germany über alles has blocked our view.

When we reached Nikolsburger Platz, all was quiet, since there were no bars or outdoor restaurants there, just new apartment buildings with tall windows and balconies, framed by linden trees. Then, on the north side of the square, one large, older building of stucco and brick stood out. It was a school. This must have been the place that housed RL 151 at the end of the war. Just then, an old woman was walking laboriously along the park. I approached her gingerly and told her about Api. When she seemed comfortable with talking to me, I asked her whether she had been here in 1945. She said that she had and confirmed that the school had served as a makeshift hospital.

That night in our hotel, shouting and firecrackers kept us awake. Germany had lost the game zero to one, but that did not stop the crowds from parading up and down Kurfürstendamm, laughing and singing and no doubt waving their flags.

# 20

# MOOD REPORTS

At the end of April 1945, three Soviet armies concentrated their attacks on the city center. Marshal Zhukov's troops fired from the Landwehr Canal, immediately south of the citadel. Stalin had given Zhukov, the liberator of Stalingrad, the honor of being the first to capture Berlin. General Bersarin, who was to become the popular commandant of Berlin, was stationed at Alexanderplatz, to the east, and Marshal Konev's troops were at Wilmersdorf, southwest of the center, the very area Api had tried to reach. Against this overwhelming force stood only scattered remnants of German units, some SS, and the ragtag Volkssturm with their *Panzerfausts*. Yet many of them, especially the Weapons SS, refused to give up and carried on guerilla warfare against the Soviets, costing both sides untold lives.

The Albrechtstrasse bunker shook as it had with the bombs. Api feared that neither the cellar nor his mind could withstand this onslaught much longer. "Gradually one collapses psychically. . . . The end of the war or my own! If only one could lead the Executioner of Berlin through this misery. If they haven't turned insane from their bestiality, if they still believe in any kind of personal responsibility, if their often praised love of the people has even a glimmer of genuineness, their decision would not be in doubt, even if they would have to give themselves up. That they cannot prevent anyhow."

It was Saturday night, April 28, when Api railed against the Nazis in his diary. That same night, not far away, Hitler married Eva Braun in their bunker twenty-five meters below ground. She wore his favorite, high-necked black taffeta dress, and everyone feverishly drank champagne. The air was sticky and oppressive, and plaster rained down on the drunk celebrants. It covered the silver trays of lobster, caviar, and goose liver pâté in a thin layer of dust. Shortly after the ceremony, Hitler retired. He spent the rest of the night writing his political testament, in which he blamed the war on a conspiracy of international Jewish leaders.

Even in this hopeless situation at the very end of the war, the Nazi organization maintained what it called a *Mundpropagandaaktion*, propaganda machinery by word of mouth that focused on a rescue of Berlin. General Walther Wenck's relief army would run down the enemy and free Berlin. This message was also spread by the *Panzerbär*, which, until its last issue on April 29, kept talking about the strength of Wenck's relief army. On April 22, the headline had quoted Hitler: "Berlin Stays German!" Posters proclaiming BERLIN BLEIBT DEUTSCH had been stuck on the ruins of buildings. In addition Goebbels's propaganda machinery put out this flyer: "Berliners! Bear up, the Wenck army is coming to your rescue, only a few more days and Berlin will be free again!" Goebbels went on to order the population to fight for every street, every house, and every ruin, to fight to the last man and the last cartridge. He urged women to step into the place of fallen Volkssturm men and boys.

Although Berliners did not believe that General Wenck would come to their aid, some of this word-of-mouth propaganda may have helped, for makeshift signs appeared on destroyed buildings, proclaiming, "Our walls are breaking but not our hearts." Perhaps, however, such sentiments are simply a sign of how ineffective the bombing of civilians is. In London after the blitz, a popular poem expressed the same sentiment, in the same words, even. Greta Brigg's "London Under Bombardment" has these lines:

> *The bombs have shattered my churches,*
> *Have torn my streets apart.*
> *But they have not bent my spirit*
> *And they shall not break my heart.*

The propaganda men were also instructed to engage in an elaborate participant observation all across Berlin and then report back on the mood of the population. In contrast with the propaganda, these reports were truthful and specific, recording conversations overheard while standing in line at stores, sitting in pubs, or waiting in stations. As early as February 13, 1945, one of the observers reported a remark in, of all places, the Kaffee Alois near the Kurfürstendamm. The coffeehouse belonged to Hitler's half brother, Alois, and was a favorite spot for Stormtroopers. A guest was overheard to say, "The situation looks bad. I have already destroyed my copy of *Mein Kampf* and Hitler's picture."

These detailed *Stimmungsberichte*, mood reports, give a fascinating picture of daily life under the bombs. Even when faced with the threat of death and disintegration, people worried about the details of everyday life. The reporters heard the understandable concerns about food, coal for heating, and the conditions in bunkers. But people also expressed their annoyance at dirt in stations, at noisy waiters during official military reports, at impolite railway employees, at streetlamps left burning by day, wasting electricity. I wonder whether this was a typical reaction of people trying to maintain a sense of normalcy amid chaos or whether it showed a characteristically German fussiness.

At the end of April, the defense of the inner city rested on three flak towers that were to protect the citadel: Humboldthain in the north, Friedrichshain in the east, and Zoo in the west. The towers were built of eight feet of steel-reinforced concrete, six stories high. They could not be blown up even after the war. The flak towers had their own water, electricity, and food, and even their own hospitals with operating theaters. The Zoo tower alone sheltered as many as thirty thousand people. And since it was closest to Hitler's bunker, it also served as Goebbels's headquarters.

On April 29, a Sunday, all telephone communication between Berlin and the outside world was broken. The city and its remaining two and a half million people were cut off. Berlin had become a no-man's-land for the invasion of the Red Army. Historian Antony Beevor gives this haunting description of the night of April 29: "In the center of Berlin that night the flames in bombarded buildings cast strange shadows and a red glow on the otherwise dark streets. The soot and dust in the air made it almost unbreathable. From time to time there was the thunder of masonry collapsing. And to add to this terrifying effect, searchlight beams moved around above, searching a night sky in which the Luftwaffe had ceased to exist."

Without any news—even Goebbels's leaflets had finally ceased—Api could rely only on his immediate senses. He heard infantry and machine gunfire nearby and saw a number of disabled tanks on Wilhelmstrasse. "There is no telephone or other means of communication with other battle units. A situation report for our district—even our remaining military command knows nothing of the others!!—is only issued on the basis of presumed eyewitness reports."

Api felt hopeless and alone, cut off not only from us but even from his job as military doctor, which had been a main reason for his return to Berlin. He relieved his anger and frustration by berating those responsible. "Never before have there been such sadistic, heartlessly brutal tyrants. . . . I am mentally and emotionally completely at an end, broken by the inexpressible mental and bodily misery which irresponsible people, without sense or purpose, have brought to over two and a half million desperate citizens. They better watch out!"

As always in his most desperate moments, Api opened his diary, took out the little pencil that was attached to it by a loop at the front, and began to talk with us. "This morning at eight," he wrote late on April 29, "I had the distinct feeling that you, my world, were very close to me." In his thoughts, he looked out of the cottage window with us and saw the peaceful landscape with the Blue Mountain in the distance. He visualized it for as long as possible as a means of calming his nerves.

Reality, however, intruded all too soon. "Just now I have been looking for spaces where one can at least have the sick sit down or lay them on the ground for the night, without doors or windows, but at least protected from rain and safe from grenade splinters, although cold without padding. Corpses lie in a chapel of the Ziegelstrasse Clinic, for the most part without clothes, men and women together in layers! . . . I hope and pray that you have no idea of our situation. . . . Therefore, despite everything, I wish the end!!"

# 21

# HUMANS ARE FIERCER

At 10:50 on Monday night, April 29, Marshal Zhukov's troops raised the hammer-and-sickle flag on the crumbling Reichstag. Stalin had kept his promise and allowed the much decorated Victory Marshal, and not his rival, Marshal Konev, to be the first to reach the Reichstag. The hero of Stalingrad was a particularly relentless adversary. He told his troops to show no pity for the Germans. "If you kill one German, kill another—there is nothing funnier for us than a pile of German corpses."

Ironically, the building that once had housed the German Parliament had not been in use since 1933, when part of it burned down. From his apartment window, Api must have seen the flames shooting up from the Reichstag on that February 27, 1933. Hitler had accused the communists of arson and solidified his position as the one to fight international communism. I wonder whether in 1945 Api noticed the Reichstag in flames once again, this time from Soviet artillery. The Third Reich had begun, and now it was ended, with the burning Reichstag.

The attack on Berlin had cost the Soviets seventy thousand men in house-to-house fighting among the ruins, and even now SS troops continued to attack from the basement of the smoldering Reichstag. According to their statistics, Soviet losses of Operation Berlin were 304,887 men.

Journalist Vasily Grossman described what was happening just a few blocks from where Api was. Although Grossman had gone through the terror of Stalingrad, he was overwhelmed by conditions in Berlin, the wasteland of smoking ruins, the mountains of dead, the tens of thousands of refugees. At the zoo in the Tiergarten, he struck up a conversation with the primate keeper. The gorilla, supposedly the largest in Europe, lay dead in her cage, as did most of the other animals. Grossman asked the keeper, who had looked after the ape for thirty-seven years, "Was she fierce?" "No," he replied. "She just roared loudly. Humans are much fiercer."

Although Berliners had longed for an end to the war, they were deathly afraid of the Soviets. Refugees from the east had come with horror tales of murder and rape. The Soviets had suffered so much and so long at the hands of this enemy, whom they at last had conquered. When they were finally in control of Berlin, they went on a rampage of rape and looting that terrified Berliners no less than the bombing had done. In the Soviets' own impoverished state, they saw everyone in Berlin as a capitalist, what with their watches, radios, carpets, and toilets. "*Uri, Uri,*" they shouted, in their version of the German word *Uhr*, meaning "watch." Soon their arms were covered in watches all the way above their elbows. Wherever they spotted a bottle of liquor, they drank it. And when there was no schnapps, they made do with pure alcohol and even tried the German cologne called Kölnisch Wasser. The promise of the Soviets as liberators was further undermined when they arrested any German in a uniform, even that of a fireman or railway worker. Long lines of ragged prisoners of war were marched through the streets on their way to the east.

An estimated one hundred thousand women were raped in Berlin during the early days of the occupation. Women blackened

their faces with coal and dirt; they dressed in rags; they did everything they could to make themselves look old and ugly, but nothing
worked. They were unable to lock themselves away in the ruins in
which they lived, and the soldiers broke in on them wherever they
tried to conceal themselves. Even nurses in hospitals did not escape.
Soviet soldiers checked the beds of the sick to make sure no nurse was
hiding under the covers. Ursula von Kardoff, a journalist who worked
as editor for the culture section of the *Deutsche Allgemeine Zeitung* in
Berlin, recorded in her diary what a young woman told her: "Twenty-
three soldiers, one after the other. I had to be stitched up in hospital.
I never want to have anything to do with any man again."

Among all the shocking experiences Api recorded, he never once
mentioned rape. I do not know whether he thought this too horrible
to share with us or whether, although this seems less likely, he had no
immediate personal knowledge of rape.

# 22

# YOU NOT LIE

Berlin had fallen, but the fighting continued. As Api moved between the bunker and the clinic, he still saw plenty of violence. On Tuesday, May 1, he wrote hastily in his diary, often crossing out lines because he was too exhausted to find the right words. "Toward 1:30 a.m., terrible carpet bombing. Our quarter is burning on all sides and on all ends. Nowhere are the streets passable because of rubble, smoke, and flames. We are imprisoned by the fire." A little later, he voiced his anger and frustration: "And the executioners in their bunkers," as he called the Nazi leadership, "criminals!! Rome, Milano, and other foreign cities were given up to spare them, and they allow their own people to perish like dogs with hunger and fire and fratricide. The houses already are looted by civilians or tramps. Several times a day we have to destroy weapons and munitions, which our own troops drop off by our building, since we have no communication with any department." Api was referring to one of the first orders the Soviets put out, that all weapons had to be turned in immediately. He even gave up his old ornamental sword from World War I.

That afternoon, on his way to the clinic, a grenade splinter hit Api. Fortunately, it merely grazed his hip, a light injury, soon forgotten in his journey through a nightmare. He was shocked to see starving people carve up a horse that had died days earlier. He himself was hungry most of the time. His daily rations consisted of one slice of bread with margarine and two cups of coffee substitute in the morning, two bowls thin pea or carrot soup at lunch, and more soup and two slices of bread for dinner.

At five thirty that afternoon, the first Soviets showed up to check out the clinic and question the staff. *"Du nicht lügen"*—"You not lie," they demanded. They inquired about the number of beds, the surgical equipment and medications. They were particularly interested in how many and what kinds of weapons the clinic still had, since hand-to-hand fighting continued. The Soviets also wanted to know who was a member of the Nazi Party and whether any of them ever fought on the Eastern Front, where Germans had committed so many atrocities against Russians, both military and civilian. Finally, they asked about a place to live for their captain and, last but not least, about schnapps.

Like all medical personnel in Berlin, Api had to register with the Soviet authorities, who compiled a list of all doctors in order to set up meetings of health professionals. Api hoped that as a result they would at least find space for the sick on the first story of buildings, no matter how damaged. "Otherwise they are lying there without care and without a roof over their heads. Doctors are still available, only no places to work!"

On the next day, May 2, the report of the Army High Command issued this announcement: "The Führer has died at the head of the courageous defenders of the Reich capital." That same day at 3:00 p.m., General Weidling, whom Hitler had appointed commander of Berlin on April 23, submitted the official capitulation. Weidling stated unequivocally that the Führer had committed suicide and thereby abandoned all who had sworn loyalty to him. He went on to urge anyone to cease resistance at once. Cars with loudspeakers conveyed this message along deserted streets: "Every hour that you continue to fight only prolongs the terrible suffering of the civilian population and of our wounded. Anyone who still dies fighting for Berlin makes this ultimate sacrifice in vain." General Weidling, who was not a member of the Nazi Party, ultimately became a Soviet prisoner accused of war crimes and died in a Soviet prison in 1955.

On that same May 2—although I doubt that Api knew this—ten men who were to play a decisive part in the city's future for decades to come arrived in Berlin. These were the Gruppe Ulbricht, a group of German communist functionaries under the leadership of Walter Ulbricht. They returned from their Soviet exile, where they had busied themselves translating propaganda material into German and supporting the Soviet regime in every way they could. Now they were sent back to Germany with the commission to rebuild district administrations in Berlin under communist guidance. Eventually, Walter Ulbricht became the head of the new German Democratic Republic, the DDR, which he ruled despotically as first secretary of the Socialist Unity Party from 1950 until chairman Leonid Breshnev forced him to resign in 1971.

On May 4, Api was ordered to report to the post office bunker on Monbijoustrasse, at the end of Ziegelstrasse, where help was desperately needed for the many injured there. The next morning, he packed his rucksack with his few belongings and moved to the cellar of the post office bunker. He found conditions there even worse than what he had experienced so far. He was surrounded by 135 wounded lying on pallets on the floor. The air stank of their wounds, and not much could be done to help the sufferers. And then there were the lice. They crawled everywhere in that dark and moldy cellar, and Api scratched himself all through the night. Later, in the winter of 1945, the health department issued a poster that warned, "*Töte die Laus, sonst tötet sie dich*," "Kill the louse or it kills you." Lice carried typhus and paratyphus.

Api overheard a conversation in the post office bunker that he took down right away. An anxious patient stopped a passing Russian officer to ask, "What will become of us? Are we going to Siberia?" "Nonsense," responded the Russian in his broken German. "You go home, and you will do same work you have done so far. The Russian isn't bad and the German isn't bad, but sentimental. *Lumpen*," meaning scoundrels, "exist among Russians and Germans alike. And Siberia. With that, they only wanted to scare you. What do you think of Siberia? No one eats black bread there like yours." This officer was typical of many of the Russians who first visited the clinics. They were honest and understanding military men who felt sorry for what this war had done both to their own and to the German people.

The next day, Sunday, May 6, was the first warm day, and Api, with the day off from the post office bunker, helped to install a hospital in the former North Sanatorium nearby. It had been a small private clinic with a capacity of thirty-two beds. It felt good to get out of the dark post office bunker and see the sky. On his way, Api took time to observe, "A wonderful morning with a pale blue sky in which swim, almost transparent themselves, the ornaments of the church towers." The beginning of May was balmy, with sunny days and blue skies. The surviving linden trees were a bright green, and their blossoms covered the dust and rubble on the pavement. Api delighted, as he had always done, in the signs of nature's rebirth. And even though he felt dizzy, feverish, and sick to his stomach, just being out of doors helped him a little to cope with what lay ahead in labor, pain, and mental shock.

The staff at the North Sanatorium welcomed him with open arms. There was much to be done to ready the place for patients, so, every day after he was finished at the post office bunker, Api helped out at the North Sanatorium. There, he witnessed a much wilder group of Soviet soldiers than had come earlier to the Ziegelstrasse clinic. They were looting the little the doctors had managed to scrape together for their patients. They considered that everything in Berlin was rightfully theirs—"Private property does not exist; everything is Soviet property"—although their first edict had declared pillaging forbidden. Api found a pair of high-laced shoes to replace his army boots, but he did not dare clean them, for fear that if they looked good, they would be taken away. Over the next weeks, the lawlessness and lack of personal security added a heavy burden to his other worries.

As soon as the war had ended, Api had had one main goal: to come to us in Suderburg, or at least to let us know that he had survived. But neither was possible. Without permissions or papers, he saw no way of fleeing from Berlin and undertaking the long journey on foot. And without postal service, he could not communicate with us. Instead, Api handed letters and postcards to anyone who was trying to get out of Berlin. The first message that made it through did not reach us until September 10, 1945.

At last, on May 8, came the official declaration that beginning at midnight on May 9, all fighting was to cease. This announcement followed the signing of the military surrender with the Allies and the Red Army at midnight of May 8 in the Soviet headquarters in Karlshorst, on the southeastern edge of Berlin. World War II was finally and officially over, for the West at least. The Army High Command ended its records with this rather Prussian bow to the millions of dead: "In this difficult hour, the armed forces commemorate their comrades lost before the enemy. The dead demand unconditional loyalty, obedience, and discipline for the fatherland, which is bleeding from innumerable wounds."

The Soviets declared May 9 Victory Day, and outbreaks of shooting from machine guns, flak stations, tanks, and pistols scared Berliners anew, but they were only "salutes to peace." Today, Germans often call May 9 Liberation Day, although those who lived through it at the time did not see it that way.

# 23

# UNFULFILLED YEARNINGS

Now that the war was finally over, Api gathered what little emotional and physical energy he had left to think about rebuilding his practice. Trying to find a way to support his family forced him not to give up and even at times buoyed him with thoughts of a once-again-happy future with them. He dreamed that he could start again, as he had done in 1920. At the same time, it also drove him to despair, for he did not know how to accomplish this one supremely important goal of his life and feared that he was no longer up to the task.

The mornings and evenings were Api's hardest times, yet he always got up at six, "only so that I can give myself for one hour to my painful longing." During the rest of the day, Api had little time to worry about his situation, since hard work took up every minute. From eight in the morning, the time the curfew ended, to eight at night, without rest, he assisted in small operations, did surgical dressings, and saw patients. He was often overwhelmed by how little he could do for them. He was particularly affected by starving babies and their sick mothers, for whom he was unable to provide nourishment.

In addition to medical work, Api also labored physically. The military hospital in the North Sanatorium still needed so much. He hauled furniture and foraged for medications and dressing materials in all kinds of devastated places. He explored abandoned medical cellars and gingerly climbed broken stairs to former supply rooms. Wherever he went, he had to be careful not to step on broken glass or sharp bits of metal, which lay buried under thick layers of dust. His clothes and hair became impregnated with dust, and the pores of his skin were caked with it, plastered down by sweat. The weather had turned oppressively hot, and the plague of lice made his dirty skin itch unbearably.

On May 10, Api was given permission to leave the post office bunker and settle in the North Sanatorium. For the first time in weeks, he had a place to stay above ground; in fact, it was an attic room four stories up. Of the two small windows in his room, one was half cardboard, the other open altogether. But at least he could see the sky. He drew in deep breaths, although the air was still tinged with smoke and dust. Except for the clouds and the birds, the view that met him was depressing. He looked out on the burned rafters of a bombed-out roof directly across from him. The other buildings had no roofs at all. They were just a sea of gray ruins. Only here and there a church spire still reached out of the rubble.

On the first full day in his attic room, Api celebrated the occasion by giving himself a thorough wash, even though he had only cold water, which he had to carry in. It was difficult to rub the grime out of his pores and hair, but the wash did him good. Afterward, he put on fresh underwear, which in itself was a luxury. He brushed and shook out his army shirt and pants, which he had worn for weeks, but since he had no other clothing, he had to make do with them again. For his final layer, he pulled out of his rucksack a blue-gray sweater that had once belonged to Nyussi. It had accompanied him during the worst days of his son's death, as well as the happy moments in Suderburg. It had become to him a symbol of her love, and he never put it on without kissing it first.

Feeling clean and protected, Api sat down by the open window and took out his diary. From then on, he would spend every free minute by his attic window, dreaming of freedom and a reunion. He regularly scanned the sky, noting the shapes of the clouds, the flight of the swallows, and how the sun painted the torn and bent rafters a golden red. This became his meditative respite, even if it often ended in desperate longing. Despite his belief in always being purposeful, he also remarked that "all this conjuring up of sweetest thoughts is useless and lost time, but for me it is uplifting." He continued his observations:

"On a pale blue evening sky, big-bellied and deformed wind clouds are spread in a colorless light. Through it race, screeching, a few swifts (many don't have any possibility of nesting, since everything is rubble and ashes). Smoke columns from new fires still rise somewhere above the ruins of the roofs, sometimes thinner, sometimes thicker. The air is heavy with dust and smoke." Hearing someone across the street playing an out-of-tune piano, he continued, "We will certainly not make music anymore. . . . And yet if only the family and the enjoyment of God's wonderful nature remain for us, how I would pray and work in humble thankfulness! . . . But perhaps I love you even more now than then, that is, more consciously aware that you are my one and all in this world. . . . If only one were free!! Freedom, health, a bicycle for which I would give gold—and off to you!!!"

A map of Germany was always on his bedside table, and his eyes often measured the distance of about 150 miles from Berlin to Uelzen, the district capital. Suderburg was too small to be listed, but he marked the spot where it should be with a little cross.

In a spare moment on Monday, May 14, when the air had cleared after a heavy night storm, Api went back to the Luisenstrasse cellar to fetch the only clothes left to him, so that he could delouse what he had been living in for all that time. After the fourth-floor apartment had been destroyed, Api had stored some of his belongings in the cellar. That was also where he put his son's bike. He had made sure to take out the valves to prevent theft. Now he carefully climbed down the stairs to the cellar, crunching broken glass beneath his boots. With each step, his feet sank into the fine, chalklike dust that covered everything in the city. When he reached the door of his section of the cellar, he found the lock broken. Looking inside, he saw that everything was gone. He particularly missed the suitcase in which he had stored all his papers, poems, and diaries. I, too, am sorry that I have only a handful of letters and poems of what must have been hundreds of pieces of writing, for Api recorded everything. Most of what I have dates from after 1945: poems for our birthdays, Christmas, and New Year, and others about the seasons on the heath. Looking at the empty cellar, Api, however, was most devastated by the loss of his son's bicycle, on which he had set such hope. It was to be his way out of Berlin and to us.

However, Api knew that he could not leave and that even if, with extraordinary luck, he should get out of Berlin without being stopped or shot, he would not be able to cross the Elbe River, the wide river that formed part of the dividing line between the Soviet occupation zone and those of the Western Allies. Api had heard rumors that people either drowned in the river or were killed by the Allies on the bridge. Despite all this, the loss of the bike was a physical reminder of his imprisonment.

I remember as a child standing on the shore of the Elbe near Hamburg, not far from where it flows into the North Sea. I was on the western side, looking across to the ominous wooden watchtowers along the eastern shore. Occasionally I caught a glimpse of an armed patrol. To me, the Ostzone, the Eastern Zone, was a forbidden land of mystery and danger. Still, today, long after reunification, I cannot get used to the ease with which Mike and I drive into the former East Germany. There is just a sign on the Autobahn telling us that this is where East Germany began, and we notice that the highway is newer from then on. What was to me a forbidden country when I was growing up is now just a smooth, uninterrupted stretch of highway.

On his way back from the apartment, Api noticed signs that showed that he was not alone in his worry about relatives. People had left messages on bits of paper stuck to door frames or pinned to lampposts. Some said that they had survived and could be found at this new address. Others asked for information about the occupants of one of the flats in what was now a gaping hole or a heap of stones. Mothers were looking for their sons who had served in the Volkssturm and had not been heard from since. People had no other way of communicating than through these scraps of paper. So many messages, each with its own desperate story and little hope of a happy ending.

When Api climbed the stairs up to his attic, a patient from the North Sanatorium was waiting at his door. Knowing how much Api would enjoy it, he offered him a bouquet of lilies of the valley and a few stalks of lilac he had picked out of the ruins. Any sign of nature softened Api's despair and kindled his love, also his love of words. He was grateful that the patient had taken the trouble of bringing these gifts of spring to him. "The lilies of the valley are fragrant on my little table. The lilac stands in my attic window with the pale blue evening sky in the background, above which radiant pink wind clouds drift northeast in a barely perceptible movement, a symbol of the most distant, the most delicate, unfulfillable dreams of peace and happiness under a heaven of divine infinity and steady goodness."

Increasingly, Api slept badly and suffered from night sweats. During, the day he had dizzy spells and felt feverish. Sleep was difficult because of constant noise in the streets, where Soviet soldiers were shooting almost as if the war were still raging. Yet Api could not afford to be tired. In addition to medical work, he had errands to run. He needed a certificate to show that he was working for the public health department. And he wanted to make sure that it said, as was the case, that he was doing so without obligation, so that he could start a private practice. Perhaps Api thought back to his controversy with the Charité over setting up his own practice and wanted to avoid a similar conflict. In order to get this certificate, he first had to go to chief army physician Dr. Kleberger, who was in charge of the North Sanatorium, and then to the mayor. I am not sure but assume that this was the chief mayor of Berlin, Dr. Arthur Werner, whom Bersarin had appointed. His office was in the Neues Stadthaus, the New City Hall, a hike of about an hour. Api was glad that he did not have to go as far as Alexanderplatz, a center for black marketeers. Cigarettes were the currency that got one access to anything: old shoes, herrings, used clothes, and even a little Nescafé.

For the first time, Api noticed long columns of women, their heads wrapped in kerchiefs. They were known as the *Trümmerfrauen*, the rubble women. For eight hours a day, they passed buckets of stones from hand to hand in a human chain. They salvaged what bricks were still usable by cleaning off the old cement and stacking them in neat rows. Hundreds of thousands of bricks were restored in this way from what seemed like an inexhaustible supply. Berlin Mitte alone had 127 million cubic feet of rubble. Altogether, six square miles of the city had been leveled, creating three billion cubic feet of rubble. Except for the *Trümmerfrauen*, Api saw few people roaming around the mountains of crumbled and dusty stones.

Once he got the certificate, Api turned his mind seriously to rebuilding his practice. His young colleague Dr. Heinz Kraaz offered to come to Luisenstrasse to see what could be done there. For hours, Dr. Kraaz swept and shoveled with true joy, although they almost suffocated from the dust they stirred up. Api was grateful for the young man's help, and even more so for his encouraging presence. Alone, he would have given up in despair, especially when he came across bits and pieces of his past. He found a picture of me, which that evening inspired him to write, "Take good care of our littlest sunshine and occasionally tell her of her poor Api's heartrending longing. . . . But yet leave her some sunshine, which she needs for the development of her little soul."

From the middle of May on, about two weeks after the end of the war, his courage seriously began to desert Api. So far he had struggled on, hoping first that the war would end soon, then that the Americans would come and alleviate the Soviet occupation. When that failed, he still hoped that he would be able to travel to Suderburg and, taking us back with him, start his practice again in his old home. Instead, he was trapped in a devastated city without hope of seeing us ever again.

For the first time in his life, the thought of suicide began to haunt him, although he never called it that directly in his diary. On the Thursday night of May 17, he made the first oblique reference: "I do not know what will happen. Never before have I felt so close to this step, so compellingly close! Hopelessness, loneliness, bleakness, boundless desolation, and direct danger with 100,000 screaming and terrible voices which drown out the memory of the sweetest harmony and blissful contentment. Gone! Gone for all time." A heavy thunderstorm accompanied by such a wind that he feared his little attic would blow away seemed to echo his desperate and tumultuous thoughts. He finally took Bromural, a heavy sleeping powder, to help him through the night.

# 24

# PENTECOST SUNDAY

On Saturday, May 19, Api obtained a certificate of military discharge from Professor Ferdinand Sauerbruch, of the Charité, who from May to October 1945 served on the Berlin City Council for Health. Thus officially relieved of his military responsibilities, Api felt freer and decided to take a walk in search of a church for the following day's Pentecost Sunday, the descent of the Holy Spirit. He loved to hear an organ, but none of the ones he saw that afternoon would ever play again. Although the sky was cloudless, it was veiled in smoke and the stench of corpses brooded unbearably beneath it.

Api could not bear to be alone on Pentecost. It had always been such a bright, joyful holiday at the beginning of spring. So he went to look for his two friends Sister Briese and Sister Baesler, both deaconesses at the North Sanatorium. They were not the Nazi deaconesses who had sworn their oath of loyalty to Hitler instead of Jesus, but the traditional Protestant ones. Much like Catholic nuns, these Protestant sisters lived together in mother houses, where they shared a simple life. Each order had its own habit, although they all wore stiff white caps ruffled at the back, mostly gray or blue shirts with white collars, and a short tunic. Their only decoration was a broach or chain with a cross and the insignia of their order. Api had always felt close to the deaconesses he had known, whose mission it was to serve others, particularly the sick. He shared their strong Lutheranism and respected their dedication. At the North Sanatorium, he had come to love the two sisters who visited every day from their mother house on nearby Tieckstrasse to help out wherever they were needed.

When I lived with my grandparents after the war, they continued to befriend the local deaconesses. Many a time I came in from play to see one of these elderly ladies in her white cap having coffee with Api and Nyussi, who always served special treats for them. As I greeted the guest with a curtsy, the little cape around her shoulders always struck me. To me, it looked as if she had stepped out of a fairy tale. But then, my formal curtsy now seems part of another world as well, although I remember that I greeted adults with curtsies well into my teenage years.

Api and the two deaconesses set out to find a church that still had a playable organ. They walked to the end of Ziegelstrasse and Monbijou Park, where just a few days earlier Api had watched the chief physician drop corpses. They passed the old Jewish cemetery that the Nazis had destroyed in 1943. The adjacent redbrick syna-gogue had already been damaged in Kristallnacht. Two blocks east of there, only a fifteen-minute walk altogether, stood Sophien Church, the head church of the parish where Api had been an elder. Api was delighted when he saw that the church still had its organ intact.

The three of them sat in a pew with a small group of other ragged and careworn people, looking out of the broken windows onto black-ened trees. As the organ began, Api's thoughts drifted westward to Suderburg and a much smaller, tree-shaded church. "Oh, how close I was to you and with what desperate longing did I think of our last church visit in Suderburg. Blessed, blessed time!"

Mike and I also paid a visit to Sophien Church. It has the most beautiful baroque onion spire in all of Berlin; it beckoned us with its glistening, delicate green-and-gold-copper top. We found the church sequestered in its small yard, shaded by old linden trees—perhaps survivors from 1945. An eight-foot-high ornate iron railing separates the church grounds from the quiet neighborhood of tree-lined streets and apartment houses.

When we walked on, we found other places Api had mentioned in the diary. The large, redbrick St. Hedwig Hospital is still there, around the corner from the church, and we saw how close it was to the synagogue, also built of red brick. The whole area exuded a subdued calm and repose, but it also felt left behind the times. Part of the former East Berlin, it had not yet caught up with the busy commercialism of the West. In contrast with the streets west of Kurfürstendamm, we saw no restaurants, wine bars, and bakeries, and very few people.

After the Pentecost service, Api decided to make use of this holiday to do more cleaning in his surgery. The windows were all broken, and glass unavailable. There also was no electricity, without which his surgery could not function. Nevertheless, he was determined to hold office hours again soon. He made up his mind to look for new instruments, since the old ones had become damaged and useless. His bank accounts and savings certificates were gone, but he had some cash left. Sometime in the middle of May, I do not know exactly when, Api put most of that money into the reconstruction of his practice. In his diary, he justified his action. "I had to make the effort. That also is the reason—among others—why I decided to stay. God grant that it was right."

Although Api did not mention it, and perhaps he did not know, on that Pentecost Sunday, May 20, while he was busy in his surgery, a new Berlin city council was formed. It was dominated by the communists, who held 100 out of 230 seats. Even if he heard this news, he could not have foreseen that this was the beginning of the totalitarian rule that presided over the entire communist German Democratic Republic until the fall of the Berlin wall in 1989.

When Api returned to his attic, he found a piece of cake on his table—a gift from the nurses at the North Sanatorium. Throughout his career, Api had been on excellent terms with nurses. He was cordial, considerate, and charming. They knew how much he esteemed them, and they liked that he could make them laugh even amid the worst pressures, so they tried to look after him as well. It was their caring as much as the food that sustained Api in his loneliness. After he had eaten the cake, he fetched twelve pails of water for the special treat of a bath.

Api ended Pentecost Sunday by his attic window. He gazed at a silver half moon and wondered whether at this very moment we were enjoying the same sight out of our cottage window. As he contemplated that sliver of moon, a smile spread across his weary face. He was thinking about an argument he had had with his daughter, my mother. She was small, not yet in school. Looking out their living room window, she saw a bright and fully rounded moon lighting up the courtyard. She ran quickly to the kitchen at the front of the apartment, and, yes, there was another, just as round and bright, shedding its silver light on the street below. With such incontrovertible evidence, she refused to believe her father's explanation that there was only one moon in the sky.

# 25

# A LITTLE LIGHT

On Pentecost Monday, Api arranged with Herr Küssner to have a special memorial for his son, Dieter. Api often mentioned Küssner in his diary in connection with the Charité chapel, but I had no luck finding him in the chapel's extensive archives. Finally, Dr. Karin Köhler, archivist at the *Landeskirchliche Archiv*, helped me out. She met me in her office with a stack of papers, saying she hoped I would find what I needed there. It didn't take me long to see Küssner's name. Not surprisingly, he had been the minister at Philippus Apostel Church, where Api had been an elder. The pastor had known my grandparents since 1924, when they moved to Luisenstrasse and he was an assistant minister. Ernst Küssner was born in Berlin in 1878, ten years before Api, and like Api had studied at Friedrich Wilhelm University. He was ordained in 1905 and appointed at Philippus Apostel Church in 1916, first as assistant, then as second pastor, and in 1935 as first pastor. In the records I even found Api's name as a member of the church council, which met at Albrechtstrasse 15, not far from the bunker and my mother's elementary school.

The church archives had pictures of the church both as it had been before the war and as it looked after the bombing. Today, no trace of that church is left. It was an unremarkable neogothic stone building from the end of the nineteenth century. The one thing that struck me as unusual was its square spire. After the bombing, only the bottom of the tower and one crumbling wall were left. This explained why Pastor Küssner held services in the Charité chapel, yet I was unable to locate him through the archives. In the immediate postwar days, pastors could preach in any church that was still intact enough to allow it, so Pastor Küssner helped out in the nearby Charité chapel, which, although damaged, could still be used.

The memorial for my uncle was not all Api discussed with his pastor friend. He also broached the question of whether a Christian was ever allowed to take his own life. Api did not record the pastor's answer, but I can imagine that it was an absolute no. Api ended by telling Pastor Küssner that if things went badly, he would make sure Küssner got the diary to preserve for us.

On Tuesday, May 22, Api was buoyed by small bits of progress, and not even the steady rain that day could dampen his mood. He managed to get some electrical supplies and even a promise to install them from an electrician who told him that he could bring in electricity from the building next door. With electric light, Api could start to see patients. The electrician showed up the very next day, as promised. Once he had made the repairs and light came up in the rooms, Api, too, felt a surge of energy. Even better, he discovered that much of his expensive equipment still worked. The electrician wanted to be of further help and started to dismantle a cracked light above the mirror in the entrance hall. Api rushed to stop him; his son had installed the light. Clinging to the last tokens of Dieter's presence, he became almost ferocious. "I had to intervene almost with force. Every time I switch it on, I think of his love, which made him put this together for me. I see and feel his beloved little strong paws. Oh, my good boy. If I could get your advice now, I would probably follow it, since I have such great trust in your decisions as I have lost now in my own."

Api was fortunate also in his hunt for other treasures, which were so very hard to obtain. He found a bit of cardboard, a piece of glass, and even some nails. In this he was particularly lucky, for nails were almost impossible to get, even on the black market. The apartment, however, still had no running water. He had to carry water in from the nearby police barracks, whose yard was dug up for mass graves. As he walked his district, he now could hear a radio playing here and there, although he himself still had only rumors for news.

The day of the electrician, however, also brought a crisis. Api had a row with the North Sanatorium's chief physician, Dr. Kleberger, which shook him badly. In what my grandfather thought had been an amicable conversation the day before, they had agreed that there was no longer enough volunteer work for him to do at the North Sanatorium and that he needed to find a living for himself. Now, the chief physician denied having said anything of the sort. Api felt as if his life was going in crazy circles and as if he had returned to the fight with the Charité at the beginning of his career, but now he was much less able to handle it.

Both Api and Dr. Kleberger were certain that they were right. So they looked for confirmation from the person in charge of health in Berlin Mitte, and that was Professor Sauerbruch. At the Charité, they were told that the professor was in an operation. Dr. Kleberger waited right there, but Api—unwisely, it seems—left for an appointment. When he returned two hours later, Dr. Kleberger had already talked to Professor Sauerbruch, and Api was sure that he had given a one-sided report. Trying to write away his agitation, Api recollected that Dr. Kleberger was not popular with the doctors. He remembered when Dr. Kleberger had told them that it was out of the question to appear in civilian clothes. Two days later, however, he himself did just that. "He told us that after all everyone is wearing civilian clothes now except for those who are not able to do so (probably meaning because they did not have any)." Api concluded, "At any rate, he always was uncomradely, egoism personified. But let's leave that." However, in his fragile state, Api found it hard to forget this altercation, although nothing came of it. He continued to help out at the clinic, but the uncertainty of the unresolved situation worried him for the rest of his stay in Berlin.

The end of May was as cold as its beginning had been hot. Temperatures stayed below fifty degrees Fahrenheit. New rumors raised Api's level of anxiety. One in particular upset him, reminding him of the disagreement with Dr. Kleberger. He heard that military discharges issued by Professor Sauerbruch, as his had been, were not legally binding. Api had no idea whether there was any truth to this and, if so, what it meant for his position. Would he be classified as a deserter? And if he were, what should or could he do about it? In the end, he felt too enervated to do anything or even dwell on the implications of what might after all be only empty gossip.

The futility of his existence was brought home to him again on Saturday, May 26, when the Soviets tried to blow up the bridge in front of the Kaiser Friedrich Museum, today called the Bode Museum, on Museum Island, a few blocks west of where Api was. The heavy detonations blew out the one window he just had managed to install.

That evening at his attic window, he wrote by the failing light: "If peace and rest would come at last!! An indescribably beautiful and peaceful evening sky and the poor earth torn apart in hostility and destruction, in enmity and hatred, in impossibility for life and in misery. I recognize that it is a near superhuman task to put this almost completely demolished Berlin back into operation. But what will happen if it does not succeed?" He needed an Allional to get through that night.

## 26

# LEAD US NOT INTO TEMPTATION

A chilly and rainy Sunday morning, the Sunday of his son's memorial service, put Api into a particularly sad and nostalgic mood. As often before, the day began with the sounds of the out-of-tune piano drifting over from a neighboring building. Although it was off key, he immediately recognized the melody. It was the beautiful seventeenth-century hymn, "Praise to the Lord, the Almighty, the King of Creation." As he listened, he thought back to his family's Sunday-morning coffee on the balcony above the roofs of Berlin. They would all be dressed in their Sunday best for the church service at ten. Then, with a smile, he remembered that not quite all of them were ready, for Dieter was always the last out of bed. For a moment, he lost track of time and, like his beloved son, had to hurry to ready himself for the service. Putting on his clothes, he suffered a sudden panic attack about us. Perhaps we were not even alive anymore? He had to force himself to finish dressing and hasten to the Charité. The chapel was heavily damaged. The neogothic windows were gone, and the roof with its step facade was partially collapsed. The weary and anxious congregation sat in what remained of the pews, their feet shuffling back and forth in layers of mortar and dust.

But the service offered Api some consolation. Pastor Küssner gave a moving speech commemorating my uncle, and afterward the congregation supported him with their compassion. The final hymn was "Sing, My Soul, to God Who Made Thee." Api gladly joined in this well-known song, which expresses deep faith in a God who, through everything, takes care of His children. "When I sleep His care surrounds me, with new strength and youth imbues . . ."

My grandparents' favorite hymn writer, Paul Gerhardt, often called "the sweet singer of Lutheranism," composed the text. As Api sang along with the small congregation, he thought how Paul Gerhardt himself had experienced violent times during the seventeenth-century religious wars. And he, too, had lived in Berlin, where he had served as a pastor not far from where Api was sitting just then.

I share Api's love of Paul Gerhardt, or, more likely, learned it from him. Gerhardt wrote many of the most popular Lutheran hymns, such as "Commit Whatever Grieves Thee," in 1656, and "O Sacred Head, Now Wounded," which is sung in Lutheran churches in Germany during Good Friday services. Both Api and I were particularly fond of the folk song–like evening hymn "*Nun Ruhen alle Wälder,*" "Now All the Woods Are Sleeping."

After the service, Api wrote, "I am so grateful to God and will not slacken off in my prayers to strengthen in me a true, vigorous, kindly Christianity, a childlike trust in God's providence, and a quiet and humble submission to His will." As if to reflect his momentarily lighter mood, the rainy morning had turned into a wonderfully bright and sunny, if still cool, day.

Soon thereafter, Api found two books that became a mainstay for the rest of his time in Berlin. One was a hymnal, and the other Heinrich Spengler's *Der Kleine Pilgerstab* (*The Little Pilgrim's Staff*), a book of morning and evening devotions for each day of the Christian calendar year. A popular work in Germany, it had seen many editions since its first appearance in 1888, the year of Api's birth. Api's own edition, which I still have, dates from 1927. From the moment he discovered the book, he followed the *Pilgerstab*'s messages of faith, hope, and love for each day. He opened the heavy black book, noticing how the gold ornamentation on the front cover had almost disappeared under the grime, and looked up the passage for that night. It came from his favorite Psalms, specifically 17:8, and he read, "As the apple of thy eye me keep; in thy wings shade me close."

From this point on in the aftermath of the war, Api clung more and more desperately to his faith to avoid a complete breakdown. He began and ended each day with a ten-minute reading from both books. He always looked forward to these morning and evening devotions. In the hymnal, he preferred the section on "Cross and Consolation," with hymns like "A Christian Cannot Live Without a Cross," which reminded him that everyone had a burden to bear and that God watched over all. Every morning on waking, Api also said the little prayer with which Nyussi and he had greeted each new day. It comes from a Protestant breviary of 1857, where it is designated as a morning prayer for children. He loved the lines, "*Du warst mit Deinem Schutz bei mir*"; "You were with me with your protection."

Although Api always went to church on Sundays, he was ashamed of his crumpled and dirty clothes. When Max Gerhardt, his friend and former neighbor, saw Api's shabby appearance, he gave him a pair of so-called Stresemann pants, formal gray striped pants, and a black jacket to go along with them. Now it felt good to dress up on Sundays. Api also still had the single pearl tie pin that he liked to wear for festive occasions. Despite his gray hair and gray face, he looked quite presentable, less like the shabby beggar he felt he really was. Reading about the pin, I thought how often I had seen him with it after the war. He wore it on his tie under his white doctor's coat and, of course, always on Sundays. I had forgotten all about it, but reading about that pearl tie pin conjured up happy memories of our times together.

Api divided his Sundays between the Sophien Church and the Charité chapel. He chose the former when the famous Pastor Döhring was holding services there. Since 1914, Bruno Döhring had held the office of court and cathedral preacher at the Cathedral of Berlin, across from the royal palace. He was, of course, the last person with that title, since there was no more imperial court after 1918. Döhring had been hugely popular, and his cathedral had always been crowded on Sundays. When times were hard in the 1930s, Döhring had his sermons printed to be sold after the service to raise funds for the poor. After Emperor Wilhelm II was exiled to Huis Doorn in Holland, Döhring dispatched a copy of his sermon to Doorn every week until Wilhelm's death in 1941, when the family chose Döhring to deliver the funeral oration.

The cathedral was destroyed on May 24, 1944, and when both pastors at the Sophien Church lost their lives in the last days of the war, Döhring helped out there. That was where Api heard his sermons. Pastor Döhring understood the desperate mood of his congregation and designed his sermons to comfort them. He knew that many were homeless, that they lived among the ruins in terror and insecurity, ravaged by hunger and sickness, with little hope for the future. The number of suicides increased daily. Physicians likewise were aware that at least half their patients came not to be cured but to ask for something to end their lives. Api's experience corroborates this: A number of his friends, men and women, committed suicide, and one of his patients in the North Sanatorium hanged himself.

Api often reported the gist of Döhring's sermon in his diary. Thus on Sunday, June 3, Pastor Döhring tried to assure the sad congregation that God would not forget the poor. Although these words did him good, Api's thoughts strayed to the old church in Suderburg, and he hoped God would forgive him this inattentiveness. His mind came back to the sermon just in time to hear Pastor Döhring's warning, which was so fitting for all of them: "As a Christian, one must not throw away one's life on one's own authority like a dirty piece of clothing, no matter how terribly difficult life has become. God will not forget about His poor people." Api felt as if Pastor Döhring were talking to him personally, and he prayed fervently that his faith in God's loving guidance would strengthen him to bear anything that was to come.

On another Sunday, Api recollected the pastor's having spoken about how with Christ and in Christ, all paths were possible. Api paid close attention and later quoted parts of the sermon in his diary. "These days in particular," Döhring had said, "will show that the mature Christian stands infinitely richer and firmer, and of an iron will . . . than someone who has not allowed himself to be touched by God. We cannot comprehend Him if He has not touched us. The longing for God is fulfilled only if someone says, 'I cannot live without my God.' But with Him we can bear anything, and we must continue to live until He says, 'It is enough now.' We should not urge the fulfillment of our wishes, however justified they may be." At the Charité chapel, Api heard much the same message from Pastor Küssner, along the theme of "lead us not into temptation, but deliver us of all evil."

# 27

# THE SILENCE

Sitting by his window on the evening of Tuesday, May 29, Api began to write about a topic most painful to him: his *Pg* (party member) status and the question of guilt. He reflected that he had often spoken out "with my patients and other officers with an openness which certainly could have had fateful consequences for me." Then, addressing Nyussi, he added, "You know how I and all of us have condemned those shameful measures of the Nazis." As for taking action, "Who could have done anything against this and how??" Yet he also voiced regret at his inaction. In the end, he felt that just being a member of the Party should not make him liable for persecution and punishment. It was a distressing subject for Api, and he revisited it only briefly on other occasions. But the following day, he still thought about it when he wrote a sort of farewell to us: "Should we not see each other again: thanks be to God for lovely days and that we never wanted evil for anyone or went past anyone's suffering without compassion."

Reading this today, I am confused on many levels. I understand that once Api joined the Party, he was caught, unable to do anything but complain, and even then only in secret, and that he now felt unjustly condemned in the rush to punish all former members of the Party indiscriminately. I am also reassured by his compassion for the suffering of others, which I have experienced firsthand. What bewilders me is that Api seems to talk of the war but does not mention the persecution of the Jews and the concentration camps, either here or elsewhere in his diary. He may not have known details about the concentration camps at the time when they occurred—many Germans did not. Even the well-connected journalist Ursula von Kardoff only found out about the mass murders of Jews after the war. But Api had surely witnessed many instances of persecution, had seen how Jewish businesses were ransacked, Jewish doctors disappeared, and even Jewish children were suddenly absent from the schools my mother and uncle attended. I wonder whether "those shameful measures of the Nazis" was a reference, albeit inadequate and oblique, to the Holocaust.

And whatever he did not know during the war, when Api was writing this at the end of May 1945, information about the horrors of the death camps was everywhere—in reports, news releases, and posters, and over the radio. I remember that when I was just three years old, I picked up the term *KZ* (short for "concentration camp") in the small village of Suderburg because I heard it mentioned everywhere. I knew it was important to the grown-ups, since they were always talking about it, but I had no idea what it meant. So one day I was singing "KZ, KZ" to myself when my mother rushed up and told me not to say that. I stopped. But I still did not know what was wrong, since everyone else used those letters all the time.

So why did Api say nothing? This is particularly striking when he himself suffered from persecution as a *Pg* and feared arrest at any time. He was prepared to leave at a moment's notice in the middle of the night, his clothes ready for immediate departure. Yet nowhere did he see his fate in relation to that of millions of Jews during the Nazi terror. Does his silence imply that he agreed in any way with the racism that ended up costing millions of lives? Is silence itself a sign of guilt? I cannot square this with his ethical and compassionate values. And yet perhaps he had succumbed to the prevailing anti-Semitism of his time. Kershaw notes that "latent or passive anti-Semitism was widespread." So why should Api be exempt? I have just one small, if inconclusive, bit of evidence in a letter from a Jewish colleague I found among Api's papers. I know nothing of the circumstances, only that the writer told Api that he had fled the Charité to Brazil, from where he was writing. He said how much Api's friendship had meant to him and that except for him and some members of his own family still left in Berlin, he cared for no one there. But then, I had to admit, one can like an individual and still be prejudiced against a group.

Perhaps Api said nothing because he felt as if it was too terrible to dwell on at a time when his nerves were overwrought with fear and desolation. Perhaps he was too ashamed. Or did he hide his head in the sand? What could he have done then, and what could he say now, as he was writing this? Who could have imagined atrocities of a kind and on a scale as the Nazis perpetrated? What collective guilt do the German people bear? Would I have acted any differently? Despite this torrent of unanswered questions, I simply cannot imagine that Api condoned fanatical hate and the mass murder of his fellow human beings.

Nevertheless, this silence still troubles and bewilders me, although I have learned that Api shared it with most of his compatriots. Even today, Germans of his generation are reluctant to speak about the Nazi persecution of the Jews. In his memoir, Joachim Fest quotes his father, who was a courageous and fervent anti-Nazi all along: "I did not want to talk about it then and I don't want to talk about it now! It reminds me that there was absolutely nothing I could do with my knowledge. Not even talk about it."

In fact, it is not even my generation but the one after mine that is breaking through the silence. Books are beginning to come out in twenty-first-century Germany that refer to silence in the title, such as *Silent Perpetrators, Talking Grandchildren, Silence Hurts,* and *After a Long Silence,* to name just a few. In 2009, I happened to speak on the phone with a man from a German village on the Mosel. His family lived next door to Kurt Simon, whose biography I had just finished. The man was probably in his forties, born well after the war. He admitted that his village had not yet come to terms with the Nazi period and the persecution of the few Jews who had lived there. "The old people here," he said, "still refuse to speak about the Nazis and the persecution of the Jews, even right here in our own village."

The Allies interpreted this German silence as a crass evasion of responsibility. "I have not found a single German ready to admit his personal guilt in the war," reported war correspondent Alan Moorehead. This assessment, however, appears too simplistic an interpretation of what Germans felt at that time. Moorehead's view can be explained by the shock and the horror he and the world at large felt as the truth about the death camps became known, as images of mass graves, gas chambers, and skeletal survivors appeared on newsreels. But it does not, and perhaps cannot be expected to, offer a nuanced insight into the minds and hearts of Germans in 1945, who at that point were themselves struggling to survive.

One evening, after a meal of peas and bits of meat that smelled bad, Api sought refuge from his worries in contemplating nature but ended with another oblique reference to German guilt. Despite the smoke clouds that still drifted across the peaceful evening sky, despite the vista of charred rafters and ruins, ". . . it is once again an evening of rare May beauty. A few pink evening clouds hang in the mother-of-pearl blue, almost motionless and transparently delicate like spirits of a goodness and nobility that has vanished from the earth. . . . On many such evenings our four-leaf clover sat on our little unforgettably cozy balcony, full of thoughts of peace, and in conversation about human ethics and divine providence! No one suspected anything about the brewing calamity until our leaders left the paths of lawfulness and we—well knowing but impotent—had to watch how the little boat drifted."

I am not surprised by the nostalgia Api voiced here, but I cannot understand his naiveté. Or is it a deliberate blindness? I am not sure what time Api is talking about when he says that they did not suspect anything, or at what point he thinks the Nazis left the paths of lawfulness and he felt "well knowing but impotent." This passage is one of those moments when I would love to talk with Api about that time and ask him what he meant, although I am not sure I would have done it anyway. And it is also an occasion when retracing Api's steps becomes most problematic for me.

# 28

# PROFESSIONAL DEVELOPMENT

Whenever he could get away from helping at the North Sanatorium, Api busied himself in his surgery. At the end of May, the first patients straggled in, and occasionally a Soviet officer was among them. But most of the time, he just waited. Even in the days of his earliest beginnings, he had not experienced such long hours of anxious waiting. He consoled himself with the thought that without public transport, patients had difficulty reaching him. But every time he heard a movement by his door, he jumped up with a pounding heart. If it was indeed a patient, Api would have liked to embrace him. Most often, however, there was no one there, just his wishful imagination playing tricks on him. Nevertheless, whenever a gust of wind moved the loose floorboards of the waiting room, he was there at the door, ready to receive his patient.

One day, Fräulein Herzog, his former nurse assistant, appeared, and they agreed to work together again, even if there was not much to do. She had, she said, nowhere else to go. Already middle aged, Fräulein Herzog was struggling with the loss of most of her family and trying to survive in Berlin by herself. She was a brave and resourceful woman, and she helped Api over the next weeks, just as he supported her.

To prepare himself for the resumption of his career, Api studied textbooks on ophthalmology. He feared that he had lost much expertise during the war years and needed to prepare himself once more for his career as eye surgeon. At the same time, he was afraid that as a *Pg* he would not be allowed to open a practice. Besieged by existential worries, he took refuge in the happy past. "I have to think backwards again and again; one can't look ahead yet."

At the back of his desk drawer, Api discovered a tiny picture album, a survivor from the past that helped him to think backward even more. He stroked its pretty marbled cover, decorated with a faded red stripe at the binding. It is large enough only for one small picture on each page. I still have that small album so that I can follow what Api looked at. There is my mother's first day of school, which shows her in knee socks, a short pleated skirt, and a sailor's top with stripes at the neck and wrists. These must have been fashionable at the time, but more than twenty years later I had just such a sailor outfit for special occasions. She is clutching her *Schultüte*, the large, colorful paper cone stuffed with sweets that first-graders get from their parents to help ease them into the beginning of school. She looks at once proud and afraid of this new world into which she is about to step.

On another page I see Nyussi, her long, dark hair gathered at the neck, in a slim skirt and patterned blouse. She is leaning against Api on their balcony. It must be a weekend, for he is dressed in his leisure-time vest and knickerbockers and holding a paper on his knee. Next, there is Nyussi again, this time in a cape and dark hat pulled over her eyes. She stands in front of their building with my mother crouching beside her, a big bow on her head, and my curly-haired uncle Dieter at her other side.

In the middle of the album, I come across one picture of myself in Bevensen that must have been inserted later. I am eight years old, standing in the bedroom I still shared with my grandparents and bending over a pram of which I was very proud. The Hinzpeter painting of the Chiemsee hangs over the double bed. And I notice that I am wearing just such a big bow on my head as my mother had at my age. As I flip through the pages once again, the album strikes me, as it must have Api, as being from another world than the one in which he found himself in 1945 or in which I am living today.

June began with an order that bewildered Api, as it did all Berliners. It was one of those absurd occurrences that happen in times of chaos, especially since by then there were four nations governing Berlin. On June 1, an order went out that every house that was still inhabited must fly the Russian, American, English, and French national flags in a size of at least two and a half by six feet. No one knew why this had to be done or how to accomplish it. Everyone looked for bits of red, white, and blue cloth to stitch together makeshift flags to hang out the windows. Those who still had Nazi flags hidden away quickly cut out the red part for the Russian flag. As people set about this task, Berliners worried about how many stars to put in the American flag. So, always quick-witted, they added a line to the popular German children's song: *"Weisst du wieviel Sternlein stehen?"* "Do you know how many stars are in the sky?" *"Denn du musst sie schleunigst nähen."* "For you have to sew them now."

One troubling topic at the North Sanatorium was that the Soviet occupation administration had decreed that for every Soviet who was shot by members of Operation Werwolf, fifty members of the Nazi Party would be executed. Operation Werwolf had been the Nazi's last-ditch effort at resistance, a clandestine force that was supposed to wage guerilla war against the occupiers and sabotage their installations. It never amounted to much, but the Allies took the threat seriously, believing that Werwolf activities could "hardly be overrated." Their fierce measures against the population in the early days of the occupation can be attributed in part to this fear of Werwolf attacks. Api saw no evidence of any Werwolf activity. He had never believed in the idea of Werwolf, regarding it as another terrible legacy of the Nazis, "this gang of criminals."

Early in June, an unexpected treasure arrived in his surgery: a beautiful Siemens radio. It came from his friend and former neighbor Herr Gerhardt. Api hoped that it would provide more accurate news than the rumor mill about all the new orders from the Soviets. He carefully placed it on his little table and admired the shiny wooden box. It had a brown fabric front with metallic threads woven in and two large black dials, one for switching on, the other for choosing a station.

Api turned the dial, hoping for a news broadcast or at least some classical music. But he found only the throbbing rhythms of dance music. "I cannot listen and do not want to. Dance music in this misery is perverse, paradoxical for my tortured, longing heart. Nevertheless, one has to listen in hope of any news and to find out about the constant stream of new regulations." Of vital interest to him were any clues about whether evacuees were allowed to come back to Berlin or whether Berliners could leave the city. So he kept the radio on anyway.

Professionally, Api had some good news. Starting on June 4, Professor Löhlein invited him to collaborate in his eye surgery class at the university, to be held each morning from eight to eleven. Api was delighted at this opportunity and relieved, too, that he had taken up his study again.

To make himself more presentable for his assignment, he went in search of a haircut. He found a barber on the ground floor of a roofless building. As he sat in the barber's chair, he had leisure to study himself in the mirror. He was shocked at the image that stared back at him. How much he had changed! The last weeks had turned him into an aged and lifeless old man. His face was as gray as his surroundings in this dust-covered rubble heap of a city. His once clear and usually smiling blue eyes looked too large for his emaciated face and stared back at him without light. Deep lines ran from his nose to his thin mouth, and the little laugh lines by his eyes had become invisible in his ashen face. He later wrote, "If only I could see a clear road ahead, how gladly would I work and what strength I could still muster to support us and make a new start!" That happy vision, however, was still only a dream.

The fulfillment of this dream was further threatened when Api developed intestinal problems. He was afraid of an attack of dysentery such as he had suffered at the beginning of World War I and that had had fearful consequences. Some mornings his stomach cramps and diarrhea got so bad that he was afraid of passing out. He knew from personal experience that dysentery was becoming widespread. For lack of eye patients, Api often functioned as a general practitioner making house calls. For the most part, he did not charge for his services, for many of his patients were worse off than he was himself.

# 29

# NYUSSI'S BIRTHDAY

The early days of June brought a trial of a different sort for Api's overwrought nerves. June 9 was Nyussi's birthday. At the beginning of the month, he started a letter to her, to which he added every day. He had little hope that this ever-growing message would reach her, as indeed it did not, but the very act of writing made him feel close to her. In the process, he remembered the many birthdays they had spent together. He gave them names: the first Dahlem birthday in 1920, with his mother's flowers; the Buick birthday, when they had bought their first big car, the "green one," in 1926; the rose bouquet birthday, on vacation in Bad Elster in 1943, when, on that very day, it was confirmed that my father had died; and 1944, just a year earlier, the bouquet of tiny wood flowers with the paltry little cake in Joachimsthal, where Nyussi, my mother, and I stayed briefly after we were bombed out.

Api began Nyussi's birthday, Saturday, June 9, by opening his book of daily devotions to that day, the first Saturday after Trinitatis. What he found seemed to be addressed to him directly: "Then he said to them: 'You of little faith, why are you so anxious?'" The commentary that followed these words from Matthew 8:26 sounded equally applicable. It

said that as long as Jesus is in our house and in our hearts, there can be
no ruin and no undoing. Api tried to internalize these words of consolation. And then he picked up Nyussi's sweater and kissed it. He was
well aware that this was going too far, but it was a defense strategy that
helped him to endure his isolation and assuage his fears. "Sometimes,"
he wrote, "I have such a terrible worry about you. I have worn your little
woolen jacket once more today, since it was chilly in the morning, and
have kissed it fervently. I know that this almost no longer is adoring
love but rather is a cult. But where shall I go with my sometimes really
overpowering longings for you all!"

Before church the following morning, Api took a few moments to
study the sky from his attic window. "A sky full of peace and infinity
in which a few delicate feather clouds drift silently together with an
early swallow. Otherwise a nameless stillness and devotion in God's
wonderful nature, which will also lift my eyes and heart above the
ruins and the sorrows of this poor earth." Church music from a radio
across the street drifted up to him, and he thought that perhaps his
faith was growing firmer. "One has to learn to pray. First comes the
joy in prayer and then the strength and the capacity to draw real
and powerful consolation from this search for God and the feeling
of His nearness!" But even his faith could not lessen the yearning. "I
could, I would, I should shoulder my packed rucksack and come to
you without hesitation, and without doubting my strength to master
the distance!"

Api did have one way of celebrating the day after Nyussi's birthday. He had been given a ticket for a musical matinee at the Deutsches
Theater. The Soviet occupation was trying to offer citizens a respite
from hunger and fear by supporting concerts, theater, and even opera
performances. These had begun as early as May 1945, but this was
Api's first such occasion. He had not been sure that he would be able
to attend, because of his stomach problems. However, not wanting to
miss such an opportunity, he forced himself to get ready.

From 1905 to 1930, the Deutsches Theater had been managed by Max Reinhardt, who had also given the building its present look by adding a neoclassical front. How many hours Nyussi and he had spent there, enjoying the classical German repertoire, as well as modern plays by Bernard Shaw and Gerhart Hauptmann. Most of the great German actors of the time had appeared there, among them Paula Wessely, Käthe Dorsch, Ewald Balser, and Gustaf Gründgens. As soon as Api and Nyussi could afford it, they had bought a yearly subscription to the theater for all four of them.

Turning into Schumannstrasse, Api saw the Deutsches Theater like an oasis in the devastation all around. It had remained almost completely unharmed. He stood outside the theatre for a long time, gazing at the familiar facade set back from the street. When he walked inside, he saw that it, too, looked much the same as he had known it. He greeted the semicircle auditorium like an old friend. Api did not mention what pieces he heard that afternoon, only that the music soothed him. Music always had a powerful effect on him. Now it made him feel connected to suffering humanity and less alone.

# 30

# WALKING THROUGH A NIGHTMARE

Throughout April, Api saw many on the streets who were far worse off than he. Berlin was choked with refugees. Streams of careworn people from the eastern parts of Germany who had fled before the Soviets were limping about in the center of Berlin. About three million refugees came through the city. They dragged their few belongings in carts or wheelbarrows through the streets. Compared with such misery, he had to count himself lucky.

One day, Api noticed an old, tubercular woman lying in the gutter. She could not go on for weakness and just lay there coughing but otherwise apathetic. He went to her and tried to make her more comfortable, but she did not respond. He offered her a piece of bread he had brought along, the pasty black bread so despised by the Russian officer, which was all he had. She just left it lying there. He could do nothing for her. The hospitals were overcrowded, and there were many like her in the streets of Berlin. She was just one of "the still never-ending columns of refugees who, with their last strength and together with four-to-five-year-old children, drag, panting, two- or four-wheeled carts containing the beggar's remains of their possessions in order to reach any kind of shelter before the curfew, or at least come a little closer to an often imaginary destination!" The image of that old woman stayed with him throughout the day.

Injured soldiers, armless and legless, who moved on old margarine cartons with added wheels, were another common sight. I still remember in the early 1950s such war veterans coming to our door and offering pictures, usually greeting cards of landscapes or flowers, "painted with the foot" or "painted with the mouth." We always gave them money and food, and I was amazed at how delicate and detailed the images were.

Api knew that epidemics were inevitable without sanitation, trash pickup, or even proper removal of the dead. And as the weather grew warmer, a plague of vermin, lice, flies, maggots, and rats infested the city. Luckily, rats did not make it up to his attic room, but flies swarmed in black clouds, bluebottles as large as he had seen them only when he was a young military doctor in Macedonia during World War I. Without windowpanes, he could not keep them out. He slew at least fifty each evening before going to bed, yet swarms buzzed around him again in the morning. As I kept reading about the plague of flies, I had to think of Sartre's recasting of the Orestes tragedy in *The Flies*. Although the play had been written two years earlier, in 1943, perhaps flies had plagued Paris then as well. Or it was an eerily prophetic work, its characters haunted by the fateful insects?

Weakened by sickness, Api tried to spend ever more time on his silent communion with us and his God. He sought consolation in the idea that if all else failed him and he did not see us again, he was left at the last with his faith that "we were all united in God and that we would be granted a blessed reunion in His kingdom, where there was no separation, no worry, no anxiety, no misery." Yet he did not entirely give up hope, writing to us, "My dearest, evening has come again, another day is gone, and the heart that does not want to, and cannot, unlearn hope rejoices to have come one little step closer perhaps to the goal always floating before it, our reunion in a world at peace."

Api's intestinal problems worsened, and the charcoal tablets he took did not help any longer. Charcoal was a popular remedy against diarrhea. When, as a small child in Suderburg, I had a bout of diarrhea, my mother would give me charcoal tablets out of a little metal tin. I did not mind their chalky taste and delighted in the way they turned my mouth black.

Api's "down" mood—he used the English word—was made worse by a desolate day in his surgery. Not a single patient showed up, perhaps because severe rainstorms and hurricane-like gusts of wind were pelting Berlin. As Api walked back to the attic after his fruitless day, he had to take cover because the walls and roofs of damaged buildings were crumbling under the storm and shingles were raining down on the pavement. And the trials of that day were not over yet. Three Soviet soldiers appeared out of the ruins and threatened to arrest him. Shaking with sickness and fear, Api produced his medical papers and the soldiers let him go. That night, Api thought that sleeping pills would not be enough, and he took opium. It was the first and only time during these months that he had such recourse. I know nothing about the medicinal use of opium at that time, but his access to medication was certainly an advantage Api had over the general population.

Despite feeling weak himself, Api continued his visits to the sick. He earned a little money, but he also wanted to assist as many people as he could. At the same time, he hoped that the contacts he made might help build his future practice. With that aim in mind, he also went to see general practitioners, asking them to refer eye patients to him. Although he tried to disguise these visits with all kinds of pretenses, he suspected that everyone knew he was begging, and his pride suffered badly.

To help him recover from his stomach problem, the always

generous Herr Gerhardt made him a present of a bottle of burgundy. Api's first instinct was to save the rare treat, to *knausern*, be stingy, once again, as was his habit. But then he thought about how his son had scolded him for being too parsimonious and for not enjoying something when the occasion arose. So, hearing his dear Dieter say to him, "Dad, don't be such a skinflint," he treated himself to a glass.

Wednesday, June 13, brought a major improvement in the attic when electricity was reconnected. For the first time, Api could write his diary and read his medical texts by electric light. It gave him a little sense that a normal life might be possible again. The next day, a glazier appeared and replaced the cardboard of his windows with glass. This helped to keep the flies at bay.

Then on Friday, June 15, Api suffered a particularly severe intestinal attack. Again he was terrified of coming down with dysentery, remembering his illness in 1914. In a decision unusual for him, he stayed in bed until ten in the morning. But then he felt compelled to get up and make his way to his practice. It turned out to be a trip made in vain, since no one came. He sat idly in his office, unable to read or do anything. This in itself was a burden to a man who hated vacuity and believed one always had to do something useful and constructive.

As he had had nothing to eat and was feeling particularly faint, the walk back made a surreal impression on him and he suffered what I now think of as a panic attack. It seemed as if the shockingly blue sky was laughing at him and at the gray, charred ruins he passed. By contrast, the black window holes glared at him ominously in their deadness. He saw himself as if from a great distance, almost swallowed up by rubble and stones. Api was walking through a nightmare from which there was no awakening. When he got to his building, he had to rest often to climb the four sets of stairs to the attic. He was bathed in sweat from the effort. But once he was safely in his "swallow's nest," the familiar surroundings helped him to calm down.

Sitting by the window, he tried to recover from the nightmare, which seemed even worse than the recurring bad dreams he had when he slept. At times he feared that he could not tell horrible dreams from reality. To counteract these images and still his pounding heart, he concentrated on picturing a reunion with us. He visualized himself walking down the streets of Suderburg and knocking on our cottage window, as he had done what now seemed like an age ago. He dwelled on the happy reunion in the most vivid details: on the joy in our eyes, on holding me in his arms, on how we would sit down to a simple meal and then walk together on the sandy path outside the farmhouse with a view of the Blue Mountain.

Then his imagination switched to another scene. We had all come back to Berlin. The old apartment had been restored, his practice was picking up, and we all lived together in peace and security. He imagined his Hinzpeter painting of the Alpine woods he loved so much. He remembered how, long ago, when he had been ill, Nyussi had taken the picture off its hook in the living room and put it in his bedroom so that he could enjoy it. Then he thought of that small oil painting that Nyussi had taken to Suderburg. It had been a surprise gift from the artist, because Api had treated him for free. The painting shows St. Martin cutting his cloak in half to share with a naked beggar. I remember it well, for it held a place of honor wherever we lived. When we looked at the picture together, Api was fond of telling me the story of St. Martin, a Roman soldier who had converted to become a monk. He led a simple life dedicated to helping others. Together we looked at the wintry landscape, covered in bleak snow; the back of the spectral, naked beggar in the foreground; and St. Martin bending down toward him from his horse while cutting his cloak with his sword. My eyes were invariably drawn to the blood-red cloak, which provided the only splotch of color in an otherwise grim scene of browns, whites, and grays.

Coming back to reality, Api could only "entrust these happy

images to this little book without life or purpose or use when I don't even know whether you—or we—will ever read it. But as I said once before, for me it is an irreplaceably beautiful substitute for the community with you which I miss so painfully, one of my dearest hours in the day!!"

# 31

# LIVING IN INSECURITY

In the latter part of June, Api's physical condition improved. He could take a few more spoonfuls of the flour or semolina soup that he had not been able to keep down before. As soon as he felt better, Api, as always, made plans. Since he had been lucky to get the loan of a bike, he would ride to RL 101, the Westend Hospital, to see about the dining room set he had left in storage there after the bombing of 1943. Api was allowed to do this because of his connection to Department 17, the large eye station there. Perhaps, he mused, he could install the dining room in Luisenstrasse so that some furniture would be ready for us.

But first he had to report once again to the health department. He was never given more than an hour's notice about these meetings. This time, the Soviets were concerned about the rise in cases of dysentery. Api wondered what could be done when patients could not be isolated and there were no trash pickups, no water, and no toilet flushes. How were they to avoid an epidemic under such conditions?

Back in his attic, Api even felt a little hungry. He ate some peas and potatoes but left the meat because it smelled so bad. He had taught himself to eat meat for the calories, no matter in what condition, but, as his stomach was still shaky, he did not want to risk it. It was so difficult to catch up after an illness. But he had the luxury of finishing his meal with a glass of Burgundy.

For the first time, Api mentioned that he had a newspaper to read. Although papers had appeared for weeks already, Api may not have been able to get hold of a copy until then, or perhaps he had not wanted to read papers, since they offered nothing but the Soviet perspective and he had never been an eager newspaper reader anyway.

Amazingly, through the bombing and the occupation, Berlin had gone only fifteen days without any newspaper. Newspapers had always flourished in the city. At their height in 1928, Berlin had had exactly one hundred daily newspapers and many more weekly ones. The Nazis, of course, forbade and censored most of them, wanting only their own voice heard.

The first postwar edition in Berlin was the *Tägliche Rundschau*, the *Daily Overview*, which appeared on May 15. It was put out by the Soviets and contained mainly articles translated from *Pravda* that talked about German war crimes and Soviet people's efforts to rebuild their own country devastated by the German army. The front page on June 9, 1945, carried headlines such as "Life Reawakens out of the Ruins," and "The Soviet Union Heals the Wounds of the War." These articles did not deal with Germany but focused on the Soviet Union and its struggle to recover. They stressed that the Soviet Union had conquered Germany in the field and now was fighting a second war to undo the damage done by the Germans. "The peoples of the Soviet Union rightfully will remember that this devastation is the work of the Germans. Its complete restitution is Germany's duty." Another article boasted of the progress that had already been made. Ukrainian coal mines, destroyed by the German army, had produced on average 3,200 tons of coal per month before the war. Now, with new equipment, they produced 6,000 tons. The only news about Germany itself on this front page concerned the suicide of a former

*Gauleiter*, a district commander, and the arrest of a man who had been in charge of a concentration camp. Yet the paper claimed that it was the "Front Paper for the German Population."

The next day, Monday, June 18, General Nikolai Berzarin died in a motorcycle accident. He was only forty-one years old. The people of Berlin mourned his death. As soon as he was appointed commander of Berlin, he had tried to establish some sense of fairness and normalcy in the city. Berliners loved the youthful, dark-haired general with his passion for motorcycles and cheered when they saw him speeding past them. Api shared this general feeling and noted that Berzarin had been ". . . energetic and apparently just. A shame."

On Thursday, June 21, Api at last found an opportunity to make that trip to the Westend Hospital to check up on his dining room furniture. He felt invigorated as he began to pedal the eight kilometers to his destination and grateful to his friend for having loaned him the bike. The ride took him straight west from Luisenstrasse, and in his mind it seemed as if, with each turn of the wheel, he was coming a little closer to us. He biked along the East–West Axis, which was to be the main avenue of Hitler's world capital, Germania. However, the stink of corpses drifted over from the Landwehr Canal, and weeds and even trees had begun to grow on the rubble. Columns of pedestrians trudged through this wasteland from the Knie, where Api had had to seek cover a few weeks earlier, across the devastated Tiergarten, to the Brandenburg Gate. Many of them had to walk an hour and a half to work each day and then back the same distance at night. As the road to the Westend still stretched before him, Api was glad that he had set out early, for it soon became hot. His attic, which had been chilly at the end of May, had now turned almost unbearably warm.

Api reached the Westend Hospital at ten in the morning. He headed straight for the storage room, where he found his dining room pieces just as he had left them. Since most of his other furniture had been destroyed, this undamaged, shiny walnut set was a huge joy for him. In his excitement, he scheduled its delivery to Luisenstrasse immediately. However, as soon as he had made this arrangement, he regretted it. "Wouldn't everything be safer where it was?" He canceled the order right away. This episode was further indication of his indecisiveness, and he was once more depressed by his weakness to make any decision, even about matters that earlier would have been trivial for him. This constant back-and-forth alone was enough to wear him out.

It was early afternoon when he arrived back in his surgery rooms, where another pleasant surprise awaited him. "A nice bunch of patients" was there to greet him. Among them was Frau Grossman, an acquaintance who was to help him much in the next weeks. She told him that the middle-class suburbs of Friedenau and Steglitz, immediately south of the Tiergarten, had been spared almost completely; houses were intact and businesses open, as in peacetime. And, she added, excited about bringing such good news, there was only one eye doctor in the area. Hearing this, Api thought fleetingly that Friedenau had been the very first location he had considered back in 1924 for his own practice. Then he heard Frau Grossmann, who herself lived in Friedenau, urge him, "Why don't you move there? It would be a much better place to start a practice than in this heap of ruins."

The suggestion, kindly meant, threw Api into a new quandary. Would he get permission from the Soviet authorities for such a move? And, more important to his always grateful and sentimental mind, how could he give up this place so dear to him? Seeing his hesitation, Frau Grossman repeated her advice and even offered to talk to the local mayor.

About the same time, his colleague Dr. Hüdepohl told Api about a full-time position for an ophthalmological surgeon that just had become available at St. Hedwig Hospital. Although Api had worked there before the war, he doubted that he was going to take this kind offer. The job would grant him security, but he would have to give up his own practice, which he was loath to do. As Api debated these possibilities, he thought that at least they promised some sense of a future, but he could not make any decision.

One powerful motivation for leaving Berlin Mitte was that life in the Soviet sector was becoming ever more dangerous for a *Pg*. The Soviet occupation was vigorous in its hunt for members of the Nazi Party.

The very next day, Api heard that a friend, also a member of the Party, had had his apartment searched at night and that the little he'd had left had been taken away: jewelry, furniture, a typewriter, even an iron. Living in similar insecurity, Api listened to every step in the house, wondering each time whether they came for him. He could not be sure of any neighbor because there were so many denunciations and false accusations among the Berlin population. He was more irritated and disgusted by the behavior of the Germans against each other than by the measures, however strict or senseless, the Soviets took. "The German people behave in such a manner among themselves that Russian commandants already have imprisoned denunciators with open expressions of scorn for such a spirit between them."

Newspapers also carried denunciations of fellow Germans. "The newspaper falls all over itself in its smear campaign against *Pgs* and creates a dangerous atmosphere for everyone, whether active, inactive, or opposed!" As a *Pg*, Api now had to fill out a lengthy application and submit to a questioning at the employment office in order to be able to work as a doctor. He felt mortified by the process but knew that he had to do it. The one reassuring news item in June was that in the British and American occupation zones of Germany, the situation was not nearly as bad as in Berlin under the Russians. He hoped, therefore, that we in Suderburg were faring better than he did in Berlin.

Api would have liked to talk to us about the situation, but was afraid to discuss politics in his letters. All he wrote in his diary was that he was convinced that "peace and prosperity are unthinkable without a return to piety, of Christian brotherly love, mutual tolerance, in short, human ethics, in our enemies and in our own people. And that," he added, "still looks pretty bad, especially with our own people."

# 32

# PARADISE LOST

On Saturday, June 23, Api forced himself to make one more of his petitioner's visits in search of eye patients. This time, he decided to see Dr. Blumann in Dahlem, where Nyussi and he had started out as newlyweds in 1920. He took out his borrowed bike and rode off westward.

Along Kurfürstendamm, Api still noticed the ruins of stores and the burned-out buildings he was used to seeing on the east side of the Tiergarten. But as he turned south, things got better, and when he reached Dahlem, he found entire neighborhoods unharmed. The handsome villas shaded by large beech and linden trees looked as in peacetime. Instead of occupying troops and refugees, here civilians relaxed in their gardens. The atmosphere was so different from Berlin Mitte that he could not believe he was still in the same city.

Api found Dr. Blumann's house undamaged and elegantly furnished. It felt strange to see such comfort. Dr. Blumann was kind and friendly, and Api could talk openly to him about his fears and his need of eye patients. At one point, Api was moved to say that, given his current horrible circumstances, he was almost happy that his son was not there to live through this. But Dr. Blumann exclaimed, "No, no! I cannot imagine if I had to give mine up. Knowing what I would have given for the life of my boy, I can judge your sorrow." Despite the sympathy and understanding, Api was glad when the begging visit was over. He was not sure what, if anything, it would bring.

After he left Dr. Blumann, Api needed the company of friends. Except for his professional associations, he had been alone for too long. On the spur of the moment, he decided to visit Fritz and Mizzi Hones, who lived nearby at the edge of the Grunewald. I vaguely remember those names from Api's stories but know nothing about them, except that, judging by their location, they must have been well to do.

Leaning his bike against a tree of their garden, he knocked on their door. It was a reunion with heartfelt joy on both sides. The roses were blooming, spreading their scent to the deck chairs where the three of them sat around a white table in the middle of a green lawn. When they went inside, Api noticed a shiny piano in a corner of the living room. Touching a few chords, he saw that it was playing in tune, not like the piano he heard from his attic. Mizzi cooked a tasty dinner in his honor, and he wondered where she got all the ingredients, especially the fresh meat. Fritz fetched a bottle of wine from the cellar to celebrate. They talked much of the past and of us. For Api, who always dreaded his now empty Saturdays, this one, seated among old friends, was a wonderfully soothing respite. But it was also tiring. He had biked twenty miles, thinking with every stroke of the pedal that if he were biking to Suderburg, he would already have done about 10 percent of that journey.

Api spent the early part of Sunday taking an air bath by his attic window, talking with the swallows, with the small clouds, with us, and with his merciful God. Inevitably, his thoughts turned back to the past. He estimated that Nyussi and he had lived through about 1,300 happy and harmonious Sundays, but he worried that there were to be no more.

In better times, he would have started every morning with push-ups and stretches. Api was a follower of Dr. Kneipp's methods, which the doctor had originally publicized in 1896. Dr. Kneipp believed in naturopathy, using nature to help heal the body. His method was synergistic, based on good blood circulation and a toughening of the physique. Dr. Kneipp's methods included dipping into icy water or running barefoot through the snow. When I was with Api in the early 1950s, we never went swimming in the winter, but he told me that when he was young he used to break the ice and take a dip. After the first snowfall, he did, however, urge me to make a quick run with him barefoot across the lawn. Although I resisted at first, it turned out to be an exhilarating experience. We both laughed out loud as we caught our breath with the sudden cold. After a short run, we rushed back inside and, still laughing, dried our pleasantly burning feet.

These days, however, Api had neither the strength nor the alacrity of spirit for even the most modest form of exercise. Yet, inspired by his recent visit, he decided to use his borrowed bike to see his close friends the Sieverts. I assume that they had been friends since the 1920s, for in an address directory for 1925, both Api and the Sieverts were listed at Luisenstrasse 41.

Herr Sievert had been a director at Siemens, the famous electrical company, which had a huge industrial complex called Siemens City in the northwest of Berlin. The association with Siemens makes me wonder about Herr Sievert's role under the Nazis. I never met him, for he died soon after the war, but I still vividly remember his wife, Gerdi, a tiny woman with piercing black eyes. Seeing her, I was always surprised how her large nose dominated her face and how her smile transformed her sharp features. Even when I knew her as an elderly woman, she was spirited and full of life. Before she came to visit us, my grandmother told me that Gerdi had been something of an adventuress. She was one of the first women to study at the university in Königsberg, the hometown of Immanuel Kant. After graduation in 1914, she went on a tour of Siberia all by herself and was there when World War I broke out. Gerdi made her way back to Prussia through enemy land and seemed to have relished the adventure. In Berlin, the Sieverts, who were childless, spoiled my mother and uncle and served as a surrogate family. When Gerdi died in the 1970s, she willed what she had left in valuables—a few pieces of jewelry and a silk Oriental rug—to my mother.

The two old friends were glad to see Api and did what they could to cheer him up. They even set a picture of Api and Nyussi on the coffee table. It was taken on vacation in the Riesengebirge, a mountain range between Silesia and Bohemia that was a favorite destination for Berliners. I also have a picture from that trip, and like to think that it is the same one Api looked at so fondly. Nyussi is dashing in a long black coat with little black ankle boots and a jaunty hat. And Api is wearing, once again, his favorite knickerbockers and jacket.

It did Api good to see his wife in happier times, and it hurt him simultaneously. Seeing his pale and thin face, and remembering his sweet tooth, the Sieverts made sure to feed him bread with jam. After an ample coffee hour, they had liqueurs and even champagne.

Delighting in the company of friends and the conversation of old times, Api stayed from three thirty in the afternoon until eight thirty at night. He had always derived an almost childlike pleasure from parties and social gatherings and used to be a great one for entertaining his visitors with funny stories. Yet even here, surrounded by the warmth of old friendship, he could not escape the ominous present. When it came time to say goodbye, he gave his friendly hosts our address, "just in case," implying that he might not survive to see us again. He added apologetically, "One has to be prepared for anything."

Api biked home accompanied by the fragrance of the linden trees. It had been Nyussi's favorite time. When he reached his attic, his first glance was out the window at the sky. "The evening sky—still without moon, but of a depth and softness which could even put a less longing person into a sentimental mood—a few thunderclouds, silent and immovable, and my evening swallows." That evening, he dropped off to sleep without the aid of any pills.

The following morning, as he was thinking back over his weekend, Api appreciated how lucky he was. He still had friends who helped him out and was treated to the occasional good meal. He thought about the tired people he had seen trudging to work across the Tiergarten. They had nothing to eat at the end of it. Api understood that it was not easy to provision a destroyed city of two and a half million people, but he also believed that it should not be an insurmountable problem for the Soviets. Yet with the passing days, the food supply seemed to him to get worse, not better.

On June 25, he reflected in his diary that "tomorrow, Tuesday, it will be eleven terrible desolate weeks since our most awful goodbye in Suderburg." He had been right when he had said that the war could not last more than four weeks. But how wrong, how naïvely wrong he had been in imagining that, should we have survived, we would be reunited immediately. Api was afraid of the approaching winter. June 21, the longest day of the year, was past already. It had been a summer of rare beauty, and yet how unimaginably horrible it had been. But, he admonished us as he wrote, "Don't let your sorrow stop you from praying." Without prayer, he could not go on.

# 33

# THE LITTLE SWALLOWS PLAY

The morning of Friday, June 29, brought an unwelcome discovery when Api found that his medical texts had been stolen from the university clinic where he worked with Professor Löhlein. There was no appeal, since a *Pg* had no rights. All his beautiful leather-bound books were gone. The only textbook that was left was one he had worked through twice already.

Contradictory snippets of information picked up during the day led to nightmares at night. They all had to do with confused and failed journeys where he never reached his destination. He heard that, beginning on July 1, only a few days hence, the passage across the Elbe River would be free or that in exchange for cigarettes you could get a ferry to take you across. Then again, someone said that the Brits would send you back after taking everything you had or that there were camps of one thousand people and more waiting to cross the Elbe.

After church and a visit to his mother's grave on Sunday afternoon, Api watched airplanes fly overhead and heard the whistle of locomotives. Occasionally he even noticed a civilian car drive down the narrow middle of the street. So much motion, yet he was imprisoned and could not budge. The prospect of the following Monday's meeting at the employment office where he had to present his application worried and humiliated him. The past weeks had sapped his mental and physical stamina to a breaking point. He now wrote in his diary mainly at night, because when he got up in the morning, he was too depressed even for that.

That evening he sat by the window, took out his green diary, and wrote, "Between some rough rain clouds, the evening descends already noticeably earlier over the sad hopelessness of the fields of rubble stretching for kilometers and over bent and askew rafters that are still standing here and there and grin above it ironically. But the little swallows play, screaming happily as in my childhood, and the small high-altitude clouds which pass in front of blue islands in the sky still breathe peace and preach God's merciful father's will."

Then his mind turned to us and he became afraid. "Sometimes I imagine the worst, the thought that perhaps all my longing, my prayers, my fight against my weakness, against myself, for this my only wish for the future, is already meeting emptiness because something has happened to you, my dearest ones!! I am also unhappy that there is no possibility to release you from the same worry about me."

At this point, Api felt as if even words, which had always helped him deal with difficult and painful, as well as happy, times, were deserting him. "Oh, if I still had the concentration and the knack for language to describe to you in a poem what longing can make of a poor human soul. Such a string of wonderful days we have not had for many years. . . . Everything breathes God's peace and infinity and makes the sorrows of this world, where so many, so infinitely many, people give up and despair, appear small and trivial. If only one could flee to it!! But this world of misery forces one to take in, with each step, unimaginably sad, heartrending pictures: amidst the tortured, tired, starved, and fearful faces of almost everyone, one sees groups laden with parcels, dressed in tatters, deathly exhausted .

. . not daring to raise their eyes above the ground, devoid of any hope because they recognize that even with the best of will no one can help them in any way."

# 34

# WITHOUT THE FAINTEST GUILT

Starting in June, people had to submit requests for "denazifica-tion" in order to be able to return to their previous positions. The result, if successful, was popularly known as the *Persilschein*, the Persil certificate. Today, Persil is the brand name of a washing powder that boasts that it can make everything spotless.

Api had no *Persilschein*, and at this point did not seem to have tried for one. As a *Pg*, he lived in fear and saw no way of reestablishing himself. Yet he reflected, "And all that without the faintest guilt, but on the other hand again that is a great consolation and support." This sentence appears in his diary without preparation or further com-ment, but it is linked to other statements, scattered throughout, that stress that he never did harm to anyone and that he never succeeded because of another's misfortune.

Reading this, I am confronted again with my key quandary, this time expressed as unambiguously as never before, "without the faintest guilt." Api did not feel guilty or in any way implicated in the murder and destruction that the Nazi regime perpetrated. I realize that he was not personally responsible for any of it, that apart from having joined the Party, he did nothing further to advance its cause, that he did not hold any office in the Party or persecute anyone. Nevertheless, he was a member of the Party; he witnessed persecution and saw his Jewish colleagues disappear. I am not imagining that I would have been able to do anything more, for I know myself not to be brave. I also have no idea how far his resistance did or didn't go at the time, what little acts of courage he was able to perform. I cannot sit in judgment of a man I knew to be compassionate and tolerant. For the moment—and I know that this subject will not let me go—I feel that any sense of guilt must have been a personal matter and understand why this was not the time for Api to engage in such soul searching.

However, the immediate postwar world did not allow Api to hide from this issue of German guilt. All Party members had to fill out forms about their activities during the Nazi era. Api mentions an *Unbedenklichkeitserklärung*—literally, a "declaration of no objection." I am not sure whether he was referring to the denazification document, the *Persilschein,* or whether there was some earlier clearance form that Party members had to fill out before they could get permission to move from one occupation zone to another or leave Berlin altogether. Api had no idea whether it would help him if he applied for this document or whether, on the contrary, it would damage his prospects or draw unnecessary attention to him. He thought about this as soon as he woke up in the morning and had to pull himself together to break the pointless spiral and get up at all. Thinking of Nyussi, he wrote, "I was so spoiled by you and our beloved togetherness, where we talked about and decided everything together."

About the same time, Professor Seegert, whom Api often assisted in operations, told him that a British major was reported to have said after his visit to a concentration camp, "A people who allow such a thing cannot count on our compassion." Api commented in despair, "As if they didn't know that any rebellious word had meant death, without helping in the slightest."

To me today, both Api's and the major's reaction are understandable. Api may not have known about the concentration camps before May 1945, and he had tried to live his life helping, not hurting, others. At the same time, the major, who just had witnessed the horror of such a camp, must have been overwhelmed by that experience and thought of all Germans as monsters. A booklet handed out to British and Commonwealth troops adopted the same hostile attitude, saying that "the Germans have only themselves to blame." Similarly, the *Stars and Stripes* admonished its soldiers, "Don't get chummy with Jerry. In heart, body, and spirit, every German is a Hitler." The Allies, especially the British and Americans, wanted to make sure that no fraternization went on between their troops and the German population and that Allied soldiers did not take pity on the people's suffering. One reason for the Allies' interdiction to fraternize was their continued fear of Werwolf. Historian David Stafford, however, suggests that "the main purpose of the ban was to make it clear to the Germans that they were a nation guilty of aggression and criminality and had made themselves pariahs and outcasts of the civilized world."

# 35

# THE ALLIES ARE COMING

At the beginning of July, fifty thousand soldiers from the US 82nd Airborne Division and Britain's 7th Armored Division reached Berlin, and the city was divided into four occupation zones. The eastern part of Berlin from Mitte to Treptow stayed in Soviet hands. On the western side—all of which later would be called West Berlin—were the French, British, and American zones. The French occupied Wedding and Reinickendorf in the north; the British were below that in Tiergarten, Charlottenburg, and Wilmersdorf; and the Americans had the southwestern part of Berlin, including Tempelhof and Steglitz.

For people caught in the Soviet sector, little changed. In fact, for Api, things got worse. The hunt for Party members only heated up in July. Api lived in constant fear of arrest and deportation. Also, the Berlin magistrate dismissed all doctors who had been members of Hitler's special forces, the SS, Gestapo, or SA, or who had shown themselves otherwise "unworthy." *Pg* doctors who were still allowed to work could do so only conditionally and for limited times. They were to be paid 0.72 marks per hour, the same as workers in the rubble fields.

Api worried ever more seriously about his *Pg* status. He never mentioned the pay, but he was concerned about food. He had received the lowest ration card. Cards were distributed according to five categories. At the top, in Group 1, were heavy laborers and public officials, doctors, pastors, industrialists, and artists; Group 2 were blue-collar workers; Group 3, white-collar workers; Group 4 included children up to fifteen years; and in Group 5, "others," were *Pgs* and the unemployed. Group 5, by the way, also included housewives. The stated day's rations for Api consisted of seven grams fat, twenty grams meat, three hundred grams bread, thirty grams grain, fifteen grams sugar, and four hundred grams potatoes. But even that was guaranteed only on paper, and especially the fat rarely materialized.

On Monday morning, July 2, Api got up early and went out before breakfast to try to assess what the new resolutions against *Pgs* meant for him. First he went to see if he could move up in his ration card classification. After a two-hour wait, he succeeded and was put into Group 1, an indication that he was not on any "unworthy" list.

Api's next errand was to report to the health bureau. When he wrote about it later in his diary, he entered only "paragraph 218." He did not want to talk about this issue, even in the intimacy of his diary, just as he had not mentioned rape. Paragraph 218 referred to the law that forbade doctors to do abortions. Doctors in Berlin, however, quickly decided to perform abortions on the great number of raped women with unwanted pregnancies. This virtual suspension of paragraph 218 soon extended to many Western zones. In this, doctors had the support of the Protestant Church, but not of the Catholic. Some critics, however, have seen this measure simply as "a continuation of Nazi-sanctioned abortions in case of rape by foreigners in order to preserve the purity of the race."

After the health bureau, Api could not put off the next errand any longer. He had to appear at the employment office to register and hand in his application to work as a doctor. Despite having spent the weekend anxious about this, he received permission right away. The need for doctors, coupled with his status as an inactive Party member, allowed him to work, at least for the moment. However, he had no assurances about the safety of his equipment in his surgery. "Anyone," the official told him, "can take anything away from a *Pg*."

What annoyed Api most was that all these decrees failed to take into account the many non-*Pgs* who had been most active during the Nazi regime. Without being members of the Party, they had hurt and betrayed innocent people. The actual situation under Hitler, as in any totalitarian regime, was more complex and ambiguous than these new regulations seemed to allow. But at least the dreaded meeting at the employment office was over. It had gone more smoothly than Api had feared, and he left feeling relieved that the whole thing was behind him.

Next, Api had to go to the office of work deployment in order to obtain his release from shoveling rubble for the month of July, another chore imposed on *Pgs*. It, too, was granted right away. So, despite the time and nervous energy he had spent waiting in offices, it had been a good day.

On his errands, Api noticed a new mood of expectancy. People had high hopes that conditions would change now that the Americans were in town. "Everyone," he wrote that night, "waits and expects something from the Anglo-Americans. Not me. There is only one thing I long for with all my heart: postal service." He added, "How many times every day my heart constricts in sudden pain when the locomotives whistle, cars or airplanes roar toward the west, and the immediate thought 'imprisoned' grinds into nothing every dream of a reunion." The summer was passing, and the span of life God still allowed him seemed to melt away in loneliness. The shorter days also made him worry about the coming winter. Fire had devoured all coal during the bombing raids, and a lack of heat and food meant it would get even worse in Berlin and cost many more lives.

Rumor, which was still the main currency, had it that the Soviets were to take over the entire Luisenstrasse for their military offices. The government buildings on Wilhelmstrasse were in ruins and would not have been used anyway, since they represented Nazi rule. So the Soviets had settled on nearby Luisenstrasse for their central command. It, too, had many large buildings, even though they needed repair. They had already taken over both the Langenbeck-Virchow House at Luisenstrasse 58, just a block from Api's practice, and the nearby Leitz and Zeiss Building, for the headquarters of the GPU, the much feared Soviet secret police. The veterinary college next to the Langenbeck-Virchow House served as Soviet command headquarters. The Soviet administration had also occupied other buildings on Luisenstrasse, so Api was surrounded.

If the whole street was to be closed to locals, Api would have to act quickly. But where could he go? Seeing so many homeless every day, he wondered, "Where on earth can I find safekeeping for the last concrete remains and mementos of our sunny past?"

Sitting by the open window of his office and waiting fruitlessly for a patient to show up, Api heard music. "In a screaming irony, a jazz band drones on in a cheap bar which just has opened nearby, and people dance on the volcano either thoughtlessly or with gallows humor." Api felt once more as if he were living by day the nightmares of his chaotic travel dreams. Next, the sky turned black and a thunderstorm drenched his waiting room and surgery and turned both into a lake. All his work had been for naught. Help was impossible to get, since the Soviets employed all the masons and carpenters in the area. When he got back to his attic room, it, too, had been flooded. The five pails and washbowls he had set out could not handle the torrents of water.

The futility of everything, his continued ill health, and his constant hunger, paired with his personal insecurity, wore him down so that he could hardly drag himself about. At this stage, Api was so afraid that something would happen to him that he went to the North Sanatorium and entrusted his diary to the head nurse for safekeeping. Under no circumstances did he want it to get lost to us. "For," he wrote quickly, before handing over the book, "even if much of it is very repetitive, some of it is quite interesting." However, he retrieved it just a couple of days later, as he needed to continue his daily reports and conversation with us.

Tuesday, July 10, Api bought two red impatiens plants for his window. As he set them on the sill, he reflected how much had changed in his life and yet how nature continued on its accustomed course. "The sky is the same as before, in meadows and fields there is the same blossoming and will to life, the swallows whirr, the butterflies dance, and the colored flies stand above fragrant blossoms, just as in my childhood. And the souls of men are just as they were 1,000 years ago, full of hopes and desires, of worries and prayers. And yet now they are so totally broken!"

Gazing out his attic window, lost in such thoughts, Api felt his attention drawn to a woman across the street. She sat by her window, chewing a piece of bread. Then he noticed someone coming into the room behind her and watched as the woman quickly leaned down to hide the bread. As he wrote about this scene, he ended with two exclamation points to suggest the shock he felt about such mean behavior.

# 36

# ANOTHER DISMISSAL

On Wednesday, July 11, Api suffered a blow similar to his altercation with Dr. Kleberger. Professor Löhlein dismissed him. He explained his action by saying, "After all, you have your own practice now and no longer need this work." But then he added something that greatly perturbed Api, although he did not understand its implication. As he tried to record what Professor Löhlein had said, he could not even remember the exact words, so great had been his agitation. The professor had mentioned something about a "warlike atmosphere" and whether Api had also noticed it. Api did not understand what Professor Löhlein meant, except that it seemed like a veiled accusation. The very phrase "warlike atmosphere" was loaded, especially in July 1945, barely ten weeks after the end of World War II.

For days afterward, Api racked his brain but could not think of anything he had said or done to offend the professor or anyone around him. Two months earlier, he thought, he had been physically and mentally better able to withstand such a shock. Now, he was not so sure. The dismissal made him feel more helpless and insecure, afraid even to leave his own four walls and shy about meeting

people—about doing or saying anything at all. He trembled to get
up each morning because it was the beginning of a day that would
present all kinds of decisions—and mistakes—to be made.

Although shaken and fundamentally unsure of himself, Api
resolved not to give up. After all, he still had occasional work
assisting Professor Seegert in operations at the women's clinic of
the Ziegelstrasse complex, and he also continued to work at the
North Sanatorium, despite the row with Dr. Kleberger. In fact, he
was already scheduled to assist in an operation there to remove an
intestinal obstruction. Nevertheless, Api continued to brood on the
dismissal, which further undermined his self-confidence—so much
so that Friday, July 13, scared him because of the date alone. He
was ashamed of this fear; he believed it a sign of how cowardly he
had become, although he would not tell this to anyone except us, in
his diary. As if to confirm his worry, the morning brought a down-
pour that set his attic room afloat again. Only the impatiens on the
windowsill were glad for the water. On that inauspicious Friday the
thirteenth, Api also had to take care of a patient who was suspected
of typhoid. Although he regularly treated such people, that day he
worried about contagion.

At this low point, Professor Seegert presented Api with a ticket
for the following afternoon's performance of Schiller's *The Parasite* at
the Deutsches Theater. He knew how much Api enjoyed the theater
and was trying to cheer him up. The theater had reopened on June
26 with a performance of *Nathan the Wise*. Lessing's classic had been
forbidden under the Nazis, and now its language of humanity and
tolerance spoke directly, if painfully, to the audience. Schiller's slight
comedy of love and intrigue, however, was probably intended as just
a moment's respite.

The Sunday after the performance, Api felt a recurrence of his
stomach ailment. The short walk to the Sophien Church exhausted
him so much that he almost collapsed during the service. He had to

lower his head onto the pew in front of him until the spell passed. For once, he did not remember much of the sermon. Still, after the service, he got on his bike, as planned, and rode off in the direction of Friedenau to see Frau Grossman, who continued to urge him to move there. Unfortunately, he had a different bike, which was much harder to pedal. When he reached his destination, pretty worn out, he was rewarded with a lunch of sauerbraten and gooseberry compote, followed by coffee and cake. Although the cake was baked without fat or sugar and the coffee was *Muckefuck*, both were rare treats.

The days of summer passed in the same deadening routine. The heat was becoming oppressive again, increasing the threat of epidemics. Api saw no way to make the journey to us and feared that soon he would be too weak to set out at all, if he was not so already.

# 37

# HOMELESS

The middle of July brought dramatic changes for Germany and Api personally. It was the time of the Potsdam Conference, which Api saw as one ray of hope for the future. The meeting started the following day at Cecilienhof, the former home of crown prince Wilhelm Hohenzollern. Stalin, Truman, and Churchill met for two weeks to work out the fate of Germany and decide the future of Europe.

On Monday, July 16, as Churchill and Truman arrived in Berlin, the Sieverts happened to throw a birthday party for themselves. Api took the rickety bike again, dressed in his best clothes: the striped pants and black jacket, which he had brushed carefully after the last bike trip. Even so, the jacket was looking less black than it had when Herr Gerhardt had given it to him. He added his pearl tie pin as a final touch. Although frail and shaky, Api would not miss the party. The Sieverts offered drinks and food and, above all, companionship. They also offered advice: Api should consult a Frau Paterek at the housing bureau about possible relocation to the American zone.

Amid his misery, Api often expressed deep thanks for what he had and what others did for him—a pervasive sense of gratitude that he instilled in me as well—although he also felt guilty that he was allowed to enjoy such luxury. Yet neither here nor elsewhere did he attribute his good fortune to the always powerful advantages of class standing.

Action was forced on him sooner than he had anticipated. On Thursday, July 19, Api had to give up his "swallow's nest" because water was coming in everywhere. All the containers proved inadequate against the increasing number of leaks. And there was ever less hope of getting patients to come to Luisenstrasse, since the Soviets had requisitioned the street. Last but by no means least was Api's fear of arrest. Word or rumor had come to him that the Soviet secret police, or GPU, whose headquarters were just a few feet away on Luisenstrasse, had inquired about him. The suggestion alone was enough to terrify him.

And Api had good reason to be afraid. The GPU arrested thousands of civilians in Berlin after the war. People were interrogated in the notorious GPU cellars—so like those of the Nazis—where they were subjected to threats and torture in an effort to extract incriminating statements. As a doctor, Api might not end up in a labor camp, but arrest and transportation to somewhere in the east was a hardly less frightening prospect. He never went to sleep without the fear that they might come for him that night, and he kept his clothes ready for immediate departure.

Therefore, on July 19, with a heavy heart and great foreboding, Api scribbled in his diary, "No need to write down everything that is going on with me and within me. I will not ever forget it anyhow."

Shouldering his rucksack, he went in search of a place to stay. He had picked out his most important instruments and added some books, a shirt, a tie, his best jacket and trousers, and, of course, his tie pin. Out on the streets, he felt truly homeless, just like the streams of refugees for whom he had been so sorry. Api almost had to laugh at what a fool he had been to imagine that he could create even a small livelihood out of the rubble in the middle of Berlin.

Cut off from the provisions of the clinic and the charity of the nurses there, Api had to forage for food on his own. It was a new experience. He went from one restaurant to another, but most of them were closed. The few that were open had nothing to offer. At best, they served coffee and soda water. Dragging his heavy load, he called upon colleagues and acquaintances. At ten thirty that night, he stopped at the district housing office—in vain. After that, he begged a bed for the night from a colleague.

The next morning, Api went to Breitenbachplatz to see Frau Paterek, the person the Sieverts had mentioned to him. On his way there, he saw an old woman collapse. She was, he wrote later, "just another in the heartrending columns of misery, refugees with no place to go." He realized then that although he, too, had no home, he was still undeservedly fortunate compared with such anguish. Breitenbachplatz, four miles south of Berlin Mitte, was in comparatively good shape. Seeing building after building still standing, he felt "a moment of envious comparison: if one had lived in such an area, perhaps one could have saved one's stuff which one had grown so fond of!"

Frau Paterek offered him a room in her nearby apartment on Opitzstrasse 3, in Steglitz, but made clear that it was only a temporary arrangement. She wanted to help him out because the Sieverts had told her how much he needed assistance. Api was relieved that he had a place to stay at least for a few nights. In the evening, he went back to the friendly Dr. Blumann, whose advice was, as Api wrote, "Not in writing!" I do not know what that refers to, whether Dr. Blumann was speaking of an application for denazification or a request to move out of the Soviet sector or whether Api had asked Dr. Blumann to make some kind of statement on his behalf.

From then on, Api became ever more distraught, almost incapable of forming coherent thoughts and plans. Even his handwriting, always so neat and precise, disintegrated and became shaky and disjointed. He often scratched out words and lines. He who had always relied on banishing anxiety by putting it into words now often could not write at all.

In this shaken state, Api made his way to his new room. Frau Paterek, the landlady, met him with a warm smile. It did him good to receive such a cordial welcome. The room she had for him was tiny, but there were trees right in front of the window—real green, shady trees as had not surrounded him since Suderburg. Looking out of the window, Api felt for the first time as if peace had really come.

Api carefully smoothed out the jacket and pants Herr Gerhardt had given him and hung them over the one chair in his room. Strangely, at the bottom of his rucksack he had put two of my children's books: *Birds of the Woods*, *The Elephant Book*, which he laid on the bedside table next to his one remaining medical text. Just when he wondered what to do next, Frau Paterek knocked on his door and invited him to share her meal of fried potatoes and tea. He accepted gratefully.

Before turning in that night, Api looked at the sky. "Exquisite light-framed cumulus clouds drift above the wonderful green of the trees and above the silent village peace." As he lay down in a strange bed, grateful to have a place to put his head, he wondered what he would dream. As superstition has it, whatever you dream the first night in a new place will come true.

But Api never recorded any dreams he may have had. In fact, the next day, July 21, he did not have sufficient concentration to write at all. Before going out in the morning, he sat down briefly with his diary but could not find words for his situation. He started to put something down but immediately blacked it all out again. He felt weak and ill and very old. His foot was swollen, and he suffered from inflammation of his veins. He could hardly walk. He also noticed hunger edemas on both legs, and a bleeding sore. He thought despairingly that once again he had made the wrong decision by coming to this place. He was more uprooted than ever before, now that he had given up his last anchor.

The following day, Api went back once more to Dr. Blumann. Together, they settled on Friedenau as the best prospect for Api's practice, since Dr. Blumann knew a three-room apartment in that area. Only, he added, one inside wall was missing. So, Api thought, he might have a practice in Friedenau after all, more than twenty years after he had first considered it.

In the evening, Api realized that this had been one of very few Sundays that he had not attended church. He ended the day with a prayer of despair: "My God, my God, don't leave me, keep me close to You and save me from the last act of despair!"

# 38

# I AM AT THE END

On the evening of July 23, Api found out that the GPU had stopped Fräulein Herzog, his surgery assistant, in the street the previous day. No one knew what had become of her. Api himself had not reported to the GPU, had not been officially requested to do so, but had it through hearsay that he needed to go. Now, he tortured himself with questions. Had they arrested Fräulein Herzog because of him? What would become of his loyal assistant in the hands of these torturers? He made up his mind that he had to report to the GPU the very next day and try to find out what had happened to Fräulein Herzog. Before going to bed that night, Api entered in his diary only "I am at the end!" He needed strong sleeping pills that night.

Fräulein Herzog was released the next day without harm. The GPU had not questioned her about her employer. It had all been some sort of misunderstanding, she said. Although he seemed to be in no immediate danger, Api determined to report to the GPU anyway, but only after he got permission from the district medical officer for his move to Friedenau. However, before doing anything else, Api wanted to deliver yet another letter for us to someone who was going to Uelzen. That person, whom Api did not name, told him that in a cottage in Suderburg, one of the new arrivals was seriously ill. Api's worst fears seemed to have come true. And yet, he wrote, "How can I reach you in the face of overwhelming outside forces? Here is a decision of life and death, the most difficult of my life, perhaps for a reunion now or never at all." It felt to him "like walking close to the abyss." Nevertheless, he managed to meet the district medical officer, who approved his move to Friedenau. It seemed that July 24, my mother's birthday, had brought him a little good fortune after all.

The next morning, Api's hopes were shattered again. The housing bureau told him that *Pgs* were not allowed to rent an apartment in the American sector—they could have no more than a single room. Api felt certain that this was an idea not of the occupiers but of his "dear compatriots," as he called his fellow Germans, thinking especially of those—and he had several in mind—who had been "the wildest, most brutal and blinded Heil Hitlers right until the end." The man in the office was sympathetic, yet he could do nothing for Api. He just concluded with an apologetic shrug: "That's how it is. Just think, all the railroad workers have been dismissed. They were state employees and had to be members of the Party. Now they have lost their jobs. And the railroads aren't working."

Api left in despair. He had to do something to find a way to come to Suderburg. The night before, his familiar dreams of futility and failure had tortured him once again. By five o'clock in the afternoon, Api came to a decision: Despite his nightmares, he would try to leave by train the next morning.

Api spent the evening with another colleague who offered to put him up for the night. As he was preparing a field bed in the study, his host strongly advised Api against the trip. "It makes no sense to leave now, without any kind of foothold in Berlin and without even an identity card. You would never be able to come back." Reluctantly, Api agreed. As he had feared all along, and just as in his dreams, he had to postpone his journey to us once again.

While Api was embroiled in these personal worries, he cherished the hope that some help would come from the Potsdam Conference. But mainly what was decided was a 25 percent reduction in Germany's territory, and that demilitarization, denazification, democratization, and restitution were to become the chief aims for Germany. The Potsdam Conference did not lead to any improvement in living conditions in Berlin. In fact, the medical situation there continued to worsen. Especially for infants up to four years, the death rate was high. Api was glad that I was no longer in Berlin. Dysentery and other gastrointestinal illnesses killed eight thousand people that summer, and more died of tuberculosis. Food was scarce—even potatoes were gone—and desperate Berliners planted potatoes in the Tiergarten.

Api's only option at this point was to see Frau Winkler, the landlady of the place Dr. Blumann had mentioned. The address was Begastrasse 10 in Friedenau, three miles straight south from the center. Although he noticed that there were no windowpanes left and the gray stucco was crumbling, the building was in far better shape than almost anything he had seen in Berlin Mitte. What delighted Api most was that the linden trees that lined both sides of Begastrasse were still alive, and there was a little mountain ash in the tiny green space right in front of the downstairs window.

Frau Winkler came up with a solution to the rent problem, one that helped them both. She could sublet the rooms to him so that Api would have a place to stay and she, some much needed income. Aware that Api had a difficult time coping, she exploited his situation to her benefit. She charged him 120 marks for his three rooms. The rent for her five rooms and balcony was only 152. When Api objected, she accused him of being petty. "You doctors always have mountains of money." It must be said in her defense, and Api acknowledged this as well, that Frau Winkler's life was difficult, too. She had to fight for everything all by herself. Her husband, a fifty-five-year-old member of the Volkssturm, had died in the war. And the Americans had requisitioned whatever good furniture and carpets she had for use in their own quarters.

The rooms also disappointed Api. The windows were broken, and, as Dr. Blumann had told him, so was part of one wall. It was "a joint à la Dostoevsky." Nevertheless, he consoled himself, this would give him a foothold. And the mention of Dostoevsky made him think of his beloved son, who had avidly read the novels during his reconvalescence. When Frau Winkler revised her offer by adding that to begin with he could have only two of the three rooms, Api accepted that also. He saw no other option. It still was better than being out on the street. Frau Paterek had been most kind, but she needed her room back and he had begun to feel like a parasite. Two rooms, he told himself, would be enough to open a surgery, even if he had to sleep in one of them. He also felt a little safer away from the Soviet sector, although he worried that "perhaps they will take me away after all! I have almost no hope."

Mike and I also visited Begastrasse, taking the S-Bahn from Potsdamer Platz to Friedenau. We crossed the square in front of the station and after a few steps came to the Dürer Platz, another little square from where we entered Begastrasse. It was a short, tree-lined street just as Api had described it. We found number 10 halfway down on the right side. The gray stucco building now was well taken care of. It was three stories high, with tall bay windows in front. The front yard had a tiny patch of grass, but the mountain ash Api had enjoyed was gone.

Api's first action was to see the American commandant to get permission to go to Suderburg for a visit. Permission was denied, since *Pgs* were not allowed out of Berlin. Or, the official added, if a *Pg* somehow already was outside the city, he was not allowed to return. This brought Api's hope of a reunion with us down to zero. The commandant also changed Api's ration card back to the lowest group, known as the cemetery, or death, card.

After seeing the commandant, Api resignedly took out his diary to tell us the names of people with whom he had deposited what little mementos he had left. He entered the names in a framed square on the inside back cover of the green booklet so that we would be sure to notice them. Since it would be difficult to get in touch with anyone in the Soviet sector and even less likely to get anything out, he listed only his newly made friends in the American sector. He left his fountain pen with Frau Paterek and his gold watch with Frau Grossman. He also mentioned Fräulein Herzog, who had the most immediate information about him.

After that, Api felt at an end. He was unable to read, work, lie down, or sit up. On the streets he was restless, and in his rooms hardly capable of concentrated thought. He noted in despair, "I cannot even master writing halfway collectedly in this little book which I have always loved so much. . . . I am afraid of great physical and mental torture. And—I do not want to abandon my God."

# 39

# WE'D BE LUCKY TO
# GET IKE CLEARED

Now that Api was installed in the American zone, he realized that it had challenges of its own. He found that the Americans were also dedicated to denazification. Historian Giles MacDonogh says, "The Americans insisted that denazification be carried out with a toughness absent from the other zones." To begin with, everyone had to fill out a questionnaire that ran twelve pages with 131 questions. MacDonogh explains, "It was only once the properly completed questionnaire had been returned and vetted that a German could return to normal life. Until then he was in a sort of purgatory that left him outside the law." Americans handled almost 170,000 cases, whereas the British had only 2,296. By December 1945, 90,000 Nazis were imprisoned in the American zone. As writer Joseph Kanon has an American officer exclaim in *The Good German*: "Denazification. Those guys—we'd be lucky to get Ike cleared."

Api struggled with the questionnaire for a long time. No space, the form warned, was to be left blank. One of the questions was whether he had ever hoped for German victory. How could anyone answer this truthfully? Who in any country had never hoped for their own victory? And if you said yes, what would happen? Glancing at the other questions, Api feared that his answers would not go over well with the Americans. The questionnaire seemed to make little distinction between a Nazi and a Prussian. Api's Prussian background, to say nothing of his education at a military academy, would no doubt be held against him. Having been a member of the Stahlhelm put him, he feared, at further disadvantage. Even his membership in a student fraternity might come back to haunt him. Api shook his head in frustration. The questioners seemed to have no idea that the Nazis had been against fraternities from the beginning and had suspended them since 1935. Another perplexing question asked whether the bombing had affected health, work, or sleep. Had these questioners never experienced a bombing raid? Then he had to list every trip abroad he had ever taken, every relative who held an office, every membership in an organization. Api often picked up the questionnaire only to let it drop again. Perhaps, he thought, it was safer not to fill it out at all.

In 1951, six years after those questionnaires were issued, novelist Ernst von Salomon wrote a witty and insightful novel about them called *The Questionnaire*. He used the 131 questions to examine his life, answering even supposedly simple questions with long, discursive answers in a novel of more than seven hundred pages. For example, question number 11 asked merely for the person's address, but Salomon could not find an easy answer even to that simple inquiry, since at that time his abode was "as fleeting as the moment." His novel shows the absurdity of this bureaucratic instrument that attempts to shove everyone into clear categories. Going deeper, the questions trigger Salomon to ask himself, "How can I understand the questionnaire in any other way than as a modern attempt to make me examine my conscience?" Pondering this, Salomon has one of his chief characters remark, "Today we are all made responsible. Today we are not only asked about what we have done, but also about what we have not done." Then again, the storyteller cannot suppress his anger at the humiliation the questioners impose on him and at the moral superiority they so easily assume, which shows little under-standing of what went on during those twelve Nazi years.

I do not know whether some such thoughts also passed through Api's mind as he sat for hours in front of the questionnaire. But for the moment he was unable to complete that document and laid it down in frustration as often as he picked it up.

# 40

# ABORTED JOURNEYS

A pi did not give up his attempts to communicate with us, although he had as little success with doing so as with the questionnaire. On Sunday morning, August 5, he was once again in search of a man who, he had heard, was heading somewhere in the proximity of Suderburg. Api did not say who the man was or how he had heard about him, but mentioned that he had to walk a long way from Begastrasse to find him. When he got to the appointed address, he was told that the man was in church. So he waited outside the nearest church, hoping that it was the right one. Sitting on a bench across from it, Api saw that the shingles of its roof were gone and the stained-glass windows shattered. But he also noticed how above this ruin "arched a sky of rare beauty, a deep blue with white cumulus clouds."

Just then, the sounds of a well-preserved organ drifted over to him. As he listened intently, he felt as if he were rising up into the heavens along with the majestic harmonies. Then the congregation, which must have been large, burst into the hymn "How Shall I Not Be Grateful to My Lord, How Not Praise Him." Api listened with rapture while the organ, accompanied by the human voices, resounded through the open roof into the sky.

After the service, Api and the man managed to find each other. Api handed over his precious letter together with urgent entreaties to help it toward its destination. The man explained his route to the west, which he considered relatively safe, and mentioned a particular spot as the best place to get across the "green border" at the Elbe River, which was the as-yet-unmarked separation between east and west. Api listened carefully but did not entrust the location even to his diary.

Inspired by the stranger's initiative and in defiance of all warnings, Api bought a ticket for Suderburg, knowing full well that a ticket was no guarantee of getting on a train. He was glad that he had been able to save enough money to be able to afford this. It felt good just holding this palpable token of a reunion. If he could not make it all the way, he would somehow get across the green border at the point the man had indicated. Fräulein Herzog, who had followed Api out of Berlin Mitte, hoping to work with him again, told him that if he left, she wanted to go, too. Nothing and no one was keeping her in Berlin. Her parents were dead, her brother was missing, and her sister had died in an explosion.

With the train ticket in his pocket, Api joined a long line of people outside a grocery store, hoping to get some bread for the journey. Two men in line behind him were talking about the green border. One of them said that he had heard that locals reported difficulties at the very place where Api had hoped to cross. "Many have already lost their lives there, and many others are still waiting, hidden in wheat fields. Both the Russians and the Brits know about this spot and watch it carefully. If you're caught, you most likely are dead." Api had no idea how trustworthy this rumor was, but he felt as if a coincidence of fate had put the men in his path just at this time.

That evening, Fräulein Herzog showed up at his door, firmly committed to the journey and almost enthusiastic. The train was to leave at 11:00 p.m. The night was eerie; thunderstorms threatened all around. They debated yet again whether it was safer to leave or to stay. Api told her what he had overheard in the food line, but Fräulein Herzog brushed it off as just another wild rumor. He also feared the added burden of dragging her into danger with him. And then he had to consider for the hundredth time that even if he did get through, the British occupation authorities of Suderburg would not allow him to stay in their zone. How, then, would he ever get back to Berlin? Fräulein Herzog could say only, "My God, Doctor, if one always considers all and every possibility, one gets nothing done." He had to agree and yet could not make a move. The hours went by in fruitless discussion, and they did not leave.

August dragged on exhaustingly and hopelessly. Api hardly wrote in his diary anymore. The main writing he did was postcards and letters to us, in part, perhaps, to make up for his inability to leave. He not only asked travelers to take these messages with them but also wrote to strangers in the area of Suderburg, begging them to please let his wife and daughter know that he had survived. Most of these efforts were in vain, but in my mother's box I found proof that at least one of these notes had been successful. I was delighted when I dug out the little card. On August 25, Api wrote to Herr Frohns, owner of the Frohns Hotel in Uelzen, that a mutual friend, Herr Gerhardt from Luisenstrasse, had given him this contact and implored Herr Frohns to forward the card or send a messenger to Suderburg telling us that he was alive and had moved to Begastrasse 10 in Friedenau. He also asked another favor: Would Herr Frohns allow us to give him a postcard in return? Then, when he knew of someone at his hotel who was planning to travel to Berlin or as near to Berlin as possible, would Herr Frohns hand him the card for mailing or delivery? It would be best, Api added, if the card were mailed in Berlin or if the person delivered it to him directly. Api explained that the Wannsee train, which left from Potsdamer station and ran pretty regularly now, stopped almost immediately next to Begastrasse 10. This was a bit of an exaggeration, since his rooms were two blocks from the station, but he so wanted to hear from the messenger. He concluded that whoever undertook this task would be generously rewarded for his pains.

On August 22, when no patients appeared, he used the empty time to write another letter. He did not touch his diary. Api wrote to us about his many frustrations and few small successes. At 8:00 a.m. that day, he had reported to the magistrate of the Steglitz-Friedenau district to try yet again to obtain permission to travel. I do not understand the bureaucratic jungle of those days, but this time he was given a form to fill out. In it he stated that his reasons for seeking travel permission were to secure his medical instruments out of Berlin and to visit sick relatives. He hoped that would do.

But the form by itself was not enough. He still needed to complete the twelve-page American questionnaire. In addition, he had to provide an affidavit from the person who was in charge of the apartment building where he lived. In an attempt to organize the population, the city had assigned a foreman to each building. The job was to watch the house and its lodgers, who in turn had to address any reports or concerns to the foreman. It was a system that facilitated spying and denunciations of all sorts. The Nazis had used something similar when they had put block wardens in charge of every city block. Since Api was not yet known at his new address and was only subletting anyway, he assumed that he had to obtain this declaration from the foreman at Luisenstrasse 41. Frau Gertrud Albrecht, who had been the building manager for all the years he had lived there, was no longer in charge; in her place was a stranger who knew nothing about Api except for his *Pg* status.

There was yet another requirement before the authorities would consider the travel permission. Api had to get approval from the Soviet commanding officer in charge of Luisenstrasse. This especially frightened him. Would he not attract the attention of the

Soviet secret police, who may have been looking for him anyway? Although he could not imagine any possible denunciation against him, he feared the GPU and its unpredictable procedures. And perhaps, he wondered, his military discharge, signed by Professor Sauerbruch back in May, was invalid after all. There had been rumors that Professor Sauerbruch had been dismissed and all his decisions had been rescinded.

It seems likely to me today that these rumors were related to Sauerbruch's ambivalent role during the Nazi regime, which was typical of many people in high places who were not outright Nazis. Professor Sauerbruch, in fact, was not dismissed from the health bureau until October 12, 1945, when he was charged with having contributed to the reputation of the Nazi regime. And then he was almost immediately reinstated at the Charité. But in August Api had only rumors and knew not what to believe, so the validity of his military discharge continued to worry him. Amid all these hurdles, Api seemed to have only two options, as he always had: to attempt a secret crossing at the green border or stay in Berlin.

# 41

# HAVE I A RIGHT?

As still no patients appeared, Api's letter to us grew longer and longer. He voiced his deep sense of responsibility that it was up to him to look after us, a responsibility he could not abandon just because he felt at an end. "Have I a right," he asked, "to throw down everything here and destroy our hope for a possibly secure future?"

His starvation diet had seriously reduced Api's energy. He had become skeletal. He could not even look into the mirror anymore when he washed himself. His scrawny arms and legs were as wrinkled as his mother's had been just before her death. Yet he believed, despite everything, that "a heart, even if it lies completely in ruins, keeps on hoping, and no experience can teach it otherwise." He continued, "If only all this would be nothing more than bad memories and the most terrible experiences part of the past, it then would lose its bitterness and unbearable pain. . . . Oh, once more with you! But if God should decree differently, then you know from my unvarnished accounts of my suffering how much I needed rest, how much I loved you, and hopefully you would find peace in the thought that it was God's will."

By now, Api had filled two pages with his small script, with which he could cram forty-five lines onto a page. He felt a little lighter for having told us about his worries and ended with sending his prayers and love, folded the paper, addressed it, and crept into bed.

Two days later, on August 24, Api wrote another long letter that spilled over into the next day, in which he continued to air the tormenting dilemmas he had already confided to the diary. In all his quandaries, Api never forgot that he was by no means without friends who supported him physically, as well as emotionally. Listing the people who had helped him these past months, he was filled with gratitude. Although Api did not acknowledge this, I am struck that all of them were women, perhaps because not many men were left after the war.

He first thought of Frau Grossmann. She regularly invited him to her place and offered both food and companionship. Frau Paterek from the housing bureau had given Api the job of administering typhoid inoculations out of her home, which earned him a little money. She had put him up when he had nowhere to go, and she, too, occasionally invited him to a meal. Next, Api thought of Fräulein Herzog, his assistant. Although they had hardly any patients, Fräulein Herzog was always there to support him and cheer him up, although she herself had lost everything and was all alone in the world. He asked us, "If I should not be able to cope, thank her at least in your hearts if you cannot do it otherwise." Api also thought gratefully of the patients who shared with him the little they had, bringing him homemade jam and making sure his surgery room was never without flowers. Finally, his thoughts turned to the deaconesses who had befriended him, both there and in Berlin Mitte. These kind women comforted Api, and he could not have managed without their help.

However, he concluded that nothing could wipe away his despair or overcome his exhaustion of body and mind. His life had shrunk down to one dominant emotion, anxiety, which made it impossible for him to decide anything. One moment, he made up his mind to leave and so would start the cumbersome process of applying for the various permissions. And the very next, he had to expend an equal amount of energy to undo everything.

At the end of August, Api made one other attempt to get out of Berlin. His friends the two deaconesses had introduced him to a Herr Reese, who was leaving for Uelzen, and Api could give him another of his letters. This time, Api decided on the spur of the moment to join the man on his trip. He knew that he would not be able to go on his own, and here was a companion who traveled essentially the same way. Before leaving for the station on August 28, Api jotted just three words in his diary: "Plan for departure." Then he started the long trek to the East station to meet his fellow traveler.

They waited a long time on the crowded platform. When the train finally pulled into the station, it was so full, Api wrote later in a letter, that not even a cigar box would have fit in. A few desperate or adventurous men even clung to the steps and the roof. It was hopeless to get on. The man told Api that he himself would try again the next day, but this time he planned to go from Anhalter station, south of Potsdamer Platz. Api thought fleetingly of the many times he had taken Nyussi and the children to that station, with its huge domed hall, for their journey to Hungary. The man explained, "It's Berlin's busiest station right now. More trains are leaving from there every day. We will have a much better chance of getting into one of them, even though we'll have to change trains several times. Let's do it," he concluded.

Api watched the man leave, admiring how easily he made his decisions. Api, for his part, was once again at a loss for what to do. It was afternoon by now, and he had already walked five miles from Begastrasse to the East station. But hours of daylight still lay ahead, and he felt as if he had to do something with this day. So he made up his mind to shoulder his rucksack again and walk to Lehrter station, just west of the Charité. It must be less than two miles. He wanted to check whether he could find a more direct train from there than the roundabout route from Anhalter station. When Api reached Lehrter station, he saw signs posted everywhere telling him that as of now and until further notice, travel to the British zone was forbidden. So there would be no trains at all to Uelzen from there. He had to turn around and start the long hike back to Friedenau, having accomplished nothing. When he got home, he dumped his rucksack without unpacking it and wrote in his diary, "Missed departure." He had no strength to say anything more.

The day after that failed trip, Api was still exhausted from the disappointment, as much as from the long hike. He stayed home and began another letter, feeling that he had to explain to us, and perhaps to himself, why he had not left after all. Underlying all the arguments was a refrain of self-reproach and shame for his weakness.

That same day, the Soviet sector announced that all members of the military from lieutenants on up, as well as all *Pgs*, had to report for registration to the Soviet commander by September 25. Feeling his brain spin in a vortex around the same questions, Api felt that it was too much for him to cope with all alone. Whenever he had faced difficulties before, Nyussi had been at his side with her love and her courage, and he had been able to listen to her always level-headed and unsentimental advice. Even as he was writing to her, he said that he was so distraught that he had to jump up, rip the spectacles off his nose, stamp his foot, and curse himself as a coward. After he had finished the letter, he reached for his green booklet and quickly scribbled his last entry of the month: "If only one could at last give up!! God be with you."

# 42

# LISTEN TO THE GRASSHOPPERS

On Sunday, September 9, Api started another diary, perhaps because he had given the first into safekeeping. It was another 3.5-by-5.5-inch booklet with a green cloth cover and gold-lettered AGENDA at the top. The beginning pages had lists of patients and their payments, dating back to earlier years. The amounts Api had penciled in varied between 3 and 10 marks, with an occasional 20 or 30 marks, all of them sums that now seemed to him like a miracle.

As Api sat down to write, the first word that came to him was "destruction." But then he recalled Superintendent Pfeifer's sermon of that morning. "If all people would become God's collaborators . . . all this terrible misery could be mastered—one might say in a moment." Despite these words of reassurance, Api had to fight with himself not to be overwhelmed by fury. This was the first time that anger and bitterness became dominant, a sign, he feared, that he was losing all hope for the future. He was afraid to be conquered by such violent emotions because they stood in the way of his faith. But with each passing day, that was getting more difficult.

After church, Api biked the short distance to Frau Paterek to administer typhoid inoculations. He found several people at her home, which earned him a little money, but, as had become his habit, he charged far less than the stipulated amount. He did it gladly, but at the same time he was a little annoyed with himself. He needed the money to fix up his rooms and above all to replace the cardboard in his windows with real panes. Frau Paterek, however, rewarded his generosity by inviting him to lunch. It was his first warm food in days.

Haunted by his *Pg* status, Api wrote that the unending smear propaganda had accelerated the hatred of *Pgs* into a psychosis—if only, he admitted to himself, with the nonthinking population. Yet because he was a *Pg*, his every move was blocked. He was unable to establish himself, to rent an apartment, or to obtain permission to travel. He had the lowest ration card and no hope of getting a telephone connection for his surgery room. Perhaps worst of all, his outcast status made him feel like a second-class citizen, even a criminal, hardly human. However much Api examined his life, he was certain that his boundless happiness "did not happen at the expense of any other human being whatsoever. . . . And yet the propaganda creates a veritable psychosis of hatred against people who had the misfortune to be inscribed." Then again, he mentioned those who, "without having been *Pgs*, agitated infinitely more wildly for the aims of national socialist Germany, yes, even abused me as a poor member of the Party if I dared call things by their right names and predict our fate."

The question of political responsibility was, of course, the point with which the Allies vehemently disagreed with most Germans, and that we still debate today. Were all Germans guilty of the atrocities that the Hitler regime committed in their name? And if so, to what degree? Is Api's defense that he did not do anything politically a valid argument, or do we not think today that doing nothing carries with it a responsibility, especially since he had to have been a daily witness to persecution? Do we then have to find Germans collectively guilty, and perhaps people like my grandfather—educated, well-to-do members of the upper middle class—most of all? It is a dilemma with which I continue to struggle. However, today I can debate it all at leisure and in peace, far from the world in which Api barely survived. He had no such luxury, and so perhaps put any thoughts of guilt and responsibility out of his mind.

Alone in his rooms, Api played with the idea of selling his instruments "in exchange for no matter how primitive and uncreative a line of work." Laborers were needed everywhere, but Api was just fantasizing. He had few, if any, such skills; he had not even been able to fix a light or a dripping faucet in his home before the war. He was also well aware that the German mark was not worth much at this point and that whatever little value it had left was unstable. Therefore, selling precious medical equipment in exchange for possibly worthless marks made no economic sense. Api realized that these were nothing but desperate fantasies to survive.

Having heard that the entire town of Oranienburg, just north of Berlin, was under quarantine because of the typhoid epidemic, Api at last gave himself an inoculation. It resulted in days of fever and chills. On Saturday evening, September 15, he sought refuge in the company of a friend, the deaconess Sister Minna, who lived at Birkbuxstrasse 30 in Berlin Lichterfelde, about three miles south of where Api lived. In the large, walled garden, Api was allowed to pick the seeds out of sunflowers that were ripening by the wall. He happily chewed them for a little fat while enjoying their conversation. On leaving, she presented him with a small but heavy cardboard box. When he opened the lid to peek inside, he found two heads of cauliflower, fourteen tomatoes, four pears, and—Sister Minna was well aware of his love of sweets—a piece of cake. He thanked the generous deaconess with tears in his eyes.

As he stepped outside, Api saw that it was beginning to get dark—another sign of approaching winter. He hoped to catch the last train, which would save him about half the distance of his hike. But when he reached the station, the train was just pulling out, which he thought was typical of the bad luck that seemed to follow him everywhere. In a dejected mood, he trudged on through the darkening and empty streets. On his walk, Api listened to the grasshoppers. Their whirring and chirping drew his thoughts back to when he was a child in Marienwerder. He remembered how often, when his homework was done, he had pedaled past fields of rye, oats, and potatoes to get to his favorite spot near the wide Weichsel River. He explored the marshy meadows and little ponds ringed by hawthorns, sloes, and alders, the homes of turtles and woodcocks. In winter, the shallow ponds froze early and were excellent for skating.

But it was summer vacations Api liked best, as he could be outside all day. Above all, he loved the fat green grasshoppers as they jumped all over the sunny meadows. He thought of them as the friends of his youth. I share Api's fondness for grasshoppers and as a child loved to lie in a meadow to watch them whirring around me. If I was very still, a few settled on my hands and arms and tickled me with their scratchy little legs. Listening to them now, however, Api noticed that these city grasshoppers already "chirped autumnally voiceless." This brought him back to the present. The cardboard in his windows would not keep out the cold.

At home, resting with the companionship of his diary, Api recalled the scene of his walk, and now the beauty of the evening mellowed him. "The moon was behind clouds, the darkness was penumbrous, a warm September evening rested silently over holy, indelible, but already oh so distant memories!" He was saddened that even recollections of his happy childhood were fading. It all seemed so far away and unrecoverable. Before going to sleep, Api knocked on his landlady's door to share his gifts with her. She accepted sourly, and his hope that their relationship would become warmer was dashed right away.

# 43

# A BAD CHRISTIAN

On Sunday, Api started the day with a cold wash. He had always believed in the recuperative power of cold showers. When I lived with my grandparents in the early 1950s, he occasionally insisted I take a cold shower in the morning, to which I submitted with shrieks of terror and delight. We were one of few German families at that time who had a shower at all, since most people had only bathtubs. Our shower was a large room tiled in a cream color, in which I could jump about, alternating between letting the cold water hit me and avoiding it. Api's predilection for showers, especially cold ones, has not stuck with me; today I prefer hot and lazy baths.

As it had been in his attic room, mornings always were Api's worst times. Instead of jumping out of bed, as of old, to do exercises, he now lay awake for a long time before plucking up courage to rise. His list of fears seemed endless. He was afraid "that no patients will come, that something will happen politically, that I cannot bear up economically, that my desperate longing makes me do something stupid, that perhaps a reunion will no longer be granted us, and, if so, how terribly hopeless it will be, that perhaps you are not all alive anymore or are sick, that I will not be able to make my apartment livable for the winter, that all my errands in that regard will fail where others succeed!"

Api felt guilty that he began the day as a bad Christian. "I am shaken by spasms of horror and I have to fight with an iron will that I don't give up everything in despair, crawl under my sheets, and wait for the end—or bring it about!" Even prayer did not help, or, rather, he could not pray at all. Instead, his thoughts strayed back to the past. He thought of all those who once had been part of his life and now were gone: his mother and father, his son, his son-in-law. Then, for moments, it seemed as if his son were with him again, yet he was not dreaming. Or perhaps, he speculated, he already belonged more to the dead than to the living. He felt dead inside and was plagued by foreboding about whether his mind would hold out.

Feeling bitterness and anger overwhelm him, Api warned himself, "Only not judge and reckon with God, or say that everything is blind chance. I am certain that it is God's will, even if I cannot understand it and that somehow it must work toward our benefit." He remembered the hymn "A Christian Cannot Be Without a Cross"; he tried to console himself that "the larger the cross, the more beautiful the reward" and that he was just a small part of a large community that lived in similar misery.

Every morning, Api forced himself to break though the cycle of fear, anger, and despair, clean his rooms, and make the bed to be ready for any patients who might come. These unfamiliar household chores were a distraction, and for a little while they kept him from facing the more problematic tasks of his existence. But not for long. "When I crawl into the bathroom and shave myself, chilled, in the half light, then cook my flour soup and in between clean my boots, make the bed, and eat my breakfast while cleaning up, watch how the time for my urgent agenda increasingly shrivels up . . . , I am in the grips of the whole misery of mankind!"

# 44

# GOD'S COWORKERS?

Standing by the open window on the evening of Wednesday, September 19, Api observed, "Silently and big rises the almost full slice of the moon above the light fog across the meadows. . . . Grasshoppers sing to me of my youth, which was infinitely joyful despite rather straitened circumstances." As it was getting dark, he noticed fireworks to the southeast, from the direction of Treptow. He was amazed how soon Berlin revived the Wednesday tradition of Treptow in Flames, a weekly fireworks show near the Spree River that had been popular before the war. When my mother and uncle were small, Api occasionally took them there to watch the fireworks and afterward treated them to cakes and soda in one of the many coffeehouses along the river—"very big happiness."

As soon as the Soviets had taken Berlin, they had moved it to Moscow summer time, one hour ahead. On Sunday, September 23, Berlin switched back for the winter. Now, perhaps, Api thought that his and his family's "oh so terribly and painfully separate life can at least run somewhat more parallel time-wise." The next day, he had to report again for registration as a *Pg*, this time in the district of Friedenau. When he got there, he was told that as an officer of the former Wehrmacht, he also needed to be fingerprinted. It made him feel even more like a criminal, now also with a criminal record. Yet he knew himself to be lucky compared with many medical officers of higher rank, who were imprisoned. He had heard that this was true of Dr. Pellnitz, who had been in charge of all the military clinics in the inner city, as well as Dr. Kleberger, with whom he had fought in May. Yet neither had been a member of the Nazi Party. As Giles MacDonogh, a historian of the postwar era, says, "The Allies were obsessed with the need to stamp out 'militarism,' and any connection with the armed forces was held against the supplicant."

That evening, Frau Grossman invited Api to a warm dinner of vegetable soup and apple cookies. His walk there took him past a small park, where he spotted a little girl my age happily chatting with her mother. It was a sight that moved him to tears, but he recovered himself enough to greet Frau Grossmann with a smile. While she was busy in the kitchen, he went over to the window and looked out on her little street, the Riemenschneiderweg. It faced allotment gardens, small parcels of public land that were given to apartment dwellers to make their own gardens. On their land, some had built huts where they stored their equipment or even spent the night. But now the gardens had turned into a field grown wild. Api noticed a group of poplars crowded with hundreds of starlings. When they all flew off together with a thunderous whirring of wings, he envied them. They were free!

I was surprised to find the location of Frau Grossmann's apartment almost unchanged from Api's description. When Mike and I took the short walk from Begastrasse going past the small park where Api had noticed the little girl, we saw a row of modest one-story houses that looked out on a field of allotment gardens, which now again were neatly tended. The street had the feel of a country lane, quite different from the urban apartments on Begastrasse.

Starting September 26, Api's practice began to pick up, and

hardly a day passed without at least one patient. He still could not get windowpanes, but on September 27 he managed to obtain curtains, which at least hid the cardboard. It was a minor thing, but in his circumstances it pleased him greatly. Perhaps, he thought, it was another tiny step toward having a home again, even though the temperature in his rooms had dropped to below fifty degrees Fahrenheit.

On his way to a talk on Tolstoy's Christianity given by Superintendent Pfeifer, Api heard a man shouting for help but could not find him. During the talk, he kept thinking about what might have happened to the man and whether anyone had been able to come to his aid. The next day, Saturday, September 29, was the wedding anniversary of my grandparents in 1919 and my parents in 1941. When Api woke up, his left ear rang strongly, which, in popular superstition, meant that someone was thinking of him. He imagined that we were also rising about this time and sending our love in fervent hopes that he was still alive. The morning was cold and bleak, the sun without any warmth, just like his life. He was chilly inside and out.

At lunchtime, he saw a few patients. Among them was the man whose screams he had heard the night before, who came to get new glasses. He told Api that some drunken Americans had seized and beaten him. They had taken his bicycle, his briefcase, and even his spectacles. A few days after that incident, another group of American soldiers broke off the black-and-white enamel sign for Api's office, which he had taken from Luisenstrasse, and threw stones at the house. The following night, they knocked down and robbed a fellow lodger, right in front of the house. Api was shocked to discover that Berliners were not safe even in the American sector.

After administering typhoid inoculations, Api was back in his chilly rooms at eight in the evening. His first instinct was to crawl into bed. But then he thought, *No, I must try to give this day a small festive appearance.* He still had a bit of flour, as well as one pear from

the gift of the deaconess, so he baked pear dumplings and flour cookies directly on his burner. He had no fat and no sugar, but it was the
best he could do.

The last day of September was a Sunday, and Api especially enjoyed
that day's sermon, entitled "We Are God's Coworkers." This was, it
seems, Superintendent Pfeifer's favorite theme, his attempt to explain
the horrors of the past and at the same time hold out the prospect of
a better future. "All of us, and not only our own people, had . . . been
coworkers not of God but of the devil. Instead of using all the treasures
of His wonderful earth for love, we had perverted everything to hate
and murder and war." Inspired by the pastor's words, Api wrote about
the need for mutual love. "Pray and be strong in hope and, if that is no
longer possible, in the love among you and among all people! If love
once again dwells in all human hearts, then also will the life on God's
wonderful earth again become not only bearable but beautiful."

Api next decided that it was time to move the furniture still
stored at the Westend Hospital to his rooms in Begastrasse. A dining
room set was hardly useful to him right now, nor did he have much
space for it, but it was the only possession he had left and he wanted
to have it with him. He would be able to accommodate it better once
he had the additional room he had been promised in his sublet. The
landlady, however, had given no sign of relinquishing that room. So
Api decided to broach the matter with her once more. He knocked
hesitantly at her door. He was always afraid to confront her, because
she was so very harsh and unfriendly. And indeed she opened her
door with a grim face. When Api mentioned the furniture, she
responded that under no circumstances would she allow that stuff
to come here. After a heated discussion, Api agreed, for the sake of
peace, to pay 140 marks, instead of the original 120, for three rooms,
even though the landlady had made no move to release the third
room. She knew she could get away with this because he was a *Pg*
who was not supposed to have an apartment.

The argument had exhausted what little energy Api had left, and it had achieved worse than nothing. He had to pay 20 marks more than before and had as little hope as ever of obtaining that third room. Cold, hunger, and the stress of this futile confrontation made him almost collapse. He hurried back into his rooms and broke down on a chair. He was afraid he would faint if he got up and even had to hold on to the chair for fear of falling to the floor. It was another low point in his existence, and he wondered how many more he could endure.

# 45

# DEUS EX MACHINA

Three days later, on Thursday, October 4, when he least expected it, Api's fortunes changed all at once. That day, the mailman handed him a postcard. With a pounding heart, he recognized Nyussi's and my mother's handwriting. The card was dated September 18. Although it had taken sixteen days to arrive, it was almost a miracle that it had found its way to him. It meant that we had received at least one of his letters or postcards, and now he knew in return that we were alive. He read and reread the few words and from then on kept the card close to his heart. He treasured Nyussi's confidence and trust that they would manage somehow if only he were with them, but my always shrewd mother had penned the line that echoed most in his mind. In order not to give anything away to the censor, she had written, "Do you already know that Api certainly will come?" He understood that this was a disguised request for him to come to us. It gave him a new impetus to find a way.

During the following days, Api spent hours working with renewed energy on that frustrating American questionnaire. He needed to submit it to the American administration, and it had to be approved before he could get permission to leave. Now, however, he went about his work buoyed by the postcard in his breast pocket and full of dreams of a reunion. His practice picked up at the same time. Sometimes a patient even had to wait before Api could get to them. Even his application for undergarments was now granted. And he found an electrician who fixed his little cooker, which had given out a few days earlier.

The weather corresponded to Api's good mood. After the earlier cold spell, it had warmed up again, and Wednesday, October 10, turned out to be a beautiful day. The thrush sang again outside his window, and the sparrows whistled a tune that was better than their wintry *cheep, cheep.* Api once more could find words to describe nature and his state of mind. "My only ones, a fall day of rare beauty and mild serenity lies over the wilting leaves and the last colorful blossoms. Once again a warming sun sends its golden rays across the colored leaves of the trees, which silently nod their heads in a light wind from the east as if they were in complete agreement and content with all that has happened and is happening and will happen in their lives, also with the fact that they now have to take leave of this summer existence. Oh, if I could only bring myself to attain such calm composure!"

That day, October 10, it had been exactly half a year since Api had separated from us. Since the arrival of the postcard, however, he had lived under the spell of my mother's words. He needed to find a way! Yet he was scheduled to do public inoculations until October 26, and his help was needed everywhere. Typhus was not the only killer. People died of pneumonia, infections, and malnutrition. Recently he had treated a patient suspected of meningitis whom another doctor had been afraid to touch. Yet in order to examine him, Api bent closely over the almost delirious young man, feeling the patient's breath on his face.

October turned out to be a month of wonderful, totally unexpected gifts in the form of postcards. Out of the blue on Thursday,

October 11, another postcard arrived. This one was from a Herr Blomerius of Speerweg 26 in Frohnau, in the north of Berlin. Api read it with amazement. "Your relatives in Suderburg are waiting for you with longing. In case you intend to go there, I ask you to get in touch with me still this week. With cordial greetings, Blomerius." Api's heart sang and rang at the prospect of this so long and so desperately awaited reunion, which now, all of a sudden, seemed within reach. He had dreamed about this for so long, had tried to find a way, and now it fell into his lap without his doing anything.

The sudden arrival of Herr Blomerius's card makes me think of the often despised and parodied *deus ex machina*, "God out of a machine." A dramatic effect that has been used from Greek to modern drama, it is the unexpected resolution of a plot, a sudden rescue that in earlier times often literally fell out of the sky from a contraption above the stage and therefore was called "God out of a machine." Now, the device may have more reality than I had imagined, and Herr Blomerius—the name itself sounds strange and unreal to me—about whose identity I have not been able to discover anything, remains just such an unexpected *deus ex machina*. In a less fanciful mood, however, I suspect that Blomerius probably was a medical colleague, since there was a large hospital on Speerweg in Frohnau, from where he had written. But why he wrote to Api at this point, how he knew where to find him, and how he knew about us in Suderburg remain a mystery.

Api wrote that he visited Herr Blomerius at six the next morning, although I cannot imagine how he covered the great distance between Friedenau, in the southwest, and Frohnau, far in the north of Berlin, so early in the morning, or what Herr Blomerius thought of his dawn arrival. The only way he could have managed it is by S-Bahn, which must have been running again. When Api got there, his dreams indeed came true. Herr Blomerius told him, "I can help you obtain permission from the physicians' organization so that you can leave Berlin. I can further arrange for permission from the British authorities, which you will need in Suderburg. It can all be arranged, and you should be on your way soon."

Api was overwhelmed. He rushed back to Friedenau to pack his rucksack so that there would not be a moment's delay once the permissions came through. Still anxious about the journey and afraid that he was always making a wrong move, he now felt a new strength and confidence surge up in him. For the first time in months, he could cherish a prospect that was not based on mere fantasies.

Once the little he had was safely packed, Api sat down, opened his diary, his companion through all these months, and wrote in it for the last time, giving voice to a hope that was still a little tentative. "Perhaps even such a poor, awkward bird as I can manage to get through this? . . . God bless my plan and protect you and me in His mercy."

# 46

# STARTING OVER

When Api arrived in Suderburg on Saturday, October 13, I screamed in terror at the gaunt and haggard stranger in his crumpled and grimy clothes. My screams, however, were drowned out by the joy on all sides. He hugged and kissed us all again and again as eventually even I submitted to his embraces. We cried and laughed and talked all at once. Already as he held us close to him, Api felt his thin arms grow stronger. He greeted the Blue Mountain like a long-lost friend.

Once we had settled down a bit, the three grown-ups spent hours talking about everything they had gone through. I did not understand what they were saying but felt the happiness underlying even the most fearful remembrances. Api sketched in his months in Berlin, which seemed to recede into a strange nightmare even as he was describing them. Nyussi told him about the friends we had made, both with the people of Suderburg and even with the Brits.

A main topic to which they all came back again and again was the lost past and the loved ones who had been lost with it. In a poem Api wrote about those first days in October 1945, he used two words that probably characterized their mood: *zukunftsbang und vergangenheitdurschauert.* The two typically long German composite adverbs mean "anxious about the future and atremble about the past." The war was over, but they were hungry and cold and had only a tiny place for the four of us.

Api did not remain long in this state of anxiousness. Now that he was free and united with his family, nothing could hold him back. As he had so often pictured it, his need to become the provider once again energized him. And his path to that was clear: He had to build a practice once more. He would have to work out of the larger of the two cottage rooms. It had to make do as dining and sleeping space, but Api had learned in his Begastrasse sublet how to deal with such constraints. It felt like starting life all over again, which at his age, fifty-eight, was not an easy thing to do. But Api threw himself into the task with energy and even joy, feeling Nyussi's strength at his side.

Before he could start, however, he had to fight his way through a paper jungle. Documents were required for everything. The German bureaucracy was bad enough, but now there was an additional layer of paperwork from the occupiers. He needed a "work pass" from the employment office, a permit to practice from the health bureau, an identity card from the British zone, and even an "interzone passport." Even I, a child of three, needed a British identification card. I found that small piece of brown cardboard among the papers in my mother's box, together with Api's work pass and interzone passport.

Api did not limit himself to waiting for patients to come to his office. He made house calls right away. This was important, since villages were spread out and few had cars. Most patients were unable to reach a doctor. The local pastor, Herr Franke, loaned him an old and rickety bicycle, but it helped Api to get around. He was soon biking all over the area, which, fortunately, was rather flat, although the sandy paths and rough cobblestone roads made it difficult to keep the bike upright. Luckily, the winter of 1945 was mild.

We had to file applications for every personal and household item. Special tickets were needed for clothing, and we were grateful for any used clothing that someone's charity provided. Food, above all, was scarce. The bakers had no flour to make bread, electricity service was often interrupted, and fat was almost impossible to find. We made good use of the thick stand of nettles in the ditch outside our door. Although the watery nettle soup was neither tasty nor satisfying, at least it was warm. I have to smile at this now, since, in a time of plenty, when just about any delicacy is within my reach, I go hunting for nettles because I have learned how tasty and nutritious they are. In Vienna, Mike and I seek out a cream-laced bowl of nettle soup at a restaurant in the beautiful square of the Grosse Markt. Back then, however, our nettle soup was nothing like this pale green concoction. If we were lucky, it was enhanced with a donation from Nyussi's relations. When we visited them, farmer Heinrich Steinke's sister Doris often slipped us a piece of sausage, bacon, or speck.

In addition to his medical work, Api had unaccustomed survival chores, which he undertook with childish glee, perhaps remembering his boyhood in Marienwerder. On weekends we went foraging for firewood. Occasionally we were lucky to be given some logs by a patient, and then Api had to split the wood and store it in as dry a place as he could find. Our lack of a shed made that no easy task in the damp climate. Peat was also welcome when we could get it. It burned hot, and for a short while our room was cozy. But it did not burn as cleanly as wood, nor did it last as long.

Api's practice grew, but the prospects in Suderburg were limited. It was too small to offer opportunities for seeing more complicated cases or doing surgeries. In order to have more scope for his skills, Api contacted the nearest hospital. This was the Hamburgische Krankenhaus, Hamburg Hospital, less than twenty miles away. He biked there in the winter of 1946. At first glance it looked rather ramshackle, a collection of wood-and-brick barracks connected by sandy paths in the pine woods outside the small town of Bevensen. Yet he found that it was better equipped than anything he had dealt with recently in Berlin. It was, after all, the main hospital of the city of Hamburg. After the bombing in 1943 that had burned down much of the city in a fierce firestorm, the hospital had been transferred to the safety of the small town, where it had had almost three years to establish itself. Api was made welcome right away. The hospital needed an eye surgeon and was pleased to take on a man of Api's reputation. Becoming part of that team was a stroke of good fortune that was to help Api for the remainder of his life.

Although Api's practice was getting better, we still had little to live on. We shared this fate, of course, not only with all refugees, but with most Europeans in that immediate postwar time. Api was thrown back to his earliest years, when he had to *knausern*, be stingy, with everything. Every envelope he received was carefully turned over and stuck together inside out so that it could be used again. He urged us to unravel sweaters that had become too small and use the yarn to make something new. We saved on wood for the little iron stove that heated our rooms, since even the fallen timber in the surrounding forests was much picked over by the other refugees in the neighborhood. And above all, we used and shared punctiliously every piece of fat, although Api always saw to it, and everyone agreed, that I got more than my share.

As the weather grew milder in the spring of 1946, Api often took me along on the backseat of the bike when he made house calls. I had long forgotten that initial shock of seeing him and had come to adore my Api. With my arms wrapped tightly around his waist on the bike, I listened as he talked to me about the plants and trees we were passing. He encouraged me to look closely at everything on our way, the buds on a bush or the placid black-and-white Holstein cows in a field. Or we played the game of finding the shapes of animals in the clouds. He also told me stories. I loved to listen, although I dimly realized that Api's stories had more of a moral than did Nyussi's. A favorite of his was Aesop's fable of the ant and the grasshopper. Its lesson of saving for the future fit nicely with his own disposition. I tended to side with the happy grasshopper who chirped away the summer without a care in the world. It was not easy to get excited about the industrious ant who painstakingly prepared for leaner times. When winter came, in Api's version, the ant complacently told the grasshopper, who was starving, "Well, why don't you chirp now?" He then turned around on his bike to look at me and ask, "What do you think the story wants to tell us?" I had no doubt about Api's preference for the saving ant. I still think so, although his diary now tells me that he loved grasshoppers as the friends of his youth. Even at the time I may have sensed that Api also had a lot of grasshopper in him when he played our games as enthusiastically as I did.

With Api there, we made even stronger contacts with the Suderburg elite. Nyussi and Api played bridge with a group of local honoraries that included the mayor; Pastor Franke; the local veterinarian, Dr. Lorscheid; and Wilhelm and Aline Westermann, who lived in Weidmann's Ruh, Forester's Rest. It was Suderburg's mansion on the outskirts of the village, separated from the road by a park. Aline was the sister of a mining director, now deceased, who had retired there. For me, the big place was always surrounded by mystery because the grown-ups often talked in whispers about the "tragedy." I later found out that some years earlier the Westermanns' young grandchild had fallen into the well and drowned.

The Christmas of 1945 was our poorest ever, but Api made it festive nonetheless. He created an Advent wreath out of fir boughs he and I had picked in the woods. He had saved silver paper, which he now cut into thin strips. His homemade tinsel glittered as brightly as the real stuff. We did not have candles for each of the four Advent Sundays, but the single one in the center burned brightly for all four weeks. The wreath also served as our Christmas tree that year, but then the medieval Suderburg church had a big tree with the required twelve candles for the twelve days of Christmas and we could all enjoy its warm beauty on Sundays. Nyussi did not have a piano, nor Api a violin, but we sang Christmas carols together. I chimed in lustily, though out of tune. Yet that was the only year that Api did not write a Christmas poem.

*Suderburg cottage, 1946*

*Api making housecalls with Gabrielle in back, Suderburg, 1946*

# 47

# RETURN TO BLUE MOUNTAIN

Mike and I visited Suderburg in search of Farmer Ohlde's cottage. My son, Benedict, joined us, for he wanted to see the places he had heard so much about when he grew up. It felt good to have them with me, especially since both supported my project and had helped me with it.

I was thrilled as soon as I saw the yellow road sign that announced Suderburg, and Mike took a picture of me in front of it. Just seeing the name made all my thoughts about the place more real. We found the village much as I remembered it, although it had grown on the outskirts. The old church looked more prosperous than in 1945. Its red brick had been restored, and the windows freshly painted white. The rough gray stone tower still looked incongruous but strong, meant to last hundreds more years. The old oaks were there, too, surrounding the church. Even the weather on this day in early January was just what I remembered, chilly and damp, with a slight fog hovering above the meadows.

But the most exciting part was still ahead: Farmer Ohlde's cottage. I did not remember the streets of Suderburg, but I knew that when we found the cemetery we would be there. Sure enough, we saw the cemetery, with its oak trees and the sandy path curving up around it to the village of Holxen. Looking across meadows, I spotted the Blue Mountain. It was much less of a mountain than I had remembered, and neither was it blue. We just saw a slight wooded rise in the distance, but still the very words "Blauer Berg" gave me a sense of protection and belonging. I greeted Api's old friend, as no doubt he would have done. Farmer Ohlde's small cottage was gone, but across the road was the rich green and thick stand of nettles.

When we drove on to Holxen, we found a picturesque village of half-timbered farmhouses, many of them still with thatched roofs. It was very quiet, with not a soul to ask for directions. However, I soon recognized the Steinkes' large farmhouse, its cobbled yard bounded on one side by the house and on the other by a long barn. Walking into the farmyard, to the left I noticed steps leading up to what I was sure was the kitchen. It was the way we had always entered. We climbed the steep stone stairs and knocked hesitantly. After some time, we heard footsteps approaching, and then an elderly woman opened the door. I identified myself with a smile, and after a moment's hesitation, the woman's face lit up. She reached out to hold "little Gabi" in her arms. She was, I knew, Wilma Förster, the Steinkes' daughter. Well into her eighties, she was still a handsome woman with bright blue eyes, white hair, and rosy cheeks.

Wilma asked us to come in. Inside, not much had changed either. We came into the huge kitchen, which looked out over moist green meadows. It was sparingly furnished, as of old, with a large table in the center and a stove and sink along one wall. A smell of yeast and something freshly baked pervaded and warmed the large and otherwise chilly room. Wilma led the way to the parlor. We passed a smaller room, which a large television screen dominated, but otherwise the dark heavy furniture was that of her parents, and perhaps their parents before that.

Wilma invited us to coffee and the *Butterkuchen*, literally "butter cake," which I have always loved. That must have been the inviting smell we had noticed in her kitchen. *Butterkuchen* is a specialty of the area, made of yeast dough with butter and sugar crisped on top. But it has to be freshly baked—otherwise, it tastes dry and dull—and this one was still warm from the oven. As Mike, Benedict, and I were biting into the crusty butter-and-sugar layer of the cake and tasting the soft fluffy inside, I enjoyed listening to Wilma's North German dialect, which I had not heard in years, although Mike and Benedict, used to my high German, found it impossible to understand.

Wilma and I started talking almost at once about how I had recited Api's poem at her wedding in 1953. She brought out an old family album that showed pictures of Api and Nyussi and me sitting with many other guests in the great hall where the celebration had taken place. When Api told me it was time to go onstage, I was scared of the large audience. He reassured me that we had practiced the poem many times and that I would do a fine job. As I walked to the podium, I had the presence of mind to ask the band to play a *Tusch*, a loud sound with cymbals and drums that demands quiet. When silence had fallen and I stood alone onstage in my fancy light blue dress with ruffles at the knee, I panicked. I started to recite but soon got stuck, and Api had to help out from the hall. But I must have gotten through somehow, for Wilma said that while she did not remember the exact words of the poem, she would never forget the sentiments—not only the good wishes but also the deep gratitude for all the help her family had given the refugees in 1945. I still have the poem, which is conceived from my point of view as a ten-year-old girl and talks about my happy memories of Steinke's farm. Unfortunately, I cannot re-create the rhyme in the pattern of ABAB.

> *Here the sun was always shining.*
> *When there was loneliness and need in Suderburg*
> *House Steinke always offered open hands and hearts.*

Wilma told me that every time I visited her family with my grandparents, I soon crawled under the big dining room table with the fringed tablecloth. I did not remember that but assumed that I was continuing my favorite game of playing beaver burrow. I did recall the Steinkes waving goodbye to us from the stoop by the kitchen, and one of them handing Nyussi a little parcel of sausage or speck. The women waved their white handkerchiefs as long as they could see us.

Wilma was also able to give me information on Nyussi's relatives who had left Holxen in the nineteenth century. Luise Hinrichs, Nyussi's grandmother on her father's side, came from a prosperous farm in Holxen, and Nyussi's grandfather August Döhrmann was from the neighboring village of Hösseringen. He was a *Wiesenbau* engineer, literally a meadow-building engineer, who had studied at the only such school in Germany, which happened to be in Suderburg. *Wiesenbau*, which then was mainly drainage of meadowlands, was important in that waterlogged area, and the Suderburg school enjoyed an international reputation. After graduation, August emigrated to serve in Turkey under the sultan. His job there was the reverse of what was needed back home. He had to design and build irrigation systems. At some point, he came back home to get married and then left the sultan's employ to settle in Hungary, overseeing a horse farm. When his first son, Heinrich, Nyussi's father, was born, he sent his wife back to give birth in Hannover, the district capital. Luise's sister had remained in Holxen and married a man by the name of Steinke who owned the largest farm in the village, the place where we were now sitting. They were Wilma's grandparents.

At the end of our visit, when we had finished most of the *Butterkuchen* and exhausted our shared memories, Wilma turned to the present. She told us sad but typical stories of a dying village. All the young people were leaving, stores had closed, her old friends were sick or dead, and she saw little future for her once prosperous home.

On our way back, we drove by Forester's Rest, following Wilma's directions on how to get there. The place looked abandoned and much smaller than I remembered it. The park in front of the house was overgrown with weeds, and the fence was broken. We had come across another abyss between then and now.

# 48

# THEODOR

The Steinkes were our major support in 1945, but our social status also helped to make life more bearable. Even before Api joined us, Nyussi and my mother, who spoke fluent English, had made friends with Dave, a British airman. Dave first entered our cottage with another airman at the start of the occupation. They held their rifles at the ready, as they were engaged in a house-to-house search of the village. Nyussi literally disarmed them when, with a wave of her hand, she told them in her broken English, "Please put that down; it makes me nervous." They both laughed, and our friendship with Dave began from that moment. That was even before the order not to fraternize with the German population had been rescinded, and despite the Ohldes' vociferous disapproval of our connection with a member of the occupying forces.

With his curly brown hair and cheerful attitude, Dave reminded Nyussi of her dead son, and no doubt the young man was glad for a little motherly nurturing in this foreign country whose language he did not speak. In fact, Dave soon called Nyussi Mother and Api Father. Considering that just weeks before we had been enemies, this relationship attested to the human spirit—how quickly people can bridge that abyss created by fear, hate, and war. It may well be that this friendship was accelerated, because Dave soon began courting my mother.

I remember him as a happy and boisterous presence in our cottage. Whenever I saw him walk toward us in his airman's blue-gray serge tunic, I ran out to meet him. He twirled me in the air, and then we walked into the cottage hand in hand. His laughter filled the small room. Dave exuded health and good spirits, which stood in stark contrast with us hollow-eyed, gray, and skinny creatures. And he never came empty-handed. After an affectionate welcome, he pulled a can of meat or a bar of chocolate from his pockets. Most important, however, he brought love and acceptance.

A note he wrote to Nyussi in the hospital before his leave shows the extent of his love for our family. I copy it in full, and wish only that I could thank Dave. I will, however, do what Api suggested in relation to Fräulein Herzog: Since I cannot thank him personally, I do so in my heart. Dave wrote, "I am very happy to have your extremely nice letter from Father and I thank you so much for all you have done and said. As your son I will remain and my thoughts are with you now and ever. Margit and Father will surely tell you all about my deepest feelings for this dear family. I have so many loving memories to go home with which I will cherish always. Get better soon, Mother Dear. I go, but will return again for certain. All my love, Dave."

I wonder whether Api and Nyussi were reminded with a pang of pain of Dieter's letter, which he ended with "dead certain." Dave and Dieter must have been about the same age.

When Dave returned from a leave in London, he had a special gift for me. I looked at the parcel with great excitement. Gifts were a rarity for me. When I unwrapped it, I found a soft, light blue teddy bear with shiny brown eyes. It instantly became my favorite toy. I don't know whether I loved Theodor because he was my only new toy, because Dave had given him to me, or because he looked different from German teddies and had come from so far away. Before him, I had only one lanky cloth doll with a painted face we called Henrietta. I do not remember how she got that name, which does not sound like a name for a doll I would have liked. And I am not sure that I ever did like her, for I tended to blame Henrietta for anything I had done wrong. At any rate, after Theodor I never looked at Henrietta again and never wanted another doll. Theodor was it, as far as I was concerned. I still treasure Theodor today, although he has lost all his hair and sawdust is coming out from behind the black stitching of his nose. Now that Api is not there any longer, he cannot fix the one eye Theodor has lost, either. Still Theodor has a place of honor on my wardrobe.

After Dave was reassigned in 1947, we all missed him very much. Nyussi in particular missed "our faithful son," as she called him in English. That Christmas, we received a parcel from him that contained such precious items as coffee, cocoa, and soap. Sadly, all my efforts with the RAF failed to find out more about Dave, since I do not even have his last name. I made many inquiries and posted an announcement in the RAF magazine, but with no result. I would have loved to contact him or, if he is no longer living, his relatives, to thank them for all he did and tell them how much it has meant to my family and me.

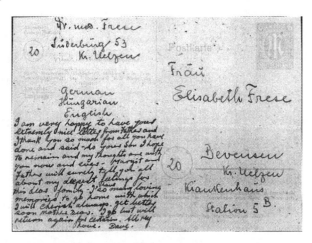

*Tri-lingual postcard, 1947; Dave's note on bottom*

# 49

# KEEP YOUR EARS STIFF

Our food supply improved when the Ohldes allowed us to use a corner of their vegetable patch. As we prepared the bed with seeds the Steinkes had given us—peas, carrots, and lettuce—the Ohldes looked on, suspicious of whether these city folk were able to make anything grow. We did, and enjoyed the results all summer long.

My mother earned a little money for the family by picking potato beetles off the potato plants for the small farmers of the area. Sometimes I was allowed to help, and we went side by side down the slightly raised aisles of potato plants. I admired the iridescent beetles crawling about on the leaves. Their little black legs stood out in sharp contrast with their many-colored bodies. We picked hundreds of them in a day. When the beetle-picking season was over, we gathered wild blueberries in the woods. They were small but much tastier than the cultivated variety. On warm days, Api put a bowl of milk on a windowsill to get sour. For some reason, he was always in charge of that job. When the milk had turned thick and creamy, we ladled it atop the blueberries. It was a wonderful meal and a special treat. The rest of the berries we sold door to door. In the fall, Api and I went hunting in the woods for lingonberries. Since I was small, it was easier for me to spot the red berries, low to the ground, hidden under their shiny green leaves. We did not have much sugar with which to cook them, but I loved their tart flavor and beautiful color.

The North German summer did not last long, and soon the weather turned wet and chilly again. Unlike the previous winter, the winter of 1946–47 was the harshest anyone could remember. Like everyone else around us, we were hungry and cold. The progress of Api's practice had leveled off. Most people were too poor to afford eye treatment. Api feared that he would never be able to provide adequately for us. After a nettle or potato soup, and perhaps a cup of *Muckefuck*, we all crawled into our beds early, trying to warm up. My place was still in the middle of Api and Nyussi in the smaller of the two rooms. It was a time, as Api later reflected, of boundless hopelessness.

But for me there were also happy moments. I'd call to Nyussi, "Let's be cozy," and we would cuddle up on the sofa. If I was lucky, she had an apple that she put on the stove to bake. While the aroma drifted through the little room, Nyussi told me fairy tales. When the apple was warm and soft, she divided it and we played dominoes while we savored the treat. Api had taught me the game early on as a way to learn numbers, and he was proud of how quickly I picked it up.

The worst part of that winter was Nyussi's illness. She had developed rheumatoid arthritis, which, coupled with poor nutrition and years of stress, caused a series of infections that affected many organs. She was always in pain and had a low-grade fever, and yet whenever she could manage, she distracted herself with her favorite pastime: reading. She had borrowed the first volume of Carl J. Burckhardt's *Richelieu*, as well as Leopold von Ranke's classic *The History of the Popes During the Last Four Centuries*. At one point, she was delighted when she caught the author out with a wrong date. Eventually she had to be hospitalized in the Hamburgische Krankenhaus in Bevensen, where she was confined for an entire year. We feared for her life and so missed her good spirits and support. Without her, the cottage was bleak.

We visited her often in the hospital to make her feel better. But it was Nyussi who tried to keep up our spirits, rather than the other way around. She did not complain about her pain. At most, she said jokingly, "How was it in my *au devant* fatherland? '*Maul halten and weiter dienen*.'" Her "former" (*au devant*—a French phrase) fatherland was the Austro-Hungarian Empire, and what she learned derives from military parlance and translates to "shut up and keep serving." While the grown-ups talked by Nyussi's bedside, I hopscotched around the wooded paths that wound between the barracks, and the nurses handed me a delicacy that I had not known before: crisp bread with a pat of butter. I kept coming back for more. Like potatoes with salt, it remains one of my favorite treats.

When we could not visit Nyussi, we wrote to her. At first it had to be postcards only, since the censors allowed nothing else. Mail from Germany and Austria was censored for years after the war. Nyussi marveled at the odd cards she received almost every day. On the top we had to note in what language, or, in our case, languages, we had written them. Api wrote in German in the same tiny script with which he had filled his diary. My mother tended to use Hungarian in her larger, forceful and slanted hand. And Dave added a few tender words in English to "Mother," scribbled in his spidery scrawl. I wonder whether these trilingual postcards attracted the censors' attention.

On Christmas Eve 1946, for the first time, I recited Api's poem of the year. I doubt I understood much of it as I voiced the lines I had learned by heart. The poem ends with:

*After most bitter blows of fate, they [angels]*
*Once again bring light into our darkness.*
*Be humble, patient, and content.*
*Have faith: that is Christmas blessing.*

When the grim winter of 1946–47 at last came to an end, Api's spirits picked up and he had a pleasant surprise. For almost a year, he had submitted applications for a new bike to use for his visits to patients. At last, after pages and pages of documents, he was granted special permission to obtain a new bike by no less than the president of Lower Saxony. He had to go to Lüneburg, the district center, to pick it up. The bike was a local brand he had never heard of, called Heidemann, but it served him well and was the envy of the neighbors—so much so, in fact, that it was stolen a few months later.

Spring once again refreshed Api in body and soul. As the elders and willows along the Hardau creek began to green, the earthy smell of the fields drifted over to our cottage, and the woods of the Blue Mountain reawakened, he wrote that "despite everything the world is immeasurably beautiful." With trust in God and hard work, he felt, he had yet hope for a more secure future. "*Ohren steif halten,*" the German version of a stiff upper lip, literally translates to "keep your ears stiff" and was one of his favorite sayings. What always followed immediately was ". . . and thank the Lord with all our hearts for what He still has left us and already given us again."

# 50

# VIENNA

In the spring of 1947, my mother left for Vienna because Suderburg had no opportunities for her. Although derelict and under Allied occupation, Vienna had more to offer. Brought up in Berlin, mother missed the big city. Her parents-in-law urged her to come, promising to help her get established. My Viennese grandfather, a former general, pulled strings from his prewar army days to get her an apartment in the Arsenal, a large complex in the southeast of Vienna near the South Railway station, now reconceived as Vienna's main station. Built in 1848, the Arsenal served as barracks and armory during World War I. Each building, or *Projekt*, as it is still called, looked like a castle built of red brick with sandstone turrets and broad stone stairways. When she first lived there, my mother had to walk through a field of rubble to get to her building, Projekt XIV. This was scary at night, especially since this part of Vienna was in the Soviet sector. But she loved her apartment on the top floor, from which she could just catch a glimpse of St. Stephen's Cathedral in the center of Vienna. With her language skills—she was fluent in French, English, and Hungarian—she soon found work, first as a secretary, then as a translator of business corre- spondence at the Abadie, a factory that made cigarette paper.

We all missed my mother, but especially Nyussi, who was still confined to her hospital room. To cheer up her daughter, she wrote letters full of funny scenes and word plays, of courage and confidence. My mother obviously cherished those letters, for she stowed them away in her lockbox, so that now I am able to hear Nyussi's voice after more than half a century. When my mother had trouble at her first job, Nyussi encouraged her not to fall victim to existential angst but to hold her head high and have faith in the future—a belief, she insisted, that was not just a sign of her Hungarian reckless spirit. She added, "In confidence, in this way I have also been able to help your dear father when he was down emotionally. Now he sits firm in the saddle again." Reflecting on the recent past, she wrote, "It is bad luck that we lost everything. So now we just have to start anew. We will make it somehow." Responding to a despondent letter from my mother, Nyussi tried to inspire courage and support, ending, "I hope I was able to write as I feel. I would have liked best to send you my old mother's heart along with this letter. Even the dear censor may have let it through." Another time, Nyussi hoped to entice my mother to visit them by saying that we would all take a vacation together at the North Sea. "After your dog's life, a few weeks of a seal's life [in German, *seal* is "sea dog"] will do you much good." When my mother could not get away, Nyussi wrote in response to that disappointing news, "I am with you so much in my thoughts that I shouldn't be surprised if you noticed my astral body crouching in a corner of your sofa."

Once my mother was established, she came to take me to Vienna with her. However, since she worked all day, I soon had to attend a boarding school. But first she had a wonderful outing planned for us. We took the bus to the Cobenzl, Vienna's local mountain—from which we could look out over the city. I had never seen so many different buildings, red-roofed houses, church spires, and large apartment complexes, and such a wide river snaking through it. My mother pointed out the *Riesenrad* rising up in the distance. She promised that we would go to the Prater, the famous year-round amusement park, and ride all the way up on the Ferris wheel. She told me that the carriages were big like railroad cars and that the Riesenrad had been built in the nineteenth century and was the tallest Ferris wheel in the world. We were resting on a grassy meadow looking out on all this marvel when my mother opened a pointed brown paper bag. It had little round and rough beige-colored shapes inside. She cracked one open and gave it to me to eat. It was my first peanut, but, try as I might, I could not open one for myself.

After I had left, Api kept up a lively correspondence with Vienna. Each letter has references to "our most beloved little Gaby, our sweetest sunshine . . . whom we remember at every step and who again and again makes our old hearts ring in painful longing." In a letter from March 1949, after visiting a fair, Api exclaimed, "O little Gaby, little Gaby, if only you could have been there with us." Or he talked about the bike rides we could take and the acorn pipes we could cut in the fall. He also wrote letters to me directly, full of love but also admonishing me to do well in school.

My new school was an Ursuline convent school, located in a dark Renaissance building on the Genzgasse in Vienna's 18th district. The nuns offered an excellent but stern education. In first grade, I learned to read and write fluently, as well as to knit and crochet. The convent rules were strict. You were not allowed to talk in the corridors and had to fold your clothes and make your bed in a very precise manner. We slept in a large hall with low ceilings on the second floor of the two-story building. My bed, ignominiously, was the only one with a rail around it, because I was small and much younger than the others. The nuns made an austere and frightening impression on me as they walked about in their heavy black serge habits, which fell in folds to their feet. Their heads were encased in a white wimple that left only their eyes, mouth, and nose visible. When I was afraid of the dark, a nun, her face framed by the stiff white linen with the starched yoke sticking out sharply at me, said in a stern voice, "It is only your own bad deeds which make you afraid." The convent rebaptized me into the Catholic faith, and later I was also confirmed in the Catholic tradition, wearing a fancy white lace dress and holding a large, decorated candle.

After less than a year with the Ursulines, I became seriously ill. It began with diarrhea and a high fever. I soiled my bed, and one of the nuns picked me up in the middle of the night and, in view of all the other students, held me under a cold-water tap to clean me off. It was not a good start, but it got worse. I became delirious, and the convent nursery could no longer handle my case. In the hospital, I was diagnosed with scarlet fever. They also suspected pneumonia and put me under quarantine for months. I could see my mother only through a glass wall, and we "touched" by placing our hands on the same spot on either side of the glass partition. When I was over the worst, I was transferred to the only place where they could find me a bed. It was at Steinhof, on a hill at the edge of the Vienna Woods. Steinhof was a hospital for the mentally ill. When I got better and could leave my room, I was both amused and frightened by the strange people I saw walking about.

On our trip in 2016, I took Mike to the Otto Wagner church on top of Steinhof after we had visited my paternal grandparents' graves just below. It was a steep climb, and once there we admired, a little breathlessly, the drama of the church, its green-and-gold mosaic cupola, the entrance of stark white columns leading to gold-studded black metal doors. The high-ceilinged and open interior, with light pouring in through tall windows, was almost blinding in its white and gold. When we left, we inspected some of the hospital buildings, called pavilions, scattered over the wooded hill below the church. Their history goes back to 1784, when a *Narrenturm*, a round "fools' tower," stood there. It was the first time in Vienna that the mentally ill weren't treated like animals in poorhouses but were beginning to be recognized as suffering from an illness.

I took pictures of a couple of pavilions halfway down the hill where I dimly remembered I had stayed in 1948. That is when I spotted a sign on Pavilion V: THE WAR AGAINST THE "MINDERWERTIGE:" HISTORY OF NS MEDICINE IN VIENNA. We walked inside. In the sunlit exhibition rooms cleared of all furniture, we focused on the wall displays and found out, with a shock, that until 1945, just three years before my stay, these middle pavilions had served as stations for physically and mentally ill children. About eight hundred perished here. Doctors did research on the brains of the euthanized girls and boys. They were *minderwertig*, of lesser worth, costly to maintain and threatening the purity of the race.

We saw posters of the time carrying this ghastly message. In one, a blond and vigorous young man was bowed down under the load of two apelike figures. In large letters, the title shouted at the viewer, "Here you, too, have to carry the load. A person with an inherited illness costs on average 50,000 reichsmark by the time he is 60." The exhibition showed that after 1938, when Austria was annexed to Hitler's Germany, Steinhof "mutated into Vienna's center for the national socialist killing medicine (*Tötungsmedizin*)." After the T4 euthanasia program ended in 1941, the killing at Steinhof continued through starvation and neglect. Adults, as well as children, became victims. Altogether, more than 7,500 people lost their lives here. A recent book shows that pediatrician Dr. Hans Asperger, whose name now designates a syndrome on the autism spectrum and who claimed innocence after the war, was part of this program and "knew that he was signing off on children's fates."

Looking at photographs of beds crowded together and children staring at the camera in bewilderment, I could not begin to imagine their suffering. Their cries and their pain must have etched themselves into the very walls, and no whitewash could ever cover them.

Did my mother know about this recent past when I was put there in 1948? I cannot say, but rather doubt it. The trials for some of the murderous doctors and nurses began only that year and were not given much publicity, and many were not tried at all. She was probably relieved to have found a place for her ill daughter. In a sense, I, too, came there as *minderwertig*, weak and sick and costly. I just was lucky that it was not three years earlier. Most likely, the nurses and doctors who still worked at Steinhof in 1948 knew about its Nazi past, even if they did not actively participate in the murders. A vast silence of fear, shame, and horror must have hung over the entire institution. Standing in the sunny rooms of the exhibit, I was struck that here was yet another way in which the Nazi past was part of my life.

# 51

# KINDERTRANSPORT

As soon as I was released from Steinhof, my grandparents pleaded with my mother to send me back to Suderburg. They believed that they could take care of me better in the country than a working mother alone in the city could. Api urged that this would help "my beloved little soul" recover more quickly, since "as is well known both in illness and in recovery the mind and the spirit have an extraordinary influence on the functioning of our organism." He added that my education would not lack the necessary seriousness, either. Nyussi, recently released from the hospital, was still in pain, and her arthritis had deformed her hands and feet, but she was determined to make a good life for us three. She wrote that the rain and wind might beat against their windows, but since she had taken over as "heat director," we would be warm inside. She added that she would cook my favorite foods to help me gain strength. A picture of me before leaving shows a pale and hollow-eyed girl with two thin braids, looking at the camera without a smile.

My mother reluctantly agreed to send me back. This time, I had to go in a *Kindertransport*. The *"Rückführungsschein,"* the document that allowed me to return to Germany, indicated that the transport would be free of vermin and infectious diseases but that I needed provisions for at least two days. We were traveling in a goods train in a wagon crowded with kids between, I think, the ages of five and fifteen. I certainly remember that, once again, I was the smallest. The floor was covered in a thick layer of straw, as there were no seats. We had an attendant who played games with us, and when we came to a long stop on the open tracks or pulled onto a side rail, we were allowed out to play. However much I wanted to join the game, I was scared to hurl myself from the high wagon into the ditch below.

Somehow, I got left behind at the station in Hannover, sixty-five miles from Suderburg. Fortunately, someone sent a telegram to the address I carried around my neck on a cardboard sign. Api jumped on a train immediately, reaching Hannover at three in the morning, but saw no sign of me. He finally found me in a women and children's bunker among other lost children. It was a happy reunion with my Api, and I clutched him tightly, afraid we would be separated. The sun was just coming up as we boarded the train for the ride back to Suderburg. Sitting on my little wooden suitcase, I fell asleep almost immediately, still holding on to him.

I was delighted to be back with Api and Nyussi. Even the Ohldes welcomed me, and I was glad to see the familiar farmyard with my old friends: the Ohlde's dog, whose name I have forgotten, and Lotte, the sheep. Once again, I watched Farmer Ohlde tend his bees, dressed all in white with a big net over his head. And although I was no longer starving, I followed him as of old when he fed the pigs.

From a letter Nyussi wrote to my mother, I learned that I continued to talk to the animals, as I had done before I left. I conversed not only with the dog and the sheep, but also with the bees, chickens, and birds, and reported our conversations to my grandmother. That day, Nyussi wrote that I had come in telling her that I had just talked to a blackbird who had told me that summer would come soon. Today, I am pleased to see that my habit of talking to animals goes back to my earliest youth; I still greet the turtle, squirrel, and rabbit I meet on my walks, and converse with the wrens in our birdhouse.

When we three were together, Api once more waxed emotional about life. "The heather which lies immediately outside our window and also already in our hearts is beautiful, and beautiful too is life, which still has left us the community of dearly loved ones and the possibility of grateful remembrance and prayer."

# 52

# DENAZIFIED

The procedure of releasing Germans from their *Pg* status continued for years after the war. Applicants had to write a detailed letter describing their activities during the Nazi period and provide corroborating testimonies. A commission looked into each case and classified the applicant according to five categories the Allies established in Directive 38 on October 12, 1946: Chiefly Responsible, Incriminated, Less Incriminated, Fellow Traveler, and Exonerated.

And here is my last discovery about Api's past: Among his papers in my mother's box, I found his denazification document, dated May 19, 1949. It said that Api had not been active in the Nazi Party and had continued to treat Jewish patients. As a result, he was classified in the lowest category, as *Entlasteter*, "Exonerated," or, literally, "Unburdened." Api no doubt felt as if indeed a burden had been lifted when he received that judgment, after years of feeling persecuted and treated like an inferior person, if not a criminal. It was a huge relief to me, too, so many years later. "Exonerated" has a good sound to it, even though I realize that these categories cannot be taken at face value. Nevertheless, it is clear that Api did not play an active part in the Nazi regime, besides, of course, having become a member on

May 1, 1933. Although I was happy to have found that document of exoneration, I realized that it would not relieve me of my need to account for our shared Nazi past.

Four days after Api's exoneration, on May 23, 1949, the *Grundgesetz*—literally, the Basic Law—came into being and the Bundesrepublik Deutschland was born. Germany wanted to make a new start committed to respecting and protecting each citizen within the state. The German Constitution, which was published that same day, begins, "The dignity of human beings is inviolable. To honor and to protect it is the responsibility of all the power of the state."

*Api and Nyussi in their arbor, 1950*

*Gabrielle and Grey Donkey, 1950*

*Api and Gabrielle, 1949*

*Api's denazification document, 1949*

# 53

# A STABLE HOME

By 1949, we felt intolerably cramped in the two rooms of the farmhouse, and the commutes to the hospital in Bevensen had grown arduous. Also, after four years of housing strangers, the Ohldes understandably wanted us out. But, try as he might, Api could not find accommodation anywhere. He wrote to the mayor of Bevensen, to the district housing bureau, to the minister of reconstruction, and even to the president of Lower Saxony in search of a more permanent place. He filled out myriad questionnaires and underwent interviews, all to no effect.

When Api was given his verdict of "exonerated," we still lived in the Suderburg cottage, but two months later we were able to move to a bigger place, in Bevensen. I wonder whether his not yet having the denazification document had anything to do with Api's prior difficulties in obtaining a place to live. The new apartment, located at Eckermannstrasse 9, was on the ground floor of a house; the owners, the Obstfelders, lived on the top floor. It was a quiet residential street halfway between the town and the Ilmenau River. Our front windows looked out on the meadows, which sloped to the river with the pine woods of the Klaubusch rising steeply on its other side. Api now had a waiting room and surgery office, and the Obstfelders allowed him to affix his black-and-white enamel sign saying DR. MED HERBERT FRESE, OPHTHALMOLOGIST to the slatted fence outside. We also had a good-size living room, although there was not enough space for me to have a room of my own. But I liked sleeping in my grandparents' room, where the Hinzpeter painting of the Chiemsee hung over their bed and I had a smaller one by the window. Nyussi was delighted that she finally had her own kitchen again. And, almost best of all, the apartment came with a tiny linden arbor in the back. My grandparents loved to sit there of an afternoon, enjoying the tranquil scene, reflecting on how fortunate they were to have such a nice home once again.

At that time, Helga Friedel joined our household. Nyussi's arthritis continued to worsen, and she needed help taking care of the bigger place we now had. She had also been used to having a maid since she was a little girl on her Hungarian estate. Helga was a strong and attractive young woman who had lost both her parents in the war. Her dark blond hair was cut short, parted on the side, and set in curls around her head. Her blue-gray eyes looked straight and fearlessly at the world. She soon became part of the family and stayed with us until Api's death. After that, we could not pay her anymore, and she eventually got married and set up a household of her own. Nyussi corresponded with her until her own death in 1958.

For me, one big event of that year was that I learned to ride a bike. All we had was an old adult bike, and I was so small that my head barely reached above the handlebars. Of course, it was Api who ran alongside my wobbly pedaling, firmly holding on to the saddle. Then he would let go for a few seconds, still running beside me and grabbing the bike when I threatened to topple. Gradually, the periods I could stay upright grew longer, and soon I was sailing along happily on the cinder paths, up and down Eckermannstrasse or down to the Ilmenau River. Despite repeated crashes, I practiced riding without holding on to the handlebars. My knees were permanently crusted with scabs.

On Christmas Eve, we discovered a beautiful Bevensen tradition, the *Siebenstern* celebration. A *Siebenstern* is a tall, seven-sided wooden candlestick, and we soon owned our own. As we entered, the church was completely dark, and the service was held without any lights. I could hear the rustle of the large congregation—everyone attended this service—but I could not make out any faces. At the end, we all lit our seven-sided candlesticks and the whitewashed walls of the simple church suddenly shone warmly in the light of hundreds of candles. It was so beautiful, I almost forgot my excitement about the *Bescherung*, the gift giving to come, and the lit tree. But on our walk back from church, I could think of little else.

It was my first stable home, and my grandparents took care of me with so much love and attention. Nyussi was a lively and spirited grandmother, and we laughed a lot together. I still see her coming back from the little town, walking slowly on the sandy path, holding a netted shopping bag. She had trouble carrying groceries in her arthritic hands, but she never forgot to add something special for me: a caramel, a piece of licorice, or a banana.

Nyussi was a wonderful storyteller. She often talked about her Hungarian childhood, which seemed so excitingly different from my world. I especially remember stories about her eccentric uncle Dionysius Farago, whom everyone called Dinybasci, Uncle Diny. He was a lifelong bachelor who lived with his valet in one wing of their villa in Nagykörös, where he and his sister, Nyussi's mother, owned an estate. Educated as a lawyer, he did not practice a day in his life, except to oversee his estate. Although he had lost a good deal of his investments in World War I bonds, enough was left to afford him a comfortable and easygoing life, which he allowed nothing to upset. When he was handed a telegram at the dinner table, he simply laid it aside without looking at it and continued his meal. Finally, his sister could not hold back any longer:

"Dinybasci, do open that telegram. It must be urgent." Dinybasci looked at her over the glass of Tokay wine he had just raised to his lips and answered, "Urgent, yes, but for the one who sent it."

He was a big man with a voracious appetite. "A duck," he liked to say, "is an inconvenient bird: One is not enough for one person, and two are too much." Dinybasci loved his horse-drawn carriages and made sure the horses matched in size and color. He would take Nyussi and, later, also my mother and uncle on rides into the vineyards for a picnic or into town for a shopping spree. My mother particularly liked to visit the shoemaker, who made her ankle boots of the softest leather that were the envy of her friends in Berlin.

I have a picture of Dinybasci's summer carriage. It has smaller wooden wheels in front and larger ones in the back, and an elegantly curved body with a turned-down hood. Nyussi is reclining in the backseat, her long legs crossed at the knee. She is wearing a dark beret and smiles at the camera. Her uncle is sitting at a small table next to the carriage, probably enjoying a snack. He has his back toward Nyussi but is looking around at her, his face turned away from the camera. He wears a bowler hat and frock coat and looks small and rotund. They must be in one of their vineyards, for in the background are two workmen standing by three large wooden wine barrels and a one-story service building. What look like fig and walnut trees shade the whole area.

Whenever Nyussi talked of her hometown, she always mentioned the sunny warmth of the broad streets and the vineyards where apricots, peaches, and almonds grew between the vines. It sounded exotic to me, for the colder North German climate produced mainly apples, gooseberries, and currants; even the strawberries had a hard time ripening. Today I wish, however, that I had asked her more questions about that time. But I preferred the fairy tales she told me at bedtime. My favorite was "Puss in Boots," which she had to repeat over and over although I already knew it by heart.

I basked in all the care and attention and enjoyed the freedom of the small town, where I could bike everywhere on my own. I loved the meadows in front of our house, full of flowers in spring, when I brought home fistfuls of anemones and primroses. In summer, I hunted for *Sauerampfer*, stacking its juicy, bitter leaves so that I could bite through many layers at once. I built forts in the tall grass near the river and in winter sledded on the steep hill in the woods across the way. There were no pressures on me as yet. Elementary school was easy. Thanks to the nuns' superior teaching in Vienna, I was well ahead of my class in all subjects. In hindsight, and even then, it seemed like an idyllic time—after all that had happened, a fairy-tale life.

# 54

# API AND ME

A s I was to discover all too soon, Api was the center of that fairy tale. He was both father and grandfather to me, spoiling me with love and laughter but also establishing firm rules and discipline. When the eyes of my teddy bear, Theodor, needed mending, I went to Api's surgery so that Theodor could receive proper treatment. I also liked to watch Api as he practiced his surgery skills using pigs' eyes. He had a standing order for them with the local butcher, and we went together to collect them, then took them back to the office, where Api started to work. When he was finished, he let me look through a magnifying glass at his operation, and I marveled at the tiny incisions. Api did increasingly more eye surgeries at the Bevensen hospital and wanted to be sure his hand was practiced and steady. Every evening before bed, he and I played dominoes or a card game for two called 66. Api liked 66 because it forced me, always a scatterbrain, to concentrate. If I wanted to compete, I had to memorize cards and learn to do quick additions. Every card had a different point value, and I had to remember how many points I had taken in my tricks. If the total added up to 66, I shouted out "66" and won.

As much as he played games with me, Api's first priority was my education. He never thought I got enough homework at the Bevensen grade school, so he gave me additional dictation or math tasks to do, always with the promise of a game afterward. He even tried to make play educational whenever possible, such as in 66, and on our outings he always found something to explain. He talked about the seasons, about the animals we saw, or about the history of our town and church. We listened to classical music together, and early on Api gave me a recorder to develop my musical ear. After church each Sunday, he expected me to give a summary of Superintendent Stünkel's sermon. I am afraid I must have disappointed him although he never let it show. All this may sound a little schoolmaster-ish, but Api made it enjoyable. I never felt lectured or talked down to. Instead, he taught me to find interest—enchantment, even—in the everyday. When we had to wait at the train station, Api helped me while away the time by asking me to draw what I saw in the waiting room. We then discussed what I had chosen, and he ended by admiring my "little work of art" and suggested that I send it to my mother in Vienna.

The one thing Api hated was vacuity. The only times I saw him angry at me were when I was neither working nor playing but just doing nothing. "You don't have to work all the time. Play is good. But do not waste your time and the beautiful day like this. If you do not know what to do with yourself, write something about why there are storms in spring and what good they do. Or read one of the books I gave you." When I did not like any of his suggestions, he often started a game that I did like. But Api never relented in instructing me not to waste time. In a letter he wrote to Nyussi when she and I were visiting friends, he suggested, "If she does not have anything at all to do in her free time, you may perhaps now and then give her an extensive dictation. You best buy an exercise book without lines so that she also learns to write straight. What is important is to write relatively quickly and clearly, and with the least number of mistakes possible. Perhaps you can bring the book back with you so that I, too, can enjoy the results."

In the fall, I loved our building a kite together in the cellar. Api selected two strips of bare wood, testing them for flexibility. He nailed them together into a cross and carefully checked the balance. It had to be exactly right; otherwise, the kite would not fly. Next came the delicate task of stretching paper across the surface. We painted big black eyes and red ears on the paper, a dragon's face, since the German word for kite is *Drachen*, or "dragon." I had to be careful not to pierce the stretched paper in any spot. It was my job also to make the dragon's tail by folding and tying pieces of newspaper to a string like a series of bow ties. When it was done, we admired our handiwork and took it upstairs to show to Nyussi.

I remember one blustery fall afternoon when we were out in the meadows in front of the house with our newest creation. Api was running as fast as he could to get the kite started. Then, for a moment, he looked up as a patient waved to him from the street. Before he could shout a hello, I saw him disappear. I ran to the spot where I had last seen him. Api had fallen into one of the many drainage ditches that dissected the meadow. He sat up in the muddy ditch, and I saw him bent over with laughter. He still held on to the string, and the wind had taken the kite high up into the sky. I tried to hold the string, but the pull was too strong. So, wet as he was, Api anchored our kite deep in the soft soil of the meadow and we watched it bouncing and surging high above us in the air. It looked so small and yet so strong. I could not believe that we had created it ourselves.

In an effort to teach me to make what he considered the right choices, Api often would give me an option: Should we first do our Latin or whatever homework I needed to finish, or should we play first? Needless to say, I invariably and without hesitation picked the latter. He always honored my choice, but today I can imagine how he must have hoped that just once I would put work before play. When

Api and Nyussi took me to Hamburg to show me the beautiful city with its two lakes and great harbor, Api again offered me an alternative to round out our day. We could go either to the opera, for Verdi's *La Forza del Destino*, or to Millöcker's light operetta *The Beggar Student*. Although I knew that Api would prefer the Verdi, I asked to see the operetta. If he was disappointed, he never let on, and we went to *The Beggar Student*.

In Bevensen, Api revived the family tradition of Sunday outings. Before we had a car, we went on hikes. A favorite walk took us to Kloster Medingen, just outside Bevensen. It was a Cistercian nunnery, founded in 1336. To get there, we passed a broad avenue lined by majestic beeches, whose beauty Api praised each time. Then he told me about the nuns who had lived there in 1235. "The first nuns who lived here had a scary and lonely time. They had no nunnery yet but lived in cottages on the heath, much like the one we had in Suderburg, remember? But Medingen also had a castle with knights. When the nuns got really scared, they sought the protection of the knights. It took them about one hundred years until they finally had their own nunnery. Then life got easier. The nunnery became famous in the area and was part of the six Nunneries of the Heath." Api ended, "Unfortunately, only a brewhouse has survived from medieval times. Everything else has burned down over the centuries. Fires were common back then, and the old places have been replaced with the newer buildings you now see." I was most intrigued by the baroque church, because it was round and I had never seen a round church before.

From Medingen, we crossed the Ilmenau River at the King's Bridge and followed a small path to the Nixengrund, the Mermaids' Hollow. I always hurried through this eerie spot and, ahead of Api, climbed to the Sängershöhe, the Singers' Hill, above the Ilmenau shore. The reward for this exertion was coffee and *Butterkuchen*.

In 1950, when cars were not yet common, Api bought his first

postwar automobile, a used gray 1948 Opel Olympia. It had thir-
ty-eight thousand kilometers and cost 3,000 marks. The Grey Donkey
was not as big or as flashy as the Buicks had been, but we all loved
it and it relieved Api of his bike rides to patients. Now, our Sunday
outings had a wider range. We drove to the nearby Göhrde, with its
sandy paths, birch trees, and stunted juniper bushes. Occasionally
we saw a shepherd outlined against the sky, standing very still and
wearing a long, dark cloak. He held a gnarled crook that was curved
at the top and so long that it extended far above his head. Api told
me that this shepherd scene had remained the same for centuries.
My attention, however, was focused on the small dog that tended the
sheep. I was amazed at how cleverly he could make them go wherever
he wanted.

   If Api did not have time for a longer outing, we visited the nearby
woods, the Riessel and the Lohn, where we looked for mushrooms
or gathered pinecones for the fire. Both were locally famous for their
tall stands of beech and oak trees. Much like the Grunewald, they,
too, had been hunting grounds of the local aristocracy and therefore
could not be cut down. Today I wonder whether they were precious
old-growth forests with their miles of underground communica-
tions, a rarity these days. Api pointed out the stately beauty of the
gray-barked beech trees and the delicate green of the larches in
spring, making me run my hand across the soft new growth. Walking
through rows of straight, tall stems, Api asked me whether I, too, felt
like being in a high-arched Gothic cathedral. I wonder now whether
he thought of his early poem in which he compared being out in
nature to attending a church service. The poem, entitled "I Do Not
Regret," contains the lines "I do not regret a single day that I have
swarmed through the hills and valleys of God's beautiful world. . . . It
was neither a church service sitting in a pew nor a day's work in the
yoke of duty, but I believe that God also holds school in His creation.
I do not regret."

Christmas was Api's special time. It was he who hunted for the prettiest tree, which he then hid away. On Christmas Eve, he decorated it in secret with tinsel, balls, and sweets. None of us was allowed to see the tree until after the *Siebenstern* service. Back home, Api disappeared into the Christmas room. I heard much rustling and listened intently for the tinkling of the little brass bell that told us we could enter. I was the first in the room and awed by the glow of the twelve candles, the glitter, and the presents around the tree.

The Christmas season also was the only time Api was busy in the kitchen. During the four weeks of Advent, he made sure that we had almonds, confectioner's sugar, and especially rose water to make marzipan. It was a sign that work was over and the holiday had begun when Api came into the kitchen to prepare the marzipan dough and knead it vigorously. Then he fashioned delicate flowers out of the mixture, using cast-off surgical instruments to make them as detailed and precise as possible. He also created little tartlets with fluted edges, which he first baked a golden brown. After they had cooled, he filled them with white icing and then decorated them with sugar ornaments, bells, boughs, and stars. After the marzipan came an egg liqueur that Api made after his mother's recipe. I, too, was allowed a little glass of the strong, creamy concoction, which glowed rich yellow in my glass.

The Christmas poem has no more echoes of terrors overcome and blows of fate but concentrates on love and faith. The last stanza I recited that year says:

> *Just as the Lord's all-encompassing love*
> *Returns to us each Christmas Day*
> *So I will pray that from above*
> *Its power remains with us to stay.*

# 55

# A HOME OF OUR OWN

pi's financial situation continued to improve during the economic miracle of the 1950s. Since the owners of the house had hinted more than once that they would like their ground floor back to themselves, we were looking for even better accommodation. After many a calculation and discussion with Nyussi, Api decided that we could afford to buy a house of our own. He soon found just the one he wanted. It was at the far end of Eckermannstrasse, at number 19, with the same vista of meadows and woods that we had come to love. Since it was the last house on the street, its view was unencumbered on three sides.

I loved the house at first sight. It looked so big and solid, its rough stucco painted gray, with a red-tiled roof and bay windows trimmed in dark wood. The house also had a terraced garden framed by a beechwood hedge, and there was a little pond at the bottom. And, even better than the arbor at the Obstfelders', this house had a tiled veranda overlooking the garden. It was open to the sun but sheltered by the house on three sides from the chilly North German winds. In summer, deep-blue delphiniums grew up the walls. The house even had a drive-in garage into the basement, a very modern amenity in

Germany at that time. Bennecke, a local architect, had built the house for himself but had to sell it before it was completed. So Api was able to purchase it for 32,000 marks. The garage was unfinished, some windows still had to be installed along with the upstairs flooring, and we needed a fence. But none of this stopped him for a moment; I think, at such a late time in life, Api was even more excited by the prospect of owning his own home than I was to live in it.

We moved in the summer of 1952. With two separate front entrances, the house was perfect for Api's surgery office and for our living space. The large living room looked out on the veranda, and along the south side of the house stretched a sunny "winter garden," where Nyussi grew her favorite cyclamens and fuchsias all year round. There was also space for a piano, although her hands were too crippled to play. And I am afraid my childish and not very talented attempts to do so were, despite regular piano lessons, no substitute. We ate in a cozy wood-paneled den off the kitchen. I spent much of that summer by the little pond, trying to train the green frogs that hopped all along its edge to jump into bark boats Api and I had made for them. On summer evenings, the frogs gave a concert by the pond, and later that winter, I skated there.

My grandparents could hardly believe their good fortune that after all they had gone through, they were now able to enjoy the evening of their lives together in such prosperity. Even Api's wildest dreams during those dark days of 1945 had not pictured anything as bountiful. For me, a child of ten, it was perfect. After being shuffled around to places where I was always a visitor with different people, after the strict convent and the quarantine hospital, I finally felt like I was home.

I even had a cat, Felix, a powerful, gray-striped tiger who spent the nights outside hunting. Early every morning, I called for him and soon saw him bounding over the high grass of the meadow, ready to share my breakfast of semolina—only he took his neat, without the layer of cocoa and sugar I sprinkled liberally over mine. Then I went off to school, and he slept on the couch.

The nuns' education, combined with Api's steady assistance, made me so far ahead of my class that the elementary school moved me ahead a grade. As a result, I was not yet nine years old when I passed the examination for the gymnasium, the highest level of secondary education in Germany. My new school was the Wilhelm Raabe Schule, in Lüneburg, twenty-five miles away. I loved the daily commute. It felt very grown-up to ride the train from Bevensen into the much larger station in Lüneburg. Once there, my friends and I had a thirty-minute walk through the medieval Hanseatic city to get to our school, an imposing redbrick building of the early twentieth century. It was much larger than my elementary school, and the broad staircases, long marble hallways, and huge arched windows made me a little afraid of what was to come. The opening ceremony took place in the neogothic *Aula*. I felt dwarfed by its twelve-foot stained-glass windows and a ceiling so high I could hardly see to the top. After the all-too-easy elementary school, I found the gymnasium difficult, especially in terms of maturity. I was two years younger than my classmates and, despite Api's training, not prepared for the seriousness of this education.

The curriculum started with Latin, and Api worked me with me on it almost every day. I still have a thick notebook that on the left side has Api's German sentences and on the right my Latin translations. Today I marvel at the complexity of what he asked of me and my ability to translate. It began with relatively easy tasks, such as, "The son jumped into the deep water of the big river and swam well." But then it goes on to complicated sentences in which I was to work out the future-conditional tense: "When you will have caught or put to flight the culprit who stole the beautiful apples from our tall apple tree, you will have been a great help not only to us but to all neighbors." Api's work paid off years later, when I was the only student in my MA class at Columbia to pass the Latin translation test right away. Api's tutoring, however, could not make up for the fact that at the gymnasium I clowned around and did not pay much attention.

When I returned from school in the early afternoon, Felix met me on my walk home from the station, running ahead with a constant stream of meows. I did not know whether he was urging me on to hurry home or whether he was just as pleased as I was to be with him. Felix was my first and only pet as a child, although "pet" seems too frivolous a term for my serious tomcat.

*Our Bevensen House, 1952*

*Margit Hevler, Vienna, 1950s*

*Nyussi with her favorite family pendant*

# 56

# A VISIT TO BEVENSEN

After Mike, Benedict, and I had checked out Suderburg and Holxen, we ended that trip into my past with a visit to Bevensen. It was only a short car ride from Suderburg on narrow roads lined with birch trees, but it must have seemed long to Api on his bike. I noticed that the town had been given the designation of a spa. The sign at the entrance proudly proclaimed SPA BEVENSEN. We looked around the flat countryside shrouded in mist and wondered how a spa could thrive there. But we soon saw that it did. The road took us directly to the spa center, which, of course, was new to me. We saw the usual trappings of a health resort, the park and long hall where patients sipped the healthful waters. Thanks to all the moisture in the air, the grass was bright green even in winter. Beyond the public amenities was street upon street of bed-and-breakfasts with names like House Rest. The larger establishments called themselves *Kur Hotels*, resort hotels. We checked into House Sabine because I liked the birches and pines that surrounded it. It was new, clean, and bright, and Frau Sabine herself welcomed us. Our rooms had startlingly white lace curtains and puffy down pillows and blankets.

As soon as we were settled, I was eager to show Mike and

Benedict the town I knew. We took a path to the Klaubusch, the little pine wood that rises up steeply from the Ilmenau River where I used to sled, often rather dangerously, between the trees. As soon as we had descended to the river and crossed the little wooden bridge, I was back in the world of the 1950s. There were the foggy meadows of my childhood reaching up to Eckermannstrasse, and the cinder path we took looked the same as well. When we came to the blue-and-white enamel sign that read ECKERMANNSTRASSE, I immediately saw that the Obstfelders' house was still there at the corner, although Api and Nyussi's arbor had gone to make way for a garden. As we walked along to number 19, I noticed that a few of the houses had been remodeled or enlarged, but on the whole the street was much like it had been.

And then we stood in front of our house. It looked the same yet also different. At first I could not pinpoint what had changed, but then I noticed that an entire wing had been added on the side where Nyussi's winter garden used to be. The two entrances, however, were still there, and the present owners also used one for business and one for living. But now, instead of a surgery office, the right entrance led to Sommer Accounting Services.

I went up to the door and rang the bell. Herr Sommer Senior opened the door. I explained who I was, and he let me in. We walked through the waiting room to his—Api's former—office. Herr Sommer told me that he remembered Dr. Frese. "In 1953, he prescribed me my first glasses." I was happy that a little connection to Api still existed in this house. When Herr Sommer showed me around, I saw that most rooms had been remodeled. Nevertheless, remaining touches took me back to my childhood with a surge in my heart: brass door handles that I had long forgotten; the two sets of stairs I had run up and down so often, the main one going up from Nyussi's winter garden, and the other from Api's office. Even the living room looking out on the veranda was much like it used to be. After I said goodbye to Herr Sommer, I could not stop talking about it all to Mike and Benedict.

From the house, we took a walk into town. The path was now paved, and houses lined one side of it, but on the other, the view across a misty meadow to the church was exactly the same. When we reached the main street, we saw the bakery where I used to buy *Bienenstich*, a yeast, custard, and nut confection I loved. Of course, the three of us needed to stop and each have a slice. Then I showed them the way to the station that I had taken every day. Again I was astonished by how little had changed, and that even many of the businesses had remained the same. I pointed out each new find. There was the paper store Schliekau, where I got my exercise books and where Api bought me my first fountain pen, the green Pelikan of which I was so proud. At the corner where we turned into Bahnhofstrasse, I spotted the tobacconist Harms, where Api had purchased his cigars. The small, wood-paneled salesroom was exactly as it had been. Then we came to the park, also the same, and beyond it the station square. The station building had two wings, each with three tall, curved windows, and a higher middle section. It must have been large for a small town where the express trains did not stop. I ran up the steps ahead of Mike and Benedict to find the station hall and the platforms just as I remembered them. I could have been rushing to catch the train to Lüneburg.

On our way back, we headed for the Church of the Epiphany, which I attended every Sunday with Api and Nyussi. We passed through a short, tree-lined square to reach the church, which was dominated by its high-pointed steeple. The interior was simple but more beautiful than I remembered it. The plain white walls now bore golden decorations around the windows, and the seat cushions in the pews were a rich red. The altar was decorated with a motif of grapes and ears of grain. I remembered that Api had told me that the church dated back to the year 833, but that a fire had destroyed it at the beginning of the nineteenth century, after which the present version was erected. At Haus Sabine, we ended the day with a game of *Halma*, pickup sticks, which we found in the lounge. Api and I often played that game, although he was more patient, and his hand, used to delicate eye operations, steadier than mine.

At night, I kept thinking about Api. I realized more than ever that his values are still with me so many years later. I have adopted his love of nature and his commitment to single-minded work and play. To this day, I do not like to watch television or even listen to music while working or reading. And even now, when I am older than Api, I still love games of all sorts. My emotional, often sentimental attitude also stems from him, as I came to realize from his diaries when he thinks nostalgically about his past or waxes emotional about his new refuge, the "swallow's nest" in the attic. I may even outdo my grandfather in sentimentality, such as my "friends" on the road. On routes I travel frequently, I have chosen some object: mile marker 270 on the way to my parents in Urbana or a red-and-white-striped smokestack, "power and light," on the southern outskirts of Indianapolis. I greet my "friends" whenever I travel past them.

I was grateful that Mike and Benedict were with me on this journey. As I drifted off to sleep, I thought that gratefulness was another trait Api had instilled in me. I was especially grateful for all he had done for me, and I hoped that this book would not have displeased him.

# 57

# GLOVES AT THE BOTTOM OF THE STAIRS

Api had such a very short time to enjoy all he had achieved after the war. He lived just two years in his new home.

Api gave me the poem for New Year's Eve 1954–55 right after Christmas. As in all previous years, I copied it out so that today I have both Api's version and mine in my rounded, childish script. I had the poem memorized a few days later, and he coached me when no one was around to hear us. It was our secret. Little did I know that this would be the last time we would do this together. Today, the poem reads like a premonition of his death, eleven days later. It certainly is a farewell, although I am not sure that either Nyussi or my mother, who had joined us from Vienna, saw it as anything other than a metaphor for bidding the old year goodbye.

*An old man wanders slow and quiet through the streets*
*Where for a year he intimately lived with us*
*Worked, suffered, laughed. Prepared now to retreat,*
*Just checking whether it's been good.*
*Troubled, I watch him leave, with almost tearful eye*

*Perhaps he notices and takes it as it's meant*
*A silent thanks. I see his gray head bow, then he is gone:*
*Farewell, be happy. Only in parting are we truly one.*

I wonder whether, when Api composed that last line, he was hearing a faint echo of those months in 1945 when, in his most desperate moments, he consoled himself with the idea of a reunion in God. Was he now again taking refuge in this sentiment because of a premonition of death?

Api died suddenly in the night on January 11, 1955, of a massive heart attack, less than two weeks before his sixty-seventh birthday. He had just managed to drive himself back from Kloster Medingen, where he tended to his aged friends in the county retirement home. The old men always looked forward to Api's visits, not so much for the eye care as for the laughter and joy he brought into their quiet lives. And Api also enjoyed their company and looked after them for free. I had often accompanied him on these visits on Saturday afternoons, following in his wake of laughter and jokes. But this time he went alone in the evening, when I was already in bed. Late at night, I heard some unusual commotion but did not find out that Api had died until the next morning.

It was the first time in my life that I had consciously come close to death, and it took me a long time to understand that I would never be with Api again. What I remember from the next morning is seeing his gloves lying at the bottom of the stairs that led up to the bedroom from his surgery. Api never left his things lying about. He had discarded them hastily the night before when he was trying to reach his bed before collapsing. The fingers of the gloves were still bent from his hand, but they looked rigid, dead. For days afterward, I saw the gloves whenever I passed the stairs, for no one took them away. The gloves with the bent fingers came to me in dreams for years after Api's death.

Api's body was laid out in the sunroom, next to Nyussi's red and purple cyclamens. Many people came to say their goodbyes. When no one was there, I stood by his body, noticing that his fingernails had turned violet blue but not really grasping that this was my Api lying there in his formal, dark pin-striped suit. In fact, sometimes I rushed into the room not even remembering that Api was there. That rigid body just could not be him.

Nyussi had put Api's death notice under the motto of "We dwell like those who always have to migrate." It is a translation from the Latin, "*Tanquam migraturi habitamus*," but I do not know its source. It seems to fit us all.

We received mountains of flowers for the funeral. In the short time Api had been in Bevensen, its people came to love and respect him. He was put to rest in the Bevensen cemetery with the heather bushes and birch trees he had come to love. The headstone was a simple fieldstone such as dotted the heath all around. It reminded me of the medieval church tower in Suderburg. His friend Superintendent Stünkel gave the eulogy, but I don't remember a single word he said. Over the years, I have understood that I will mourn Api all my life and how much of his spirit has become part of me.

The final stop on our Benensen trip with Mike and Benedict was the cemetery. When I stood at Api's grave, I suddenly began to cry, overcome by a feeling of childish abandonment. But my husband and son stood by me, and I felt their love and sought refuge in their presence and support.

After Api's death, life changed dramatically for both Nyussi and me. My mother had come back from Vienna, but she went on to Hamburg, where she studied to become a business-school teacher, as her father had wished. Nyussi and I were alone in the house. She had been advised to rent out the practice until we knew better what to do. The eye doctor we took in to run it and live with us turned out to be a morphine addict. He wandered about at night, the pupils of his eyes huge and black, talking fantastically. We hid from him whenever possible.

I still ate my porridge with Felix the cat and went off on the train each morning, but I began to fail in school. In less than a year, it became clear that Nyussi and I were unable to handle the situation. She sold the practice and the house for much less than it was worth, and in the summer of 1956 I was once again back at a boarding school, this time on the Baltic Sea, and had to repeat the grade I had just finished.

In his diaries, Api had written about how helpless and distraught he was alone in Berlin. Without us, he felt unable to make decisions and was barely able to survive. After his death, we saw how much our lives were based on his planning and provisions, how defenseless we were without him, and how much we needed him. For me, Api's death abruptly brought an end to the five happiest years of my childhood. And Nyussi survived her husband by only three years, during which time, although increasingly ill, she was my strongest support.

As I grew to be a teenager, Api began to be with and within me. After failing in school during the year after his death, I excelled in my work and became ambitious, committed to studying and learning. I then remembered what he had told me so often and tried to live up to his rule of work before play, and to do both, work or play, wholeheartedly, giving each my full attention. I enjoyed listening to classical music, as he had done. He would be pleased to know that now I, too, would choose Verdi over an operetta.

Api was the only father figure I had known, and I cherish his memory, his love, and his joie de vivre. He remains my role model, but the image I have of him is never stern and rigid—it is one filled with gladness, gentleness, and good spirits. He taught me to be grateful for whatever I have and to enjoy every moment. I feel free to preserve a childlike glee about the little things in life, as he did. Even today, I am not beyond skipping along the street when I am feeling good. Api taught me to love nature, and, yes, to wax sentimental at times. When I did well at the university, won a Woodrow Wilson fellowship, and received my PhD at the age of twenty-five, I imagined him watching me succeed and feeling proud of what I had accomplished.

And then, at the end of my career, I found the diary. First, I was surprised at how fearful and helpless Api had been in Berlin in 1945. I still had the child's image of a strong father who was never at a loss for what to do. But reading his words made me feel closer to him; I understood him as a man on his own, loving and very vulnerable. I began to think about what I knew of his life before he became my grandfather, his Prussian upbringing, which explained many of his beliefs and mental bearing. Over a gulf of many years, I felt closer to Api than ever before.

Then I discovered that Api had been a Nazi. It was a physical shock. I had lived more than thirty years in the United States and had absorbed the image of the cold-blooded, steely-eyed, and cruel Nazis as films and stories portray them. How could Api be one of them? When Mike at last persuaded me to write Api's story, I had to confront this question. Learning more about that time and Api's circumstances helped me to explain and understand, although it did not answer everything. I was often reminded of Edward Ball's account of the slaves in his family and, like he did, hoped that by recounting Api's story, I would not "dig up my grandfather and hang him," but instead would come closer to some sense of accountability.

# 58

# TRYING TO UNDERSTAND

Looking back, I have to admit that this recounting has left unanswered the questions with which I set out. How can I account for Api's Nazi membership, and how can I assess his individual guilt during the years of the Nazi terror?

Api was formed by his small-town Prussian upbringing at the end of the nineteenth century. His years of military service reinforced the lessons of discipline and obedience to authority that he had learned from his family. He was proud to wear his uniform, and proud, too, of his country. He was raised as a conservative and remained so all his life.

Coming out of World War I, Api was at odds with the world into which he was thrown. The emperor's abdication was a blow to his Prussian sensibilities, and there was no one to fill that void. The Weimar Republic was never strong enough to assert itself against the extremists on both the right and the left. President Ebert's attempts at a new, pro-democratic government were drowned in a cacophony of violence. Although Api prospered economically in the 1920s, he did not subscribe to the ethos of the roaring twenties, with its emancipated women, expressionist art, revolutionary spirit, and sexual liberation. He never made the transition into this new world.

The golden '20s did not last long. The stock market crash of 1929 triggered an economic crisis even worse than the one after World War I. By 1932, Germany had 6.1 million unemployed. Banks collapsed, and the stock market had to be closed for more than a month. Politically, the situation was no more stable. Rival political gangs from the right and the left kept fighting each other, and a total of five elections took place that year, none of them conclusive. Api must have feared that the newly won order and prosperity would disintegrate.

When Api joined the Nazi Party on May 1, 1933, he may well have seen Hitler as the best hope for a battered Germany and believed his promises of stability, peace, and Christian values. In 1933, according to historian Peter Fritsche, the National Socialists "were popular insofar as they were identified with a new national mood that emphasized national integration, social reform, and economic prosperity." Perhaps Api saw Hitler as the only one strong enough to stand up against all warring parties. He perfectly fit the profile of Hitler's supporters in the early 1930s. They tended to be older, conservative, anticommunist, and Lutheran.

Api was steeped in a pietistic Lutheranism, a religion of the heart that thrived on introspection. It taught him to be tolerant, modest, and compassionate, but it also made a clear distinction between private and public life. In his 1946 book, *The Solution of the German Question*, Wilhelm Röpke, a social theorist, argued that this Lutheranism helped pave the way for the Nazi regime. "The two are entirely separate from each other, and thus demand quite different conduct; they may even be ruled by opposite moral principles. . . . Thus this doctrine meant for the Germans a school of non-resistance against the power of the state, of political indifference, of ready acceptance of the political situation at any moment, and of submission to the authorities in all questions of public life." Therefore, the

Protestant pastor Martin Niemöller voted for the Nazis in 1933, and Richard Evans says that generally "committed right-wing but populist pastors like Niemöller were particularly susceptible to the appeal of the Nazis."

One reason for this susceptibility was that early on Hitler presented himself as a religious man. He wove into his speeches references to God's blessing, and even ended them with "amen." On February 1, 1933, he assured his listeners that Christianity was his foundation, concluding, "May the almighty God take our work into His mercy, form our will justly, bless our understanding, and gladden us with the trust of our people." Bishop Dibelius, who officiated at the Day of Potsdam, wrote that few pastors would not be heartily glad of this new direction Hitler initiated. Api may have thought that Hitler would preside over a new Christian state.

Hitler's speeches in the early 1930s also tended to stress his peaceful intentions. On March 16, 1935, although he had just instituted compulsory military service, he assured everyone in Germany and beyond, "The government of today's Germany desires only a single moral and material power: It is the power to preserve peace for the Reich and therefore also for all of Europe." MacDonogh argues, "To make all Germans responsible for the relatively docile Hitler of 1933 is to apply the Allied weapon of collective guilt."

In addition, Hitler came to power legally. According to George Mosse, a historian of racism and nationalism, that in itself turned fatal for many moderate voters like my grandfather: "If there had been barricades instead of legality in 1933, men and women would have been forced to make more reasoned decisions. The legal assumption of power, however, allowed them to drift into the open arms of the Third Reich, finding themselves in an embrace from which there was no escape, except prison or exile."

And who could have been prepared for a man like Hitler? Sebastian Haffner writes about this: "Our thinking is usually constrained by a certain civilization in our outlook, in which the basics are unquestioned. . . . [C]ertain Christian, humanistic, civilized principles [are accepted] as axiomatic." Hannah Arendt says that only a madman could have predicted what was coming. She believes that "they," and she includes not only Germans but other nations, "who were the Nazis' first accomplices and their best aids, truly did not know what they were doing and with whom they were dealing." Peter Gay, an emigrant from Nazi Germany who became a professor of social history at Yale University, echoes these sentiments in his memoir: "Hitler's threats were so utterly implausible that we regarded them as unreliable guides to future conduct." Peter Gay was born Peter Föhlich into a Jewish family in Berlin. They did not flee until 1938, and he was shocked when Jews in America battered him with suspicious questions about why his family had not emigrated earlier.

During the first years of Hitler's rule, the world at large also was not denouncing him. In 1933, the Vatican signed a papal concordat with Hitler. In 1935, the Saar region became part of Germany again; in 1936, Hitler occupied the Rhineland, but France did nothing; in 1938, he was allowed to annex the Sudetenland, part of the Czech Republic, and Austria. As Ian Kershaw says, "Internal terror and the readiness of the Western powers to hand Hitler one success after another in foreign policy had undermined the skepticism of many waverers."

No other than Winston Churchill, although not blind to Hitler's ruthlessness, found words of praise for him. In his 1935 article, "Hitler and His Choice," for the *Strand*, reprinted in his 1937 book, *Great Contemporaries*, Churchill wrote, "While all those formidable transformations were occurring in Europe, Corporal Hitler was fighting his long, weary battle for the German heart. The story of that battle cannot be read without admiration for the courage, the perseverance, and the vital force which enabled him to challenge, defy, conciliate, or overcome all the authorities or resistances which barred his path." Churchill ends, "Those who have met Herr Hitler face to face in public business or on social terms have found a highly competent, cool, well-informed functionary with an agreeable manner, a disarming smile, and few have been unaffected by a subtle personal magnetism." Two years later, in an article from September 17, 1937—published in *Step by Step* in 1939—Churchill added, "One may dislike Hitler's system and yet admire his patriotic achievement. If our country were defeated, I hope we should find a champion as indomitable to restore our courage and lead us back to our place among the nations." Journalists LeBor and Boyes show widespread support for Hitler among the financial, political, and industrial establishment of Great Britain, including the king himself. Fleet Street reflected this sentiment, from the *Times* to the *Daily Mail*.

Otto Friedrich sums up this international support for Hitler and its effect on Berliners: "For the Berliners of those early years, it must have seemed that Hitler not only achieved great successes but won the praise of the outside world. . . . When Hitler canceled all reparations, when Hitler marched troops into the Rhineland, when Hitler walked out of the League of Nations, when Hitler staged the *Anschluss* with Austria—which of the great powers of the world did anything to stop him? And what lessons should the ordinary Berliner have drawn from Hitler's triumphs?"

# 59

# AND YET . . .

And yet Hitler's 1925 book, *Mein Kampf*, already proclaimed his racist worldview, his anti-Semitism, his hatred of communism, and the need for more *Lebensraum*, space for life, for the "master race." Astute political observers did understand Hitler's true nature and aims, even in the early 1930s. Thus, the writer Erich Ebermayer acknowledged Hitler's moderate and statesmanlike behavior immediately after 1933 but refused to be taken in. At most, Ebermayer expressed the hope that Hitler would be as good as his word. But at heart he never doubted that Hitler was lying. For there were also signs in Hitler's speeches, and especially in the rhetoric of Joseph Goebbels, his Reich minister of public enlightenment and propaganda, that should have made Api refuse to vote for a man who, more than any other politician, stood against everything Api held dear.

Moreover, Hitler created neither his racist ideology nor his territorial expansion out of thin air but built on existing German prejudices and longings, especially among conservatives. I have to ask myself if Api shared either in the racism or in the desire for *Lebensraum*, or both. He may well have wanted Germany to regain the part of Prussia that was now Poland. He grew up there, after all.

And could his diaries' silence about the persecution of the Jews be any indication of anti-Semitism? I do not like to jump to this conclusion but have to admit I just do not know. Richard Evans, one of the foremost historians of that period, says, "Anti-Semitism was rife in the upper levels of society and in conservative politics." So this prevailing prejudice may well have affected Api.

In the end, I cannot get around the fact that Germans who joined the Party bear a responsibility, even if, like Api, they took no further part in its activities. And that responsibility lies perhaps most heavily not only on Api personally but on his class of educated professionals, who should have known better and not given in to Hitler's lure so easily. That is why Professor Peter Fritsche concludes, "The brutal terms in which all nationalists regarded the enemies of Germany and the correspondingly imperious way they defined its future made most Germans complicit in the crimes of Nazism."

This brings to mind Daniel Goldhagen's haunting book *Hitler's Willing Executioners: Ordinary Germans and the Holocaust*, which claims that all Germans, whether Nazis or not, espoused a century-old eliminationist anti-Semitism. Reading this, I have to ask myself once again whether or to what degree this sweeping bias affected Api. Goldhagen finds strong anti-Semitic bias at all levels of German society and in all parts of the country, from Bavaria in the south to Api's beloved Prussia in the northeast. It was rampant also, he argues, in the Protestant church and in the clergy, from pastors to bishops. He indicts the Lutheran theologian Karl Barth, as well as Pastor Dietrich Bonhoeffer, whom Hitler had executed in 1945. In their obsession with "eliminationist" anti-Semitism, Goldhagen paints Germans as different from all other civilized people—and it made them capable of genocide.

Although Goldhagen's book was an immediate best seller in Germany, German, as well as international, historians have hotly contested his thesis. Scholars like A. C. Grayling, Omer Bartov, and

Clive James have testified to the questionable character of Goldhagen's scholarship. Richard Neuhaus takes issue with Goldhagen's view of the German churches as eager members of Hitler's willing executioners: "It is simply not true to say that the churches welcomed the ascendancy of the Nazis." While recognizing "the absolute centrality of violence, coercion, and terror to the theory and practice of German National Socialism," Richard Evans notes, "It is impossible to understand the terror vented by the Nazis . . . upon the Jews . . . unless we grasp the fact that they had already vented it . . . on millions of their fellow citizens, indeed at one level or another . . . on the great majority of them."

Above all, scholars have rejected Goldhagen's attempt to keep alive the notion of the collective guilt of the Germans, who are unlike the rest of the world. In fact, they see such a view as dangerous, since it nullifies the moral significance of the Holocaust. "If Goldhagen is right about the uniquely German cause of the Holocaust, the rest of us need never again say, 'Never again'!" Wilhelm Röpke fought the idea of collective guilt well before Goldhagen. He believes that blaming an entire nation implies a betrayal of the principle of personal responsibility, a cornerstone of our civilization, in favor of a collectivist notion that eliminates individuality. And in 2013, the Serbian American poet Charles Simic wrote, "Collective guilt . . . has to be one of the most evil notions the human brain has concocted, most likely the cause of more suffering of innocents than any other vile belief in history."

Ian Kershaw offers a balanced view of the Goldhagen controversy that resonates with my own struggle. He agrees with Eberhard Jäckel that, based on its scholarship, Goldhagen's is "simply a bad book," but then adds, "Whatever its deficiencies, Goldhagen's book poses important questions which . . . still need answers."

# 60

# INNER EMIGRATION

In an effort to come to grips with the troubling question of Api's guilt, I sought other testimonies of the time. Writing from Nazi Germany, journalist William Shirer noted the effect of living under a totalitarian regime. "No one who has not lived for years in a totalitarian land can possibly conceive how difficult it is to escape the dread consequences of a regime's calculated and incessant propaganda." Shirer admits, "I myself was to experience how easily one is taken in by a lying and censored press and radio in a totalitarian state." Unlike most Germans, Shirer had access to foreign newspapers and radio broadcasts. Despite this, he felt, "It was surprising and sometimes consternating to find that notwithstanding the opportunities I had to learn the facts . . . a steady diet over the years of falsifications and distortions made a certain impression on one's mind and often misled it."

Looking back on the Third Reich from the perspective of the twenty-first century, historian Tobias Jersak sees a related effect of Hitler's propaganda. "The first norm which Hitler and his followers changed was logic itself: they did so by introducing a *new* logic, i.e., new rules of right thinking." It created profound self-doubt that "consisted precisely in doubting the rightness of one's own thinking. And when that is in question, active protest is impossible." This made me think of Api's paralyzing self-doubt, and I wondered whether this not only was the result of his immediate situation but had been building during the years of the Nazi regime.

In her book, *On the Other Side*, dedicated to her children, Mathilde Wolff-Mönckeberg tries to explain what it was like living under the Nazis. Neither she nor her husband, a professor and Hamburg city senator, had been Party members and hated the regime. Yet they felt helpless to do anything. After the war, however, British occupation officers told her that all Germans were responsible for the atrocities of the Nazi regime. She tried to make them understand ". . . it was totally impossible to form an opposition, spied upon as we were from all sides, telephone conversations listened in to, people standing behind us and alongside us listening and denouncing. It would have cost us our lives, or we should have ended up in concentration camps."

Physician and poet Gottfried Benn, who, like Api, had been educated at Kaiser Wilhelm Academy and served as a doctor in both World Wars, wrote from Berlin in a letter of March 19, 1945, "He who wants to talk and judge Germany must have stayed here." Benn, however, had been a Nazi supporter. Theodor Heuss, who in 1949 was to become the first elected president of the Federal Republic of Germany, likewise said, "[O]nly he who has lived twelve years under the Nazi terror can judge how enormous this pressure was and how much heroism and political insight were required to resist it." He was trying to urge restraint in American denazification procedures. Even if such statements sound self-serving or one-sided, they give me pause about easy judgments and unilateral condemnation.

I remember well a phrase that was much used after the war: *innere Emigration*, "inner emigration." I often caught those words as my grandparents listened to the radio, although I had no idea what they meant. Germans argued that they had not supported Hitler's brutal regime, but since they were powerless to act against it, their only option was withdrawal, or inner emigration. It has indeed been observed that after 1933, many people withdrew from politics and focused all energies on their private lives. This also was the case in Joachim Fest's family, in which his father was a fervent anti-Nazi. In a review of Fest's memoir, *Not I*, Neal Ascherson writes, "So, like countless Germans at the time, he left the toxic public sphere altogether and fell back on the Christian home barricaded against the outside world." And not only apolitical people like Api engaged in this, but ". . . even politically minded people withdrew into privacy in face of the constant pressure to conform, the perpetual need to demonstrate loyalty, the thought control and the bureaucratic routine that marked public life under National Socialism." Yet again, inner emigration seems too easy an excuse, a willed and partial blindness to what was happening. In the end, it entails a passive consent and acceptance of Nazi atrocities. Richard Evans sees the notion of the unpolitical German as "an alibi for the educated middle class."

The philosopher Karl Jaspers, who lived in Germany during the war, faced this responsibility squarely. Writing in 1946, he states without prevarication that "we Germans, every German, is guilty in some way." Or, "In view of the crimes which were committed in the name of the Reich, each German is co-responsible. We are all collectively liable." Yet Jaspers also recognizes the limits of this political responsibility. "Germany under the Nazi regime was a penitentiary. The guilt of getting into this penitentiary is political guilt. But once the gates had fallen shut, it became impossible to break out of this penitentiary from within."

Jaspers finds all Germans, himself included, guilty not only politically but morally and metaphysically. Everyone in Hitler's Germany made some gestures of accommodation; they may have attended meetings and rallies, given the Hitler salute, or, faced with threatening bodies like the Gestapo, pretended, if they did not feel it, loyalty. "We did not go into the streets when our Jewish friends were led away; we did not scream out until we, too, were destroyed. We preferred to stay alive on the feeble, if correct, ground that our deaths could not have helped in any way. The fact that we live, that is our guilt."

If we accept Jaspers's uncompromising view of political responsibility, we are all responsible for the acts of our government. And Jaspers acknowledges this: "Politically everyone acts in the modern state, at least by voting, or failing to vote, in elections. The sense of political liability leaves no one a way out."

Api, a member of the Nazi Party, was responsible. By that argument, however, so are we, if we allow our government to engage in torture and war or, even closer to home, stand by when we know racism and social injustice is destroying lives around us. We become guilty just by being silent bystanders.

However, to avoid painting with too broad a brush, Jaspers makes clear that this responsibility is an individual matter and has to be considered case by case. Otherwise, the very notion of guilt and responsibility becomes meaningless. Jaspers therefore gauges this liability not collectively but sees the degree of guilt as different for each individual. When and why someone joined the Party, how they supported the regime, what even small acts of resistance they risked in their daily lives, all have to be taken into account. Between the extremes of murdering people in concentration camps and risking one's life by hiding Jewish friends lay so very many degrees of choice for everyone.

As I ponder this, I am nagged by questions about what I would have done, how far I would have been willing to adapt, to go along, to commit small acts of cowardice and submission. Like Api, I am not particularly politically interested or engaged and could easily have become as withdrawn into my private world, ready to compromise, as he seems to have done. Similar questions have troubled many people of my postwar generation. As one writer put it, "In how far can a human being be sure of her- or himself?" In his 1981 preface to *Popular Opinion and Political Dissent in the Third Reich*, Ian Kershaw muses, "I should like to think that had I been around at the time I would have been a convinced anti-Nazi engaged in the underground resistance fight. However, I know really that I would have been as confused and felt as helpless as most of the people I am writing about."

In a 1945 essay, Hannah Arendt argues that the measure of guilt "can be determined only by the One who knows the secrets of the human heart, which no human eye can penetrate." Arendt, who fled Nazi Germany, first to France and then, in 1941, to the United States, grew up in Königsberg, Prussia, and Berlin, and wrote her dissertation under Karl Jaspers. She goes on to say, "[W]here all are guilty, nobody in the last analysis can be judged." Arendt distinguishes between guilt and responsibility, saying, "[T]here are many who share responsibility without any visible proof of guilt." She includes in this group leaders from other countries and ultimately every human being. "For the idea of humanity, when purged of all sentimentality, has the very serious consequence that in one form or another men must assume responsibility for all crimes committed by men and that all nations share the onus of evil committed by all others." Thus, the Jewish genocide entails the crisis of our humanity and our morality.

Observers have noted that at the end of the war, most Germans were like my grandfather and did not reflect on their national guilt. Reverend David Cairns, member of a Scottish regiment, told a meeting of the British Council of Churches that German civilians were obsessed with their own survival and that of their families and friends. He was particularly bothered by "the lack of understanding for the suffering that Germany has caused other people" and that a sense of guilt was "rather lacking." General Lucius Clay, who was

Eisenhower's deputy and after the war was military governor of the US zone of Germany, voiced the same sentiment: "The German masses seem totally apolitical, apathetic, and primarily concerned with everyday problems of food, shelter, and clothing. . . . No general feeling of war guilt or repugnance for Nazi doctrine has manifested itself. Germans blame Nazis for losing war, protest ignorance of regime's crimes, and shrug off their own support as incidental and unavoidable."

General Clay's summary of German attitudes rings true, even expressed without much sympathy. Lack of sympathy for Germans was, of course, understandable right at the end of a war that had cost the lives of millions of Allies. And yet it does not seem quite as surprising as these observers thought that, during a time when they had lived through an inferno, had lost many members of their families, and their own survival was in doubt, Germans did not dwell on the problem of collective guilt. As Jaspers notes, "The horizon has become narrow. One does not want to hear about guilt, about the past . . . one simply wants the suffering to cease."

I can also imagine that it was not only their own suffering that made people apathetic. The deaths of millions of people—soldiers in the field, women and children in cities and towns, a quarter million civilians during the atom bomb attacks on Japan, and six million in concentration camps—had been too much to take in and effectively deadened people's feelings.

In the end, I cannot measure whether and to what extent Api individually is politically responsible, even if he himself felt innocent. Given that doubt, should we then discount his suffering or even see it as just deserts? Or should we discount it because others suffered even worse? This makes me think of the article by Columbia professor Mark Anderson that helped me to overcome my reluctance to tell Api's story. Anderson says that after the war, "German victimhood became politically incorrect." But with the passing of the generation that lived through the war, that is beginning to change. "Unacknowledged suffering claims its due," and, "Individual suffering, not a simple tallying of perpetrators and victims, is beginning to emerge in striking historical detail and complexity." This by no means implies a lessening of the horror and unexceeded brutality of the Holocaust. Instead, Anderson concludes, stories of German war experiences tell us, "the importance of individual historical experience that resists the either/or of victimhood. In a sense, arguing over whose victims can be counted is another way of continuing the war—a war that may truly be over only when we stop feeling the need to deny the Germans their stories of suffering and loss."

In that sense, Api's individual historical experience has value without in any way reducing that of millions of victims of the Nazi regime. Perhaps it can help us to understand not only the past but also our present situation and make us each feel accountable for what happens around us, even if we are in no way directly responsible. Understanding experiences like my grandfather's also may temper accountability with compassion and, perhaps, lead to a better future.

# 61

# A WIDE FIELD

And yet, and yet . . . the questions won't go away. Layers and layers of them keep ricocheting in my mind, compelling me to go over the same ground again and again. I cannot forget the living hell of Api's daily struggle for survival in Berlin—the inferno of flames and the stench of corpses. Api lost his only son, his livelihood, and his home. He was surrounded by people dying from hunger and illness. And even though he was a doctor, he could do little to help them.

Then again, in 1933 he joined the Nazi Party and continued his successful career under the Hitler regime. Yet he had established most of it—his practice and apartment in the premier medical district of Berlin, even his eight-cylinder Buick—well before the Nazis took over. His Prussian values of hard work and thrift led to his success. He started out poor, and it took him years to buy his instruments and furnish his office. He sent his family on vacations while he himself stayed in Berlin to work. But perhaps his Party membership helped him to prosper in a way he would not have without it.

Api was a member of the Nazi Party and did not revolt against the regime, but no other member of his family was a Party member. I am certain—and his denazification classification as "Exonerated" confirms this—that he maintained his personal integrity, but he tried to do so outside politics. Arguably, at a time when one's country is engaged in unparalleled atrocities, there is guilt in trying to live in such a way. It means that one has to turn a blind eye, even if many of us would not do so otherwise, for protest was life-threatening and everyone had good reason to be afraid. As Richard Evans says, the regime turned its violence on its ordinary citizens as much as on the outside world: "Fear was all pervasive in the Third Reich." In 1945, Api did voice regret at his inaction but believed that there was nothing he could have done. He saw himself as "well knowing but impotent."

Living under a totalitarian regime, Api focused on his immediate family, and as a doctor he dedicated his life to helping people. This is also how I knew Api. In Bevensen in the 1950s, he looked after people in an old folks' home for free, and at his death many of his patients who were grateful for what he had done for them came forward. From the Berlin times, I have only one account, from a patient Api treated from 1928 to 1944. She wrote after the war that her life would have been sadder and poorer had it not been for the care Dr. Frese had given her. Although, she wrote, he was known as one of the best eye doctors in Berlin, he took the time to befriend her. In times of trouble, he was almost like a second father to her. I do not know the circumstances but am pleased that this woman's testimony confirms my sense of my grandfather.

Of course, without trying to become an apologist for his actions or lack of action, I find my judgment inevitably influenced by my love for my grandfather, who, in the 1950s, gave me the only home I had known up to then. So I am not able to judge Api. He was battered by history, one of the almost uniquely unfortunate generation that had to serve in two World Wars and endure a frightening and brutal totalitarian regime.

Overwhelmed, I take refuge in old von Briest's response to his bewildering world in Theodor Fontane's 1894 novel, *Effi Briest*, the very book behind which I discovered the diaries. Whenever he was confronted with the fearful complexities of his life, so different from the strict discipline and morality in which he was raised, Briest shrugged his shoulders in helpless resignation and said to his wife, "That is a wide field, Louise." In this way, he avoided becoming judgmental of a world he no longer understood.

Briest's life is similar to Api's in that both experienced a fundamental upheaval of their world. Old Briest was anchored in the nineteenth-century conservative ethos of the Prussian *Junker*. The end of the century brought profound social and cultural changes that were antithetical to his straitlaced *Junker* tradition. Yet Briest does not judge or condemn a world so different from the one he holds dear. He simply lives his life in private, away from the new ethos of his times. Old Briest's "wide field" expresses both a sensitive understanding of the fatalities and irresolvable dilemmas of life and a sad resignation to understand them. The only thing he will not question or give up is his love for his family, including or even especially for his "fallen" daughter, Effi.

Perhaps the intimate details of Api's life also are such a "wide field." They allow a glimpse into the fate of his generation, churned up by "the almost uninterrupted volcanic tremors of our European world," but they provide no answer other than compassion and love.

Yet as I consider this, even my appreciation of von Briest's position is brought up short. I have to wonder whether, in a strange way, von Briest is not a forerunner of the transformation of the family man, as Hannah Arendt describes, "from a responsible member of society, interested in all public affairs, to a 'bourgeois' concerned only with his private existence and knowing no civic virtue." For it is such good family men, Arendt argues, who made Nazi mass murders possible by following orders in an effort to secure their own families. Seen in this light, the "wide field" suddenly appears as an evasion of Briest's own responsibility in his daughter's tragedy, since, in the tradition of his class, he married her off to the stodgy Instetten. And when she rebelled by having a rather desperate affair, Briest refused to question the social system that he himself had affirmed and promoted and that eventually led to her death. Instead, he hid behind this notion of a "wide field."

# 62

# THE PARTIALITY OF EVERYTHING

In an effort to find my way through this "wide field," treacherous with its hidden mines, I remember lines from Bertolt Brecht's poem, "To Those Who Follow in Our Wake."

> *What times are these where*
> *A conversation about trees is almost a crime*
> *Because it includes a silence about so many misdeeds.*

Brecht's Theater am Schiffbauerdamm was just minutes away from my grandparents' apartment but miles apart from them spiritually. They did not like Brecht's plays, full of cheating and violent underworld creatures, nor did they sympathize with his Marxist politics. Nevertheless, Brecht's poem expresses something that is relevant to my perplexity about Api's life.

A silence that is almost a crime is a chilling specter that lays its finger on many, if not all, of us and makes innocence impossible. I am reminded again of Martin Luther King Jr.'s "Letter from Birmingham Jail," in which he condemned not only the actions of bad people but the silence of the good. Yet, in telling Api's story, I did not want to condemn him. I wanted to be one of those who break the silence, sometimes referred to as the Germans' "second guilt," and recount and account as clearly as I could. I found that this led to unwelcome discoveries and an uncomfortable questioning of my family history. But it also brought up kernels of insight from the buried past.

Api's story not only raises disturbing questions about me and my family but also helps stitch together some sense of history, however fragmented and incomplete. "There exists no position within an epoch from where one can view the history of that epoch," Goethe once wrote. "Indeed," added Ernst von Salomon in his novel *The Questionnaire*, "there was only a personal position, and only the sum of reports from such positions had to be the material in unlimited amounts for writing history, since 'truth lies partially in everything.'" I might be so bold as to add that truth lies in "the partiality of everything." Both my love, my partiality, for my grandfather and my open questions and partial truths have become part of this story and its history.

In the end, when I am left with many explanations but no complete answer, is it too glib and simple-minded to conclude that compassion and love, or call it "partiality," should not be selective and cannot be separated from any accounting of Api's story and of history? If we accept the notion that we are all responsible for the acts of our government, that we are all politically guilty, we need to become more humane toward all around us and learn to forgive others, as well as ourselves. This does not release even my postwar generation from being accountable for what was done during the Third Reich and from living with that history. But if love and compassion can help us understand, though not excuse, what happened to people like my grandfather, then perhaps they can help us see and accept our common humanity and appreciate how it binds us together across nationality, race, and gender.

Love and compassion feature prominently in Api's postwar poems. I remember a line from his Christmas poem of 1952 that I recited when I was ten. It says, "Love is man's most beautiful strength." Amid the crimes of the Nazi regime, and the horrors of two World Wars and their millions of dead, remains the question whether this is wisdom or evasion. Does it show a Panglossian resignation and denial of responsibility or a profound understanding of life through humanity and compassion? I still cannot find any solid ground upon which to stand in this "wide field."

# SOURCES

## 1 Oh My God!
Suicide statistics: Kershaw, *The End*, 356.

## 2 You Made Soap out of my Aunt
"was a prize specimen": Mann, *Dr. Faustus*, 59.
"Passivity and cooperation": Kershaw, *The Nazi Dictatorship*, 208.
"To do this is to condemn": Ball, 63.

## 3 A Clash of Memories
"a most fruitful": Kershaw, *The Nazi Dictatorship*, 218.
"Decisions that influence": Haffner, 182–183.
"Behind and amid": Stafford, xiv.
"The guilt felt": Grayling, 115.
"The descendants": Grayling, 1–2.
"the importance": Anderson, 38.
"the broadest": Evans, *Third Reich in Power*, 222.
"We will have to repent": King, 92.
"We're not responsible": Ball, 416.

## 4 Growing Up Prussian

"each one of us": Zweig, 7.

"media monarch": Clark, 589.

"What a man has drawn": Zweig, 18.

## 5 Seven Kilometers of Documents

Statistics of applicants: Schmidt, 14.

"of thorough knowledge": Schmidt, 72.

## 6 The Shot Heard Around the World

"We saw war": Morton, 10.

## 7 Track 17

"the quintessential": Evans, *Third Reich in Power*, 222.

"No other nation": Haffner, 52–53.

"the fundamental quality": Otto Friedrich, 126.

## 8 Better Times

Statistics of doctors' gross income: Kater, 260 and Evans, *Third Reich in Power*, 222.

"Along the entire Kurfürstendamm": Zweig, 59.

"the whole nation": Zweig, 360.

## 9 May Day, May Day, May Day

"turbulent instincts": Domarus, I, 1, 192.

"the marriage between": Domarus, I, 1, 227.

"in order to underline": Evans, *Third Reich in Power*, 222.

"Notoriously, a joint statement": Franklin, 72.

"no excitement": Shirer in Noakes, ed. 510.

"You may call me Meier": Read and Fisher, 53.

## 10 Wedding Bells

"Jewish vagabondism": Mosse, 72.

"there was a scent": Read and Fisher, 86.

## 11 Little Noodle

"as completely insane": Osterkamp, 369.

"11:27 attack": *Kriegstagebuch III*, 1, 593.

## 12 Christmas Trees

"No other Second World War": Middlebrook, 306.

"We can wreck": Sir Arthur Harris in Wheatcroft, 80.

RAF losses: Middlebrook, 306–307.

"from Alexanderplatz": Benn, 353.

"A gargantuan force": MacKinnon, 194–195.

"an overture": Boree, 33.

"the regime was sustained": Kershaw, *The End*, 393.

## 14 A Death in Prague

"Stalingrad is burned down": Grossman, 125.

## 16 Russians at the Gates

"Politics!": Bahm, 113.

"Berlin itself": Bahm, 31.

"powerful and full-blooded": Bahm, 25.

## 18 Blocked on All Sides

"The path which": Schenck, 140.

## 20 Mood Reports

"*Berliner!*": Beevor, 315.

"The bombs have shattered": Briggs in Price, title page.

"The situation looks bad": Wette, Bremer, Vogel eds., 259.

"In the center of Berlin": Beevor, 366.

## 21 Humans are Fiercer
"If you kill": Simic, 22.

Losses of "Operation Berlin": Le Tissier, 225.

"Was she fierce?": Beevor, 394.

"Twenty-three soldiers": Kardoff, 217.

## 22 You Not Lie
"The *Führer* has died": *Kriegstagebuch* IV, 2, 1274.

"Every hour": Rürup, 37.

"In this difficult hour": *Kriegstagebuch* IV, 2, 1282.

## 23 Unfulfilled Yearnings
127 million cubic feet of rubble" Bahm, 48.

## 27 The Silence
"latent or passive": Kershaw, *Hitler: Nemesis*, xliii.

"I did not want": Fest, 362.

"I have not found": Stafford, 506.

## 28 Professional Development
"hardly be overrated": Stafford, 136.

## 34 Without the Faintest Guilt
"The Germans have only themselves to blame": Stafford, 129.

"Don't get chummy with Jerry": Stafford, 128.

"the main purpose": Stafford, 130.

## 35 The Allies are Coming
"a continuation": A. Grossmann, 200.

### 39 We'd be Lucky to get Ike Cleared

"The Americans insisted": MacDonogh, 243.

"It was only once": MacDonogh, 348.

Americans handled almost 170,000: MacDonogh, 355.

"Denazification": Kanon, 265.

"as fleeting as the moment": v. Salomon, 52.

"How can I understand": v. Salomon, 8.

"Today we are all made responsible": v. Salomon, 225.

### 44 God's Co-Workers

"The Allies were obsessed": MacDonogh, 347.

### 50 Vienna

Statistics: From the exhibition at https://www.uvm.edu/~lkaelber/
children/amspiegelgrundwien/Steinhof-Folder_screen.pdf

"knew he was signing off": Appignasi, 32.

### 58 Trying to Understand

"were popular in so far as": Fritsche, 228.

"The two are entirely separate": Röpke, 140–141.

"Committed right-wing": Evans, Third Reich in Power, 222.

"May the almighty God": Domarus, I, 1, 194.

"The government of today's Germany": Domarus, I, 2, 494.

"To make all Germans": MacDonogh, xiii.

"If there had been barricades": Mosse, 367-368.

"Our thinking is usually constrained": Haffner, 102-103.

"they who were the Nazi's": Arendt, 126.

"Hitler's threats": Gay, 112.

suspicious questions: see Gay, 124.

"Internal terror": Kershaw, *Hitler: Nemesis*, 184.

"While all those formidable": Churchill, *Great Contemporaries*, 228.

"Those who have met": *Ibid.*, 232.

"One may dislike": Churchill, *Step by Step*, 143–144.

widespread support for Hitler: LeBor and Boyes, 176.

"For the Berliners": Friedrich, 391–392.

## 59 And Yet . . .

"Anti-Semitism was rife": Evans review of *Broken Lives*, *The Nation*,
Oct. 29, 2018, 35.

"The brutal terms": Fritsche, 209.

"It is simply not true": Neuhaus, 4.

"the absolute centrality": Evans, *Third Reich in History and Memory*,
117.

"If Goldhagen": Neuhaus, 4.

fought the idea of collective guilt: Röpke, 221.

"Collective guilt": Cimic, 22.

"simply a bad book": Kershaw, *The Nazi Dictatorship*, 255

"whatever its deficiencies": *Ibid.*, 258.

## 60 Inner Emigration

"No one who has not lived" and "I myself": Shirer, *Rise and Fall*,
247.

"it was surprising": Shirer, *Rise and Fall*, 247.

"The first norm": Jersak in Echternkamp, 337.

"It was totally impossible": Wolff-Mönckeberg, 136.

"He who wants to talk": Benn, 388.

"Only he who has lived": Heuss in MacDonogh, 348.

"So, like countless Germans": Ascherson, 18.

"even politically-minded people": Peukert, 77.

"an alibi for the educated . . .": Evans, *The Coming of the Third
Reich*, xxv.

"we Germans"" Jaspers, 65.

"In view of the crimes": Jaspers, 56.

"Germany under the Nazi regime": Jaspers, 73.

"We did not go": Jaspers, 65.

"Politically everyone": Jaspers, 56.

"In how far can a human being": Carole Stern in v. Arnim, 229.

"I should like to think": Kershaw, *Popular Opinion and Political Dissent in the Third Reich*, viii.

"can be determined": Arendt, 123.

"where all are guilty": Arendt, 126.

"there are many": Arendt, 125.

"For the idea of humanity": Arendt, 131.

"the lack of understanding": Stafford, 506.

"The German masses": MacDonogh, 356.

"The horizon": Jaspers, 29.

"German victimhood" and "Unacknowledged suffering": Anderson, 32.

"the importance of": Anderson, 38.


## 61 A Wide Field

"Fear was all pervasive": Evans, 128.

"from a responsible": Arendt, 129.


## 62 The Partiality of Everything

"There exists no position": v. Salomon, 391.

# BIBLIOGRAPHY

Diaries, Interviews, Eyewitness Reports: Berlin 1945

Andreas-Friedrich, Ruth. *Schauplatz Berlin: Tagebuchaufzeichnungen 1945 bis 1948*. Frankfurt am Main: Suhrkamp, 1984.

Anonymous. *A Woman in Berlin: Eight Weeks in the Conquered City: A Diary*. New York: Henry Holt, 2005.

Benn, Gottfried. *Briefe an F.W. Oelze 1932–1945*. München: Limes Verlag, 1977.

Bielenberg, Christabel. *The Past Is Myself*. London: Chatto and Windus, 1968.

Boldt, Gerhard. *Hitler: The Last Ten Days*. New York: Coward, McCann & Geoghegan, 1973.

Boveri, Margret. *Tage des Überlebens: Berlin 1945*. München: R. Piper and Co. Verlag, 1968.

Diem, Liselott. *Fliehen oder bleiben? Dramatisches Kriegsende in Berlin*. Freiburg: Herder, 1982.

Doernberg, Stefan. *Befreiung 1945: Ein Augenzeugenbericht*. Berlin: Verlag Dietz, 1975.

Ebermayer, Erich. *Denn heute gehört uns Deutschland: Persönliches und politisches Tagebuch.* Hamburg: Paul Zsolnay Verlag, 1959.

Fest, Joachim. *Not I: Memoirs of a German Childhood.* New York: Other Press, 2012.

Findahl, Theo. *Letzter Akt: Berlin 1939–1945.* Hamburg: Hammerich und Lesser, 1946.

Gay, Peter. *My German Question: Growing Up in Nazi Berlin.* New Haven, CT: Yale University Press, 1998.

Gosztony, Peter, ed. *Der Kampf um Berlin 1945 in Augenzeugenberichten.* Düsseldorf: Karl Rauch, 1970.

Haffner, Sebastian. *Defying Hitler.* London: Weidenfeld & Nicolson, 2002.

Höcker, Karla. *Die letzten und die ersten Tage: Berliner Aufzeichnungen 1945.* Berlin: Bruno Hessling, 1966.

Hunt, Irmgard. *On Hitler's Mountain: Overcoming the Legacy of a Nazi Childhood.* New York: Harper Perennial, 2006.

Junge, Traudl, and Melissa Miller, ed. *Until the Final Hour: Hitler's Last Secretary.* New York: Arcade Publishing, 2004.

Knoke, Heinz. *Die grosse Jagd: Bordbuch eines deutschen Jagdfliegers.* Rinteln: C. Bösendahl, 1952.

Köhler, Jochen. *Klettern in der Grossstadt: Volkstümliche Gechichten vom Überleben in Berlin,* 1933–1945. Berlin: Das Arsenal, 1979.

Koller, Karl. *Der letzte Monat. 14. April bis 27. Mai 1945. Tagebuchaufzeichnugen des ehemaligen Chefs des Genralstabs der deutschen Luftwaffe.* München: Bechtle, 1985.

Lange, Horst, and Hans Dieter Schäfer, ed. *Tagebücher aus dem Zweiten Weltkrieg.* Mainz: v. Hase & Koehler, 1979.

MacKinnon, Marianne. *The Naked Years: Growing Up in Nazi Germany.* London: Chatto & Windus, 1987.

Menzel, Matthias. *Die Stadt ohne Tod: Berliner Tagebuch 1943–45.* Berlin: Carl Habel, 1946.

Schäfer, Hans Dieter. *Berlin im Zweiten Weltkrieg: Der Untergang der Reichshauptstadt in Augenzeugenberichten.* München: Piper, 1985.

Schenck, Ernst-Günther. *Ich sah Berlin sterben: Als Arzt in der Reichskanzlei.* Herford: Nicolaische Verlagsbuchhandlung, 1970.

Vassiltchikov, Marie. *Berlin Diaries 1940–1945.* New York: Vintage Books, 1985.

von Kardoff, Ursula. *Diary of a Nightmare: Berlin 1942–1945.* London: Rupert Hart-Davis, 1965.

von Studnitz, Hans-Georg. *While Berlin Burns: The Diary of Hans-Georg von Studnitz 1943–1945.* London: Weidenfeld & Nicolson, 1964.

Wolff-Mönckeberg, Mathilde. *On the Other Side: To My Children: From Germany 1940–1945.* London: Peter Owen, 1979.

# SELECTED GENERAL BIBILOGRAPHY

Anderson, Mark M. "Crime and Punishment." *The Nation*, October 17, 2005, 32–38.

Appignanesi, Lisa. "Dr. Death." Review Edith Sheffer. *Asperger's Children: The Origins of Autism in Nazi Vienna. New York Review of Books*, Junly 19, 2018, 30-32.

Arendt, Hannah. "Organized Guilt and Universal Responsibility." *Essays in Understanding 1930–1954*. New York: Schocken Books, 1994.

Ascherson, Neal. "A Gutter Subject." Review of *Not I: Memoirs of a German Childhood. London Review of Books*, October 25, 2012, 17-18

Bahm, Karl. *Berlin 1945. The Final Reckoning*. St. Paul, Minnessota: MBI Publishing Company, 2001.

Beck, Earl R. *Under the Bombs: The German Home Front 1942–1945*. Lexington, Kentucky: University Press of Kentucky, 1986.

Beevor, Antony. *The Fall of Berlin 1945*. New York: Penguin, 2002.

Bessel, Richard, ed. *Life in the Third Reich*. Oxford: Oxford University Press, 1987.

Boree, Karl Friedrich. *Frühling 1945: Chronik einer Berliner Familie.* Darmstadt: Franz Schneekluth, 1954.

Borkowski, Dieter. *We weiss, ob wir uns wiedersehen: Erinnerungen an eine Berliner Jugend.* Frankfurt am Main: S. Fischer Verlag, 1980.

Braumüller, Maximilian. *Geschichte des Königin Augusta Garde-Grenadier Regiments Nr. 4.* Berlin: Ernst Siegfried Mittler und Sohn, 1901.

Brunner, Claudia, and Uwe von Seltmann. *Schweigen die Täter, reden die Enkel.* Frankfurt/Main: Fischer Verlag, 2006.

Burkert, Hans-Norbert, Klaus Matussek, and Doris Obschernitzki, eds. *Zerstört Besiegt Befreit. Der Kampf um Berlin bis zur Kapitulation 1945.* Berlin: Stätten der Geschichte Berlins, Band 7, 1985.

Childers, Thomas. *The Nazi Voter: The Social Foundations of Fascism in Germany, 1919–1933.* Chapel Hill, NC: University of North Carolina Press, 1983.

Churchill, Winston. *Great Contemporaries.* New York: G. P. Putnam's Sons, 1937.

Churchill, Winston. *Step by Step, 1936–1939.* New York: G. P. Putnam's Sons, 1939.

Cimic, Charles. "Oh, What a Lovely War!" Review of Buruma, Ian. *Year Zero: A History of 1945. New York Review of Books*, October 10, 2013, 21–23.

Clark, Christopher. *Iron Kingdom: The Rise and Downfall of Prussia, 1600–1947.* Cambridge, Massachusetts: Harvard University Press, 2006.

Davidson, Martin. *The Perfect Nazi. Uncovering My Grandfather's Secret Past.* New York: Berkley Caliber, 2010.

Diehl, James M. *Paramilitary Politics in Weimar Germany.* Bloomington, Indiana: Indiana University Press, 1977.

Dinter, Andreas. *Berlin in Trümmern: Ernährungslage und medizinische Versorgung der Bevölkerung Berlins nach dem II. Weltkrieg.* Berlin: Verlag Frank Wünsche, 1999.

Doehring, Bruno D. *Mein Lebensweg: Zwischen den Vielen und der Einsamkeit.* Gütersloh: Bertelsmann Verlag, 1952.

Domarus, Max, ed. *Hitler: Reden und Proklamationen 1932–1945.* Würzburg: Schmidt, 1962–63.

Echternkamp, Jörg, ed. *Germany and the Second World War, vol. IX/I: German Wartime Society 1939–1945.* Oxford: Clarendon Press, 2008.

Engelmann, Bernt. *Berlin: Eine Stadt wie keine andere.* München: Bertelsmann, 1986.

Evans, Richard J. *The Coming of the Third Reich.* London: Allen Lane, 2003.

Evans, Richard J. *The Third Reich in Power.* London: Allen Lane, 2005.

Evans, Richard J. *The Third Reich at War.* London: Allen Lane, 2008.

Evans, Richard J. *The Third Reich in History and Memory.* Oxford: Oxford University Press, 2015.

Falconer, Jonathan. *The Bomber Command Handbook 1939–1945.* London: Sutton, 1998.

Fest, Joachim. *Not I: Memoirs of a German Childhood.* New York: Other Press, 2014.

Franklin, Ruth. "Forced Into a Double Life." Review of Cohen, Roger. *The Girl from Human Street. New York Review of Books,* August 13, 2015.

Friedrich, Jörg. *Der Brand: Deutschland im Bombenkrieg 1940–1945.* München: Propyläen Verlag, 2002.

Friedrich, Otto. *Before the Deluge: A Portrait of Berlin in the 1920s.* New York: Harper & Row, 1972.

Fritsche, Peter. *Germans into Nazis.* Cambridge, Massachusetts: Harvard University Press, 1998.

Giordano, Ralph. *Die zweite Schuld oder von der Last Deutscher zu sein.* Hamburg: Rasch und Röhring Verlag, 1987.

Goerke, Heinz. *Die Militärärztlichen Bildungsanstalten von ihrer Gründung bis zur Gegenwart.* Zürich: Edition Olms, 1986.

Goldhagen, Daniel Jonah. *Hitler's Willing Executioners: Ordinary Germans and the Holocaust.* New York: Vintage Books, 1997.

Grayling, A. C. *Among the Dead Cities.* New York: Walker & Co., 2006.

Grossmann, Atina. "The Debate Will Not End: The Politics of Abortion in Germany from Weimar to National Socialism and the Postwar Period." In Manfred Berg and Geoffrey Cocks, eds. *Medicine and Modernity: Public Health and Medical Care in 19th and 20th Century Germany.* Cambridge, UK: Press Syndicate of the University of Cambridge, 1997, 193–212.

Grossman, Vasily. *A Writer at War: A Soviet Journalist with the Red Army, 1941–1945.* New York: Vintage Books, 2005.

Isherwood, Christopher. *The Berlin Stories.* New York: New Directions, 1963.

Italiaander, Rolf, et al., eds. *Berlins Stunde Null.* Düsseldorf: Droste Verlag, 1979.

Jameson, Egon. *Berlin so wie es war.* Düsseldorf: Droste Verlag, 1969.

Jansen, Christian, Lutz Niethammer, and Bernd Weisbrod, eds. *Von der Aufgabe der Freiheit: Politische Verantwortung und bürgerliche*

*Gesellschaft im 19. und 20.* Jahrhundert. Berlin: Akademie Verlag, 1995.

Jaspers, Karl. *Die Schuldfrage.* Heidelberg: Lambert Schneider, 1946.

Kannapin, Norbert. *Die deutsche Feldpostübersicht 1939–1945.* Osnabrück: Biblio Verlag, 1980–82.

Kanon, Joseph. *The Good German.* New York: Henry Holt, 2001.

Kater, Michael H. *Doctors Under Hitler.* Chapel Hill, NC: University of North Carolina Press, 1989.

Kater, Michael H. *The Nazi Party: A Social Profile of Members and Leaders 1919–1945.* Cambridge, MA: Harvard University Press, 1983.

Kershaw, Ian. *Popular Opinion and Political Dissent in the Third Reich: Bavaria 1933–1945.* Oxford: Clarendon Press, 1983.

Kershaw, Ian. *Hitler: 1889–1936 Hubris.* New York: W. W. Norton, 1998.

Kershaw, Ian. *Hitler: 1936–1945 Nemesis.* New York: W. W. Norton, 2000.

Kershaw, Ian. *The Nazi Dictatorship: Problems and Perspectives of Interpretation,* 4th ed. London: Hodder Arnold, 2000.

Kershaw, Ian. *The End: The Defiance and Destruction of Hitler's Germany, 1944–1945.* New York: Penguin, 2011.

Kettenacker, Lothar, ed. *Ein Volk von Opfern?* Berlin: Rowohlt Verlag, 2003.

King Jr., Martin Luther. *I Have a Dream: Writings and Speeches That Changed the World.* San Francisco: HarperSanFrancisco, 1992.

Kiaulehn, Walther. *Berlin: Schicksal einer Weltstadt.* München: Biederstein Verlag, 1958.

Kraatz, Helmut. *Zwischen Klinik und Hörsaal: Autobiographie.* Berlin: Verlag der Nation, 1977.

Kronika, Jacob. *Der Untergang Berlins*. Flensburg: Christian Wolf, 1946.

LeBor, Adam, and Roger Boyes. *Seduced by Hitler*. Naperville, IL: Sourcebooks, Inc., 2001.

Le Tissier, Tony. *The Battle of Berlin*. New York: St. Martin's Press, 1988.

MacDonogh, Giles. *After the Reich: From the Fall of Vienna to the Berlin Airlift*. London: John Murray, 2007.

Madison, James H. *What We've Learned About World War II*. Bloomington, IN: Institute for Advanced Study at Indiana University, 2006.

Mann, Heinrich. *Der Untertan*. Berlin: Claasen, 1958.

Mann, Thomas. *Dr. Faustus*. Berlin: Suhrkamp, 1947.

Middlebrook, Martin. *The Berlin Raids: RAF Bomber Command Winter 1943–44*. London: Viking, 1988.

Morton, Frederic. *Thunder at Twilight: Vienna 1913–1914*. Cambridge, MA: Da Capo Press, 2001.

Mosse, George L. *Nazi Culture: Intellectual, Cultural, and Social Life in the Third Reich*. New York: Grosset & Dunlap, 1966.

Nelson, Walter Henry. *The Berliners: Their Saga and Their City*. New York: David McKay Company, 1969.

Neuhaus, Richard John. "Daniel Goldhagen's Holocaust," *First Things* 65 (August–September 1996).

Noakes, Jeremy, ed. *Nazism 1919–1945, vol. 4: The German Home Front in World War II: A Documentary Reader*. Exeter, UK: University of Exeter Press, 1998.

Osterkamp, Theo. *Durch Höhen und Tiefen jagt ein Herz*. Heidelberg: Kurt Vowinckel, 1952.

Pehle, Walter H., ed. *Der historische Ort des Nationalsozialismus.* Frankfurt/Main: Fischer Verlag, 1990.

Pehle, Walter H., and Wolfgang Benz, eds. *Encyclopedia of German Resistance to the Nazi Movement.* New York: Continuum, 1997.

Pem. *Heimweh nach dem Kurfürstendamm.* München: Blanvalet, 1952.

Plievier, Theodor. *Berlin.* München: Verlag Kurt Desch, 1954.

Peukert, Detlev J. K. *Inside Nazi Germany: Conformity, Opposition, and Racism in Everyday Life.* New Haven, CT: Yale University Press, 1987.

Price, Alfred. *Blitz on Britain: The Bomber Attacks on the United Kingdom 1939–1945.* London: Ian Halland, 1977.

Read, Anthony, and David Fisher. *The Fall of Berlin.* New York: W. W. Norton, 1993.

Rein, Heinz. *Finale Berlin.* Berlin: JHW Dietz Nachf., no date.

Richie, Alexandra. *Faust's Metroplois: A History of Berlin.* New York: Carroll & Graf, 1998.

Röpke, Wilhelm. *The Solution of the German Problem.* New York: G. P. Putnam's Sons, 1946.

Rürup, Reinhard, ed. *Berlin 1945: Eine Dokumentation.* Berlin: Verlag Willmuth Arenhövel, 1995.

Ryan, Cornelius. *The Last Battle.* London: Collins, 1966.

Schmidt, Hermann. *Die Kaiser Wilhelm Akademie für das militärärztliche Bildungswesen von 1895 bis 1910.* Zürich: Edition Olms, 1995.

Schoeps, Julius. *H. Ein Volk von Mördern?* Hamburg: Hoffmann und Campe Verlag, 1996.

Schramm, Percy Ernst. *Kriegstagebuch des Oberkommandos der*

*Wehrmacht*, vols. 1–4. Frankfurt/Main: Bernard und Graefe Verlag für Wehrwesen, 1961–65.

Schultz-Naumann, Joachim. *The Last Thirty Days: The War Diary of the German Armed Forces High Command from April to May 1945*. Lanham, MD: Madison Books, 1991.

Sebald, W. G. *On the Natural History of Destruction*. New York: Random House, 2003.

Senfft, Alexandra. *Schweigen tut weh: Eine deutsche Familiengeschichte*. Berlin: Ullstein Verlag, 2008.

Serge, Victor. *Unforgiving Years*. Translated by Richard Greeman. New York: New York Review of Books, 2008.

Shirer, William L. *End of a Berlin Diary*. New York: Alfred A. Knopf, 1947.

Shirer, William L. *The Rise and Fall of the Third Reich*. New York: Simon & Schuster, 1960.

Sichrovsky, Peter. *Schuldig Geboren: Kinder aus Nazifamilien*. Köln: Kiepenheuer und Witsch, 1987.

Simic, Charles. "Oh, What a Lovely War," *New York Review of Books*, October 10, 2013, 21-23.

Singer, Peter. *Pushing Time Away*. New York: Ecco, 2004.

Slowe, Peter, and Richard Woods. *Battlefield Berlin: Siege, Surrender and Occupation, 1945*. London: Robert Hale, 1988.

Stafford, David. *Endgame, 1945: The Missing Final Chapter of World War II*. New York: Little, Brown and Co., 2007.

Steinhoff, Johannes, Peter Pechel, and Dennis Showalter, eds. *Deutsche im Zweiten Weltkrieg: Zeitzeugen sprechen*. München: Schneekluth Verlag, 1989.

Studier, Manfred. *Der Corpsstudent als Idealbild der Wilhelminischen Ära*:

*Untersuchungen zum Zeitgeist 1888–1914.* PhD dissertation, Friedrich-Alexander University, Erlangen, 1965.

Surminski, Arno. *Vaterland ohne Väter.* Berlin: Ullstein, 2004.

Trampe, Gustav, ed. *Die Stunde Null: Erinnerungen an Kriegsende und Neuanfang.* Stuttgart: Deutsche Verlags-Anstalt, 1995.

Trevor-Roper, H. R. *The Last Days of Hitler.* New York: Macmillan, 1947.

von Arnim, Gabriele. *Das grosse Schweigen: Von der Schwierigkeit, mit dem Schatten der Vergangenheit zu leben.* München: Kindler Verlag, 1989.

von Salomon, Ernst. *Der Fragebogen.* Hamburg: Rowohlt Verlag, 1951.

von zur Mühlen, Bengt. *Der Todeskampf der Reichshauptstadt.* Berlin-Kleinmachnow: Chronos, 1994.

Werner, Bruno E. *Die Zwanziger Jahre.* München: F. Bruckmann, 1962.

Wette, Wolfram, Ricarda Bremer, and Detlef Vogel, eds. *Das letzte halbe Jahr: Stimmungsberichte der Wehrmachtpropaganda 1944–45.* Essen: Klartext Verlag, 2001.

Wheatcroft, Geoffrey. "One Hundred Years of Destruction." *New York Review of Books*, December 20, 2018, 74–81.

Williamson, Murray. *Strategy for Defeat: The Luftwaffe 1933–1945.* Maxwell Air Force Base, AL: Air University Press, 1983.

Wippermann, Wolfgang. *Wessen Schuld? Vom Historikerstreit zur Goldhagen-Kontroverse.* Berlin: Elefanten Press, 1997.

Zweig, Stefan. *Die Welt von Gestern: Erinnerungen eines Europäers.* Berlin: S. Fischer Verlag 1982.

# INDEX

# ACKNOWLEDGMENTS

The archives of Humboldt University Berlin provided two volumes on my grandfather's career as a medical student and young ophthalmologist, and archivist Ilona Kalb uncovered yet uncatalogued materials about his work at the Charité. Dr. Karin Köhler at the Landeskirchliche Archiv in Berlin traced the pastor of my grandfather's church and Pastor Ingrid Hamel sent me materials about the Charité chapel. Dr. Mauersberger shared detailed information from his archive about the history of Berlin-Mitte, and Dr. Manfred Stürzbecher helped with insights into the workings of auxiliary military hospitals in Berlin. Most recently, Clint Mitchell, administrator of the Luftwaffe Research Group, provided amazing details about my father's life and death as a fighter pilot. I am grateful that he shared both his photos and his expertise with me.

In She Writes Press and its staff I was blessed with staunch supporters throughout the process. Publisher Brooke Warner shared materials related to publishing and promoting that helped me find my way through that jungle. More than that though she listened and responded to all my concerns. I am grateful for her patience. Annie Tucker did a superb and thoughtful job as copy editor. Editorial manager Lauren Wise was my first resource and helped me with her quick, efficient, and informative responses. Together they make a great team.

For help with my website and its design as well as navigating social media I am grateful for the help provided on many a week end by software developer Romaric Zounlome. With great skill and patience, artist and website designer Kay Westhues helped with my website and videos. Publicist Hannah Robertson of Books Forward was indefatigable and creative in finding new ways to promote the book. Her positive attitude was a boon at times of stress. Gigi Toth of Gigi Toth Consulting rescued me from several computer crises and generously shared her knowledge on marketing.

Sadly, my mother Dr. Margit Schönfeld had already passed away when I started the book, but my stepfather, Dr. Hanns Martin Schönfeld, was able to fill in some gaps. He also gave me that invaluable lockbox of documents. My most loyal and supportive companions throughout both the hard cover version and this new revised paperback were my son Dr. Benedict Robinson and my husband Dr. Mike Keen. My son, an English professor at SUNY Stony Brook, referred me to related literature and critiqued the manuscript. He also helped with copyediting problems, and was supportive even when he himself was swamped with work. My husband was an indefatigable collaborator on the original manuscript where the sixty-two chapter organization is largely the result of his insights that helped me to re-vision the book. Both joined me in trips back to Germany and their loving and enthusiastic support sustained me throughout this journey.

# ABOUT THE AUTHOR

Peter Ringenberg Photography

Gabrielle Robinson was born in Berlin in 1942. Her father, a fighter pilot, was shot down in 1943. After her family was bombed out twice, they fled Berlin, the beginning of a string of migrations that ended in the US. She holds an MA from Columbia University and a PhD from the University of London, both in English Literature, and taught at US universities and abroad. Robinson has won a number of awards for her writing and community service. She now is settled in South Bend, Indiana, with her husband, a sociologist turned sustainable neighborhood developer, and their cat Max.

# SELECTED TITLES FROM SHE WRITES PRESS

She Writes Press is an independent publishing company founded to serve women writers everywhere. Visit us at www.shewritespress.com.

*Surviving the Survivors: A Memoir* by Ruth Klein
$16.95, 978-1-63152-471-4
With both humor and deep feeling, Klein shares the story of her parents—who survived the Holocaust but could not overcome the tragedy they had experienced—and their children, who became indirect victims of the atrocities endured by the generation before them.

*Jumping Over Shadows: A Memoir* by Annette Gendler
$16.95, 978-1-63152-170-6
Like her great-aunt Resi, Annette Gendler, a German, fell in love with a Jewish man—but unlike her aunt, whose marriage was destroyed by "the Nazi times," Gendler found a way to make her impossible love survive.

*The Beauty of What Remains: Family Lost, Family Found* by Susan Johnson Hadler $16.95, 978-1-63152-007-5
Susan Johnson Hadler goes on a quest to find out who the missing people in her family were—and what happened to them—and succeeds in reuniting a family shattered for four generations.

*The Butterfly Groove: A Mother's Mystery, A Daughter's Journey* by Jessica Barraco $16.95, 978-1-63152-800-2
In an attempt to solve the mystery of her deceased mother's life, Jessica Barraco retraces the older woman's steps nearly forty years earlier—and finds herself along the way.

*Implosion: Memoir of an Architect's Daughter* by Elizabeth W. Garber
$16.95, 978-1-63152-351-9
When Elizabeth Garber, her architect father, and the rest of their family move into Woodie's modern masterpiece, a glass house, in 1966, they have no idea that over the next few years their family's life will be shattered—both by Woodie's madness and the turbulent 1970s.

*Don't Call Me Mother: A Daughter's Journey from Abandonment to Forgiveness* by Linda Joy Myers $16.95, 978-1-938314-02-5
Linda Joy Myers's story of how she transcended the prisons of her childhood by seeking—and offering—forgiveness for her family's sins.